Ireland at the United Nations

Ireland at the United Nations

Memories of the Early Years

Noel Dorr

INSTITUTE OF PUBLIC
ADMINISTRATION

First published in 2010
by the Institute of Public Administration
57–61 Lansdowne Road
Dublin 4
Ireland
www.ipa.ie

© Noel Dorr, 2010

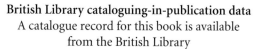

ISBN 978-1-904541-87-5

British Library cataloguing-in-publication data
A catalogue record for this book is available
from the British Library

Cover design by Slick Fish Design, Bray, Co. Wicklow
Typeset in Minion 11/14 by Carole Lynch
Printed in England by MPG Books, Bodmin, Cornwall

The cover photograph shows the Minister for External Affairs,
Frank Aiken (third from left) in discussion with members of the Irish
Delegation to the UN General Assembly, autumn 1957. The officials
are (from left): Eoin MacWhite, Sean Ronan (back to camera),
Eamon Kennedy (bending forward), the Permanent Representative
Ambassador Freddie Boland, and Conor Cruise O'Brien (courtesy of the
UN Photo Library, New York).

The photographs within the book are used with kind
permission of the UN Photo Library, New York.

Contents

Acknowledgements

I thank the publisher, the Institute of Public Administration, and particularly Hannah Ryan of the IPA Publications Division and Eileen Kelly (now retired).

I would like also to thank former colleagues of mine in the Department of Foreign Affairs – Noel Fahey, who read the text and offered comments at an earlier stage; and Anne Anderson and her colleagues, Jenny Thomas and Brian Cahalane, in the Irish Mission to the UN in New York, who helped in obtaining photographs from the United Nations along with permission for their use. I also thank Dr Michael Kennedy of the RIA and UCD, who provided appropriate footnote references to documents in the National Archives of Ireland for an earlier version of Chapters 10 and 11 that appeared in *Obligations and Responsibilities*, a book of essays which he co-edited with Deirdre McMahon in 2005. The IPA as its publishers kindly allowed me to draw on my essay in that earlier publication for the two final chapters of the present book.

I am very grateful to the editor chosen by the IPA, Brendan O'Brien. He not only did a very professional job of editing the text but also gave me help and encouragement along the way.

My greatest debt of gratitude is to my brother, Donal, himself an experienced author, who helped, supported and encouraged me at all stages from writing to publication. Without his support, his help and his gentle but constant pressure, I doubt if I would have continued to write or offered my recollections to the reader in this book.

Of course I take full responsibility for any errors or omissions in the text.

I would like to dedicate this book to my wife, Caitríona.

Introduction

This is a book about the role that Ireland played as a Member State of the United Nations, as I saw it, over the decade of the 1960s. It is, for the most part, a personal memoir which draws on my own recollections and occasional notes as well as on documented sources – apart from Chapter 1, which outlines the historic background and explains how Ireland came to be a Member State of the UN.

I joined the Irish Department of External Affairs as a junior diplomat in January 1960. On my first day in Iveagh House I was assigned to the Political section on the top floor, which dealt with Ireland's membership of the United Nations. Ireland had been admitted to the UN four years earlier, after a long wait, and it had been little more than three years since an Irish Delegation travelled to New York to take part in the work of the General Assembly for the first time.

That was a heady time for the small group on the top floor, of which I was now the most junior member. We worked under the direction of Conor Cruise O'Brien, who at that time was still a middle-level Irish diplomat in the Irish Foreign Service with the rank of 'Counsellor'. Frank Aiken, who was the Minister for External Affairs, had become a prominent figure at the UN General Assembly where he spent lengthy periods each year. Freddie Boland was Ireland's Permanent Representative (i.e. Ambassador) to the UN in New York, and soon to be President of the General Assembly. Six months after I joined, Ireland embarked on its first major venture in UN peacekeeping in the Congo, and we in the Political section were deeply involved in the arrangements.

Some fifteen months later I moved to another area of work in the Department. Later still, after further experience at home, I was sent to serve in Embassy posts abroad, first in Brussels and then in Washington, DC. Over the following thirty-five years, however, I found myself involved for extended periods – at various levels and with varying degrees of intensity – in aspects of Ireland's membership of the United Nations. A high point was the two-year term that Ireland served as an elected member of the Security Council in the early 1980s, while I was the Irish Permanent Representative in New York. I retired from the Irish Foreign Service in the mid-1990s but even after that I remained involved on behalf of Ireland, for another five years, in an informal discussion group of sixteen countries chaired by Sweden, which focused on the possibility of UN reform.

They say that young ducklings become 'imprinted', which is to say, they tend to follow faithfully the first moving object they see after they have hatched. Too bad if it is not their mother. I have a private theory that something similar happens in the life of a young diplomat. Those of us who spend a career in the foreign service experience great variety as we alternate between home and abroad and move to a new post every four years or so. But we still tend to think of the work we were first assigned to – be it political, economic, trade, cultural, consular, press relations, protocol, or any other – as centrally important, if not indeed as the 'real' work that should preoccupy the Foreign Ministry and its diplomats.

Perhaps that has happened to me. In any case, though I have been involved in a variety of other issues during a thirty-five year career in the Irish Foreign Service – not least in Anglo-Irish relations and Northern Ireland – I have always maintained a particular interest in the work of the UN and in the role that Ireland has played there. In this memoir I would like to draw on that experience in order to give the reader a personal view of some of the more interesting issues in which Ireland became involved in the 1960s.

I should start by offering my view of the United Nations itself. I believe it is weak, fragile and inadequate. It is often exasperating. It is also indispensable, and if it did not exist it would be necessary to invent it. But I seriously doubt whether it would now be possible to do so. So the best we can do is to support the UN as we have it, with all its inadequacies, and work incrementally to strengthen and adapt it so that it can address the problems of this new world of the twenty-first century.

The best argument for the UN that I know of rests on a single sentence in a report issued by the previous Secretary General, Kofi Annan, in the Millennium Year 2000:

> In addition to the separate responsibilities each state bears towards its own society, states are, collectively, the custodians of our common life on this planet.[1]

For the most part, States can be relied on to be aware of the responsibilities that they bear to their own societies – even if some fail in those responsibilities. But how are States to exercise, collectively, their other responsibility as 'the custodians of our common life on this planet'? It seems to me that it can only be through a universal organisation of States such as the United Nations, working in conjunction with the family of related organisations that have grown around it.

The UN was established in 1945, towards the close of the Second World War. A draft Charter, largely inspired by the US, was agreed between the four major Allied Powers – the US, the UK, the Soviet Union and (Nationalist) China – in negotiations in Washington, DC in the autumn of 1944. Outstanding details were settled by the three principal Allied leaders – Roosevelt, Churchill and Stalin – at their Summit Conference in Yalta in early 1945; and in June 1945 the final text of the Charter was approved by representatives of all fifty Allied States at a conference in San Francisco. The new organisation came into being on 24 October 1945.

The founding States, all of which were at war with Germany

---

1   *'We the Peoples': The Role of the United Nations in the Twenty-First Century.* Report of the Secretary General of the United Nations, 2000.

and/or Japan at the time, seem to have thought of the new organisation as essentially a continuation of their wartime alliance. They believed that if they remained united they could act, forcefully if necessary, to maintain international peace and security in the post-war world. In the event, because of the Cold War split between 'East' and 'West', this did not happen. But over the second half of the twentieth century a fundamental change took place in international life as colonies and dependent territories everywhere asserted their right to self-determination and achieved independence. Over those decades, the world in effect transformed itself and became what it is today – a global society of sovereign independent States. Each newly independent State joined the United Nations when it became independent. This meant that the UN, too, was transformed: no longer merely an alliance, it became a universal organisation of States, the first such organisation in human history.

Since each State joining the UN was required to accept the Charter, the result was that each new State in turn was 'socialised into' the international system; the UN Charter became a kind of constitution or set of basic rules for international society. Today, even if it is not always observed, the Charter is, nevertheless, accepted universally as a primary source of international law and a basic text setting out fundamental principles for relations between States. Furthermore, centred on the UN, there is now quite a dense network of other bodies and specialised agencies that coordinate international action between States in a wide variety of fields.

It is true that the United Nations as it exists today often seems far from adequate to its intended role as a structure for the maintenance of world peace; and it certainly needs to be reformed and strengthened if it is to function effectively as an international security organisation. But, even while admitting this, we ought to recognise the importance of the two aspects of the UN that I have just mentioned: the UN Charter as a universally accepted code of rules for State relations imposes a measure of order on what would otherwise be the essential anarchy of international life; and the 'family' of specialised agencies centred on the UN serves, though still imperfectly, as the means through which 200 sovereign independent States can exercise, collectively, their responsibility as 'custodians of our common life on this planet'.

The UN is now well into its second half-century: it will celebrate its sixty-fifth anniversary in 2010. It has already lasted more than three times as long as its predecessor, the League of Nations.[2] But its future cannot be taken for granted. President Obama has a very positive attitude to the UN but for a time under the previous Bush Administration it looked as if the US, the major world power which was largely responsible for creating the organisation in the mid-twentieth century, had lost interest in sustaining it. US policies in those years sought to bypass the UN, as was evident when it went to war in Iraq in 2003, and the overall attitude of the US Government at that time seemed to range from indifference to something very close to hostility.

The smaller and less powerful of the world's States, on the other hand, have come to value the UN, imperfect as it is, as a structure that brings a measure of order, if not always of justice, to inter-State relations. It is of interest that, at a time when the US was turning increasingly to unilateral action to advance its interests and maintain its security, many other States reacted by looking instead for a multilateral approach organised through the UN. They came to see this as the only way to ensure international legitimacy, particularly in those cases where it may become necessary to consider the use of force for the maintenance of international peace and security. So, paradoxically, the very fact that the US, the UK and some other countries bypassed the UN by going to war in Iraq in 2003 without specific authorisation from the Security Council, and the resulting lack of widespread support in the world community for what they did, helped in some degree to establish the

---

2   The effective life of the League, which was founded in 1919, was about two decades. As a legal entity, however, it continued in existence until it was formally wound up in 1946.

importance of the UN as a source of international legitimacy. More generally it created a better understanding of the need for a multilateral approach to major international problems of all kinds.

The outlook and psychology of the people of any country are shaped by their country's past – or rather by the narrative constructed from those aspects and events of their history which, as a people, they choose to remember. The peoples of a large and powerful State may well feel that their country has created its own history and successfully established its place in the world. Smaller and weaker nations, in contrast, may see themselves as objects of history, buffeted by the ebb and flow of its tides across their territories. In consequence they are more likely to value international systems that bring a measure of structure and order to international life. As the American writer, Robert Kagan, puts it:

> In an anarchic world, small powers always fear they will be victims. Great powers on the other hand, often fear rules that may constrain them more than they do anarchy. In an anarchic world, they rely on their power to provide security and prosperity.[3]

Ireland is a good illustration of this: its relative weakness as a State and its perception of its own troubled history have given it a strong sense of the importance of order and the rule of law in international affairs and the need for a multilateral approach to international issues.[4]

It could be said indeed that the attitude of Irish people to international affairs has been formed and shaped by a historical

---

3   Robert Kagan, *Paradise and Power*, p. 38.
4   The Irish Constitution, Article 4 states that 'The name of the State is Éire, or in the English language, Ireland'. In this book, in accordance with standard usage, I will use the term 'Ireland' to refer to the State, in the sense of the Republic of Ireland, and where I wish to refer to the whole island of Ireland I will so indicate.

narrative that emphasises their country's long struggle in an earlier era to assert its independence against heavy odds. In some larger countries the narrative may focus on the central, not to say dominant, role their peoples have played – politically, economically and culturally – in the creation of the modern world and on what they have contributed to civilisation and to the spread of enlightenment. In Ireland our past is complex but we tend to remember our history as that of a submerged people seeking independence and looking to support from elsewhere to achieve it. In consequence, in our approach to international affairs today we draw naturally and easily on a language and rhetoric of 'rights' and 'justice'.

This does not at all mean that, where its own interests are concerned, Irish foreign policy is necessarily more moral than that of its European neighbours. But it does tend to give at least a 'moral tone' to Ireland's international discourse – though there are times when we need to remember that there is a difference between being 'moral' and being 'moralistic'. It means, too, that Irish people tend to have sympathy for the idea of 'self-determination' for other dependent peoples – even though a reflection on the recent history of this island would suggest that the effort to apply that principle to a particular population or area can be contentious and may lead to conflict.

This general outlook was evident in the active role that the then Irish Free State played as a Member State of the League of Nations in the 1920s and 1930s. But since it was neutral in the Second World War and did not join as a belligerent on the Allied side, Ireland was not invited to the San Francisco Conference in 1945. So it did not become a founder member of the United Nations. Ireland did apply to join the new organisation in July 1946, but the Soviet Union used its veto in the Security Council to block the admission of Ireland and that of a number of other countries. Nine years passed before the veto was lifted and Ireland was formally admitted to membership on 14 December 1955. It was nearly another year before a full Irish Delegation, led by the Minister for External Affairs, Liam

Cosgrave, arrived in New York to take its seat for the first time in the UN General Assembly. I deal with these events in Chapter 1.

In later chapters I will draw on my own memories of years in the 1960s when I was a junior member of successive Irish Delegations to the UN General Assembly. In a later period I served as Ireland's Permanent Representative to the UN and sat in the Irish seat on the Security Council over a two-year term in the early 1980s. That is a story to be told elsewhere and I will not cover it in this book.

Later still, after I had retired, Ireland served a very successful term as a member of the Security Council for the two-year period 2001–2002. I leave the story of those later events to be told by those who were active at that time after I had moved on to other things. I hope that they will do so in due course.

The official files for the 1950s and 1960s, the period that I will cover here, have long been open to researchers under 'the thirty-year rule'; and academic studies and papers of various kinds have already appeared. What I write here will not be an academic study but I would like to make it something more than a purely personal memoir. I will certainly draw on personal memories – including memories of what I might call the 'lore' picked up from my seniors in what was then the Department of External Affairs in regard to the years immediately before I joined the Department in 1960. But, where I can, I will also try to fill out, and document to some extent, the wider background to the issues that I cover.

In concluding this Introduction, I feel that I owe it to the reader to explain in rather more detail how I came to be involved in UN issues over such a relatively long period.

I first took a serious interest in the United Nations in the autumn of 1956. I was living in Galway at the time. I was no longer a student and, after a year spent teaching, I had just taken up a job in the Civil Service. In late October and early November of that year the world went through two serious crises simultaneously: Israel, abetted secretly by France and the UK, attacked Egypt; and the Soviet army forcefully suppressed a nationalist uprising in Hungary. I have a vivid memory of listening apprehensively late at night in my flat to the crisis debates in the UN Security Council and the General Assembly, which were broadcast by the BBC World Service. I remember particularly my fear that the world could be close to nuclear war; and my thought as I went to bed at night that it might have started by the morning.

I never expected at that time that I would find myself joining the Department of External Affairs a little over three years later – still less that I would be working on issues relating to the United Nations. However, in late 1959 some posts as 'Third Secretary' in the Department were advertised. I sat for the exam and I was called to join the Department in January 1960. It was quite a small Department at the time. A number of diplomats recruited well before me had grown senior in years of service but remained junior in rank, and they saw little prospect of promotion. The notable expansion that came in the early 1970s as the Department took on important functions in regard to both Northern Ireland and the EEC was still far in the future.

It was my great good fortune that my first assignment to the small Political/United Nations section of the Department in that long-ago January of 1960 fitted well with the interest I had already developed. Furthermore, I now found myself working with colleagues who had a deep commitment to the United Nations and who had had an active role as members of the Irish Delegation under Frank Aiken over the previous three years.

I worked in a room alongside Bob McDonagh, who was very much my senior. Our section was headed by the late Paul Keating, who worked next door and spent as much time in our room as in his own. Later, each in turn served abroad in Ambassadorial posts and each in turn became Secretary of the Department. I learned a lot from both. Above Paul again in the small hierarchy of the system was Conor Cruise O'Brien, still at that time a civil servant. He was, to say the least, refreshingly different. Our section was responsible, through Conor, for advising the Minister on UN issues, and for maintaining close liaison with Ireland's Permanent Mission to the UN in New York, headed by the Ambassador, Freddie Boland. Next door to us worked Máire Mhac an tSaoi, a renowned Irish poet, who later married Conor, and also, like the others I have mentioned here, a regular member of the Irish Delegation to the UN General Assembly each autumn.

In later chapters I will recount in more detail some memories of those early years. For the moment, in this Introduction, I simply want to trace briefly the thread of my own involvement with UN issues over a period of more than forty years.

In 1961, after just a year and a half in the Department, I was sent to New York as the junior member of the Irish Delegation to the three-month annual session of the UN General Assembly. The practice in the Department during this period of particularly heavy work each autumn is to augment the small permanent staff based in the Irish Permanent Mission to the UN in New York by drawing in other officials from Dublin or from other Embassies on temporary assignment.

I arrived in New York in September 1961 at what proved to be a rather dramatic time. I awoke in my hotel to startling news on the first morning after my arrival: the UN Secretary General, Dag Hammarskjöld, had been killed overnight in an air-crash in what was then Northern Rhodesia. I will talk about this at greater length in Chapters 3 and 4. Later in the 1960s I was sent regularly again to the General Assembly over four successive years. At the time I was based in the Irish Embassy in Washington and each September I left my Washington apartment and moved for three months to New York to join the Delegation and sit on one of the Assembly's Committees. By the end of the decade I had accumulated some fifteen months' experience of the General Assembly.

That period from 1960 to 1969 is essentially the period I will cover in this book, with a glance back at times to the three or four years before I joined the Department. But my involvement in issues related to the United Nations did not end there. I spent the 1970s at home in Ireland. For the last six years of that decade, I was what, following the European model, we came to call 'Political Director' – that is, head of the Political Division of the Department.

In that capacity I again encountered the UN in a very active way, since the Political Division was responsible, among many other things, for following closely the work of the UN and helping to shape Ireland's policy there. On the basis of reports and recommendations from our colleagues in the delegation in New York, we advised the Minister on the draft resolutions before the Assembly and then transmitted voting instructions back to them. There seemed to be an enormous number of these resolutions each year. They were usually clustered towards the end of the session in December; and instructions were always needed urgently and at short notice. I recall a particular day when something like thirty-seven resolutions on various aspects of disarmament were voted on. On that subject at least, the number of resolutions was inversely proportional to the level of success they achieved.

By now Ireland had joined the EEC, as it was still called at the time, and, under an arrangement known as 'European Political Cooperation', had accepted a commitment to try where possible to coordinate positions on international policy issues with the other Member States. This commitment was still quite a loose one at the time. Nevertheless, it meant that we in Dublin, and our colleagues in New York, had also to consult regularly with our opposite numbers in other Member States to try to work out what the representative of the State that held the Presidency could say in important UN debates on behalf of the EEC as a whole. This effort to 'speak with one voice', where possible, also meant that, at times and on certain issues, Irish representatives spoke less frequently to set out a purely national position – though it was always open to us to do so if we wished. On the other hand, as most other UN Member States saw it, there was a new seriousness to Ireland's voting position since we were now an active member of the most important group economically, and one of the most important politically, in the

General Assembly. Furthermore, since the Presidency role rotates around the table every six months among Member States, Ireland itself has had to take its turn from time to time in coordinating policies and presenting a common EEC (now EU) position in UN bodies.

In 1980 I was transferred to New York to take up the post of Permanent Representative – which is to say Ambassador – to the United Nations at its headquarters there. (I should explain that Ireland, like most other countries, also maintains a Permanent Representative at the European office of the UN in Geneva. The holder of that post is also the Irish representative to a wide variety of other important international organisations in that city.) 'Permanent' is something of a misnomer for such postings, but I did stay there for the next three years. When I arrived in New York in September of 1980 I was plunged straight into an intensive campaign that my colleagues there, supported by the Minister, the late Brian Lenihan, and the Department at home were already running for election to a seat on the fifteen-member Security Council. In the event when the election took place later that autumn we were successful and, as a result, Ireland served a two-year term in 1981–1982 as a 'non-permanent' – that is to say, an elected – member of the Council. During most of those two years I sat in the Irish seat on the Council, supported by a small team of excellent colleagues. This was another intense experience: a two-year period at what could be seen as the heart of the UN system. I hope, elsewhere and at another time, to recount some memories of those two years.

I left New York in the autumn of 1983 to take up the post of Ambassador in London, and my career in the Department for a number of years thereafter focused largely on other issues – particularly Northern Ireland and Anglo-Irish relations. Later I returned to Dublin as Secretary of the Department (a post now described as Secretary General). For over eight years in that post, I still had occasion to follow events at the UN regularly – though not, of course, in as detailed a way as before – and I usually travelled with the Minister to attend the first week or two of the General Assembly session.

Later, still, in the mid-1990s, now in retirement, I was nominated by the Taoiseach[5] to represent him on an informal discussion group convened by the Prime Minister of Sweden, Ingvar Carlsson. Carlsson had been co-Chairman of a body called The Commission on Global Governance which included such eminent figures as Jacques Delors, the former President of the European Commission; Sadako Ogata, formerly UN High Commissioner for Refugees; and Sir Brian Urquhart, who, for years, had been one of the most senior figures in the UN Secretariat. The Commission had recently produced an excellent report entitled *Our Global Neighbourhood*, and Prime Minister Carlsson hoped to achieve some follow-up to their work through our group.[6] So he invited fifteen other Heads of State or Government to nominate personal representatives. Together we constituted an informal discussion group that was chaired throughout by our Swedish colleague. We met some four or five times a year from 1995 to 2001 – either in New York or in one or other of our capitals. Throughout that period we discussed various aspects of UN reform and from time to time we were able to agree on a statement for issue by our principals, the Heads of State/ Government, or a paper to be submitted to the Secretary General. Discussion in the group in its closing stages focused in a particular way on what might be achieved at the Millennium Summit that was to take place at the UN in the year 2000, and our work as a group petered out once that Summit meeting had concluded successfully.

Our work was useful enough – and worth doing – and great credit is due to Sweden for having brought the group together and steered its meetings. I would like to be able to go beyond that and say that our group had some real influence in advancing the more formal discussions on reform of the UN that were then under way

---

5   Actually two successive Taoisigh – first John Bruton in 1995 and then Bertie Ahern when he came to office in 1997.

6   Commission on Global Governance. *Our Global Neighbourhood.*

in New York. Perhaps it had. But it was not always easy for us to agree on just what needed to be done. The trouble was that Prime Minister Carlsson had selected too well. Our little informal group of sixteen representatives drawn from various continents and regional groupings of States, though congenial in its own way, was the UN in microcosm: too often it reflected on a smaller scale the very disagreements that had divided the organisation as a whole and made progress on reform so difficult to achieve.

I have spoken here of this particular experience because it was a salutary reminder to me of just how difficult a task reform of the UN can be. The organisation is now a universal organisation of States: it mirrors the world. Reforming it amounts to working out how what is now a planet-wide international system should organise itself to face the problems of the new century. That is a daunting task.

We may not always have been able to reach a high level of agreement in what we called informally 'the Carlsson Group', but one thing did unite us: a firm belief on the part of all sixteen Governments represented that only a 'multilateral' approach, involving cooperation between the nearly two hundred sovereign States that now share the globe between them, could address the multifarious problems of the world of the twenty-first century. Certainly, all of us were convinced that unilateral action by major States, however strong and powerful, was unlikely to do so.

It is well not to exaggerate the role a small country can play in international affairs, but Ireland's commitment to 'multilateralism' and to the concept of international organisation is something more than lip-service: it has been a continuous thread of the policy of successive Irish Governments since the 1920s. That policy, already well established in the League of Nations, was picked up again when Ireland was eventually admitted to the United Nations in the mid-1950s, as I will explain in Chapter 1.

Over the first fifteen years of its UN membership Ireland established a very creditable record as a Member State. I hope that this book will be of interest in explaining in some detail some issues in which it was involved. In the General Assembly, the Security Council and other UN bodies Ireland was seen as a small, active Member State, concerned to make the organisation work as it should; and a reliable and effective contributor to UN peacekeeping forces in many of the world's most troubled regions. It is an approach that was maintained in later years and that, I am glad to say, continues today.

In the preface to a book on UN peacekeeping that he wrote in retirement,[7] the late Sir Anthony Parsons, a former British colleague on the Security Council in New York whom I much admired, made a comment that I have taken very much to heart. He explained that he had 'brooded long before deciding to write'. In the end his daughter, an academic, had tipped the scale: 'She told me that I must write the book so long as it was one which only I could write, not another rehash of known historical facts and interpretations'. I doubt if I can claim such originality, and I know that there are at least some others who might perhaps have written from personal experience about the period I have covered in this book. But it does not look as if they will do so now. That is why, as someone who was around – in a junior capacity – for many of these events, I have decided to try.

But first I must begin with a chapter of what I would call 'pre-history' in order to explain the background to Ireland's admission to membership of the UN in late 1955.

---

7   Anthony Parsons, *From Cold War to Hot Peace.*

1

How Ireland Joined the UN

The founders of the United Nations began by thinking of it as an alliance: the fifty States that attended the Conference in San Francisco where it was founded in 1945 were all at war with either Germany or Japan by 1 March 1945. In wartime, as in other disputes in human affairs, those who stay out of a quarrel are seldom popular with either side: States such as Sweden, Portugal and Ireland that had been neutral during the war were not invited to the Conference and had no say in the establishment of the new organisation.

The Charter of the UN, however, looked beyond the founders to a future wider membership: it provided that:

> Membership in the United Nations is open to all other peace-loving States which accept the obligations contained in the present Charter and, in the judgment of the Organization, are able and willing to carry out these obligations.[1]

The phrase 'all *other* peace-loving States' (emphasis added) is interesting. The use of the word 'other' here seems to imply that the founders, the wartime Allies, which were still at war with Japan at the close of the Conference, were by definition 'peace-loving'; and it would be for them to judge whether other States were sufficiently 'peace-loving' to join them in the new enterprise.

Ireland, which had remained neutral during the war, did not apply immediately to join the new organisation but, nearly a year

---

1   Article 4.1 of the UN Charter.

after it was founded, the Taoiseach, Éamon de Valera, arranged for the Dáil to debate the question of Irish membership. In late July 1946, he introduced a motion that would have the Dáil recommend that the Government apply for admission to the United Nations 'as soon as they consider it appropriate to do so'; he spoke in the debate himself at some length to explain what membership would entail.[2] The motion was adopted after two days of debate; one month later, in August 1946, Ireland applied to join the United Nations.

The Charter provides that the admission of new Members to the organisation is to be 'effected by a decision of the General Assembly upon the recommendation of the Security Council'. In practice this leaves the decision in the hands of the Security Council since the General Assembly cannot act until the Council has first made a recommendation. This in turn means that the decision rests largely with the five Permanent Members of the Security Council: all five must at least acquiesce before any decision can be taken, and any one of the five can block an applicant if it uses its veto.

The Irish Government must have been taken aback when this happened in 1946 and its application for UN membership was met with a rebuff. The Soviet Union used its veto on the Council to block the admission of Ireland and a number of other States that it thought of as 'pro-Western'. The United States, for its part, then blocked the admission of States allied to, or supported by, the Soviet Union and used its influence in the Council to ensure that such States would not gain the seven votes needed for approval of their applications. The result was what was described as 'a policy of competitive exclusion'. The deadlock persisted until late 1955, when a 'package deal' was worked out between 'East' and 'West' and Ireland, along with fifteen other States, was admitted to membership.[3]

---

2   See Maurice Moynihan (ed.), *Speeches and Statements by Eamon de Valera 1917–1973*, pp. 484–490.

3   See Inis L. Claude, Jr, *Swords into Plowshares*, pp. 79–92. The other States admitted at the same time were: Albania, Austria, Bulgaria, Cambodia, Ceylon, Finland, Hungary, Italy, Jordan, Laos, Libya, Nepal, Portugal, Romania and Spain. See Joseph Morrison Skelly, *Irish Diplomacy at the United Nations 1945–1965*, pp. 25 fn.

This sequence of events more than half a century ago gives rise to some interesting questions. First, why should Ireland, which had maintained its neutral status with great difficulty through the six years of the Second World War, want to join the new 'collective security' organisation founded by the Allies, so soon after the war came to an end? Joining such an organisation would involve a commitment by all Member States to act forcefully together to stop aggression and to maintain international peace and security. But Ireland had chosen to opt out of the war just ended, which was indeed a war against aggression: a war that could be said to have more nearly fitted the definition of a 'just war' than any in history. Why should it now want to commit itself so quickly to the principle of 'collective security'?

De Valera touched on several reasons when he spoke in reply to the debate in the Dáil on 25 July 1946. One, which may now seem a little strange, was a belief that membership would help to preserve Ireland's independence.

We need to remember, however, that at that time an independent Irish State had been in existence only for a generation. A central issue for successive Irish Governments over previous decades had been how best to consolidate the independence that had been achieved and gain international recognition for the State. In the 1920s, Cumann na nGaedheal had worked within the Commonwealth structure to loosen the constraints of membership of that organisation; de Valera himself had gone further in the 1930s through a series of radical steps that loosened many of the legal/political ties with Britain that the Anglo-Irish Treaty of 1921 had imposed. Like other leaders of the generation that had brought the country to independence, he still felt this 'existential' question of the independence of the State to be of central importance, and he had it in mind when he came to consider membership of the new international organisation. In his speech to the Dáil on the issue in July 1946, he touched briefly on the question of Irish unity. But he did so only to say that he did not believe that UN membership in itself would help to bring it about– although he thought that, at least, it would not hinder it. For him, the issue was, rather,

> in what way, either by joining or not joining, are we most likely to preserve the independence of this country? That is really the net question. Is the independence and freedom to which we aspire for the whole country likely to be better guaranteed by our being a member of this organisation or by our not being a member of it?[4]

A related issue that he raised was whether joining the new organisation or staying out would better help to preserve an independent Ireland's capacity to remain neutral in war. The preservation of Ireland's neutral status had been his central preoccupation for the previous seven years, but he understood quite clearly that, in time of war, it was not enough for a small country simply to declare itself a neutral:

> Our people sincerely desire to remain out of war. I am perfectly convinced of that. The question they have to ask themselves now and the question we here have to ask ourselves is: are we more likely to keep out of war by joining an organisation of this sort, or are we more likely to keep out of war by remaining outside such an organisation?
> … We should bear in mind that it is not sufficient for a nation to wish to remain out of a war, that, even though they may wish it sincerely and though they may declare their neutrality and do everything in their power to maintain that neutrality, yet that does not prevent them from being attacked.

His belief that Ireland as a Member State of the UN would be better able to stay out of war is somewhat at odds with the detailed explanation that he gave to the Dáil in that same speech of the

---

4   This and following quotations are from Moynihan (1980) pp. 484–490.

commitments that membership could involve. He was realistic and honest enough to recognise that it could involve the country in forceful collective action – indeed in war – at some future date, and he wanted Irish people to be aware of this:

> our people should realise that, when we enter into an organisation of this sort, we are committing ourselves to take collective action with other people. The difference between a war such as may arise under the obligations of the Charter and other wars is this: that that type of war would be a war of enforcement, enforcement of obligations and also enforcement of rights. If there is ever to be a rule of law, nations must make up their minds that they will take part in such enforcement, because, if there is not enforcement, then, of course, the duties and the rights that are guaranteed will all be thrown aside.
>
> … the difficulties generally in building up an organisation of this sort, lie in the fact that there seems to be a kind of dilemma involved. You have to face the waging of war in order to prevent war. It seems a strange thing, but there is no way of enforcement against large nations, particularly enforcement of the rule of law, except by military action, which means war. Therefore, when you enter an organisation of this sort, if you enter it with any hope that it will be successful, you must enter into it with the firm conviction that, if enforcement is to be effective, it has to be achieved by the loyal co-operation of all the members and by you also doing your part.

He was clear, too, about the limitations of the new organisation, and he was realistic in his view of the need to live with its shortcomings, including the right of veto that it would grant to the five Permanent Members of the Security Council:

I have to admit that possibly it is as good as can be got at the moment. If one of the great powers says 'We will not enter this organisation unless on the condition that we have a right of veto', what can you do? You start with the best you can get.

De Valera's willingness in July 1946 to live with the limitations of the new organisation is in contrast to the much more critical view that he had taken a relatively short time before. In a Dáil speech on 26 June 1946, he compared the UN unfavourably with the League of Nations; and in November 1944, after the Dumbarton Oaks proposals became public, he said that what was being substituted for the League was 'a dictatorship of the great powers'.[5]

Now, however, despite what he called the 'defects' of the UN, he was hopeful about the future – and indeed prescient, in some respects at least, in his view of how the organisation would develop:

My own hope is that this organisation will ultimately embrace all the nations, both those who were on one side and those who were on the other, and that we will really have a world organisation of the large states and the small states, with no discrimination against peoples ...

I have quoted at some length from de Valera's speech to the Dáil over sixty years ago because I think it was a very clear-eyed assessment, at a very early stage, of both the new United Nations organisation itself and what Ireland's membership could entail; and it was an assessment that the Dáil seems to have accepted in voting in principle to approve the application for membership. But none of the reasons that I have quoted so far seems to me to be a wholly adequate answer to the question I have raised: having persevered so strongly in maintaining its neutrality for six years of war, why should Ireland,

---

5   I draw here on an interesting 1986 essay by Professor Ronan Fanning on the attitude of Britain and of the US at this period to the Irish application for UN membership. See Fanning, 'The Anglo-American alliance and the Irish application for membership of the United Nations', pp. 35–61.

eleven months later, with eyes open, want to join a 'collective security' organisation that would commit it for the future to joining in possible military action to maintain international peace and security?

A more complete answer, I think, is to see the decision not as an inexplicable break with the logic of the country's policy over the previous six years, but rather as evidence of a deeper and much longer-standing continuity that went back to the foundation of the State and beyond. It is true that in his speech to the Dáil, de Valera devoted only two sentences to arguing for the consistency of his approach:

> I am not conscious of any change of mind with regard to this matter of whether we should or should not join a world organisation designed to maintain peace. I have always stood for that.

But de Valera's activities and policies at the League of Nations throughout the 1930s would have been well known to his listeners. So too, indeed, would the active approach of the previous Government in the 1920s. The continuity over those two pre-war decades had not been only that of de Valera himself – it was a characteristic of the State as such from its earliest days.

Already, even before Irish independence was recognised, the First Dáil, in its *Message to the Free Nations of the World* of 21 January 1919, had raised the issue of membership of the new international organisation that was being planned at that very moment in Versailles. In rather flamboyant language, the Dáil:

> demand[ed] to be confronted publicly with England at the Congress of the Nations, in order that the civilised world having judged between English wrong and Irish right may guarantee to Ireland its permanent support for the maintenance of her national independence.[6]

---

6   See Ronan Fanning *et al.*, *Documents on Irish Foreign Policy 1919–1922*, document no. 2, p. 2.

A month later, Sean T. Ó Ceallaigh, 'the accredited envoy of the Provisional Government of the Irish Republic' wrote in a more diplomatic tone to the French Prime Minister, Georges Clemenceau:

> Accordingly, I have the honour, Sir, to beg you to be good enough to fix a date to receive the delegates above-named, who are anxious for the earliest possible opportunity to establish formally and definitely before the Peace Conference and the League of Nations Commission now assembled in Paris, Ireland's indisputable right to international recognition for her Independence and the propriety of her claim to enter the League of Nations as one of its constituent members.[7]

Since the League was not yet in existence, this must be seen as a very early request indeed for Irish membership. The Peace Conference at Versailles had opened just the month before, and the final text of what was to become the League of Nations Covenant was not agreed until two months later – on 28 April 1919. At this stage, the primary interest of the Dáil and its envoy in Paris seems to have been in the use that might be made of membership of the new organisation as a way of gaining international recognition for Irish independence.[8]

Unfortunately for Ó Ceallaigh and Irish Republican aspirations at the time, US President Woodrow Wilson, the most important leader at the Peace Conference, refused to meet the Irish Delegation, despite pressure from Irish-America. His refusal played some part later in increasing the opposition to the Peace Treaty in the US Senate. The other Great Powers took a similar position. As Dr

---

7   Ibid., document no. 4, p. 5.
8   'Sinn Féin hoped to gain legitimacy for their actions in Ireland and to publicise their case abroad through the League of Nations. Ireland's position within the League was not considered; it was the League's use to Ireland that conditioned Sinn Féin's approach to the new world organisation' (Michael Kennedy, *Ireland and the League of Nations 1919–1946*, p. 19).

Michael Kennedy puts it in his study of Ireland's role at the League of Nations, 'The Great Powers were at Paris to deal with the defeated Alliance powers. No favourable notice was given to the Irish Delegation. The Irish manoeuvres were an irrelevant distraction to the Great Powers and ended in failure.'[9]

Nevertheless, despite that rebuff from the Allies in Paris, the first Dáil passed a resolution on 11 April 1919 expressing Ireland's readiness 'to enter a World League of Nations based on equality of rights' and 'to accept all the duties, responsibilities and burdens which inclusion in such a League implies'. This sounded very positive indeed, but it was a qualified commitment to a League of a particular kind: it seems from a speech in that Dáil debate by its President, Éamon de Valera, that the resolution did not necessarily commit the Dáil to support the actual League as it seemed to be emerging at that time. Unfortunately, the verbatim minutes of the Dáil debate for that day no longer exist, but according to a contemporaneous report in the *Irish Independent* that seems to have been accepted as authoritative, de Valera told the Dáil that:

> They were ready to enter any League of Nations in which each nation would be under the obligation not to resort to arms against another nation in the League without first submitting the matter at issue to a court of arbitration. But they were not prepared to enter the League as it was appearing at present.[10]

The negotiations at Versailles on the League, chaired by Woodrow Wilson himself, still had some weeks to run at this point and the detailed shape of the League was not yet settled. It would be too much to suppose that Wilson knew of de Valera's speech and took it to heart. After all, the speech was made in Dublin and delivered

9   Ibid.
10   See Moynihan (1980) p. 26. A footnote in that book reads as follows: 'In the Dáil *Minutes of Proceedings* (p.71) a note on the record for 11 April 1919 states: "The minutes of the proceedings of this day were destroyed owing to enemy action." The text which follows is a press report from *The Irish Independent* of 12 April 1919.'"

in Irish. Nevertheless, the text of the Covenant that was eventually pushed through by Wilson at the Peace Conference in Versailles on 28 April 1919 did indeed meet de Valera's point to a remarkable degree. One Article required Member States of the League to submit 'any dispute likely to lead to a rupture ... either to arbitration, or judicial settlement or to enquiry by the Council' and not 'to resort to war' until three months after the award, or decision, or report by the Council.[11]

Over the following years, Ireland was preoccupied at home, first with the independence struggle and then with the civil war. However, the question of possible membership of the League, and the help that this might give in consolidating independence, was not forgotten. Erskine Childers mentioned it, for example, in a memorandum on Irish defence that he drafted in late July 1921 in the interval between the calling of the Truce and the opening of the Treaty negotiations.[12] The issue continued to be a subject of internal discussion and of memoranda when the Free State Government was formed. Eventually, following a debate and the passage of a Bill in both Dáil and Seanad, the new Government applied formally for admission to the League. On 10 September 1923 its application was approved unanimously by the League Assembly.[13]

In his speech of thanks to the Assembly on that day, the President of the Executive Council of the Irish Free State, William T. Cosgrave – understandably, perhaps – allowed himself some high-flown, not to say exaggerated, rhetoric:

Ireland has to-day formally, yet none the less practically, entered into a new bond of union with her sister nations, great and small, who are represented in this magnificent world concourse ... [Ireland] joins to-day in a solemn covenant to exercise the powers of her sovereign status in promoting the

11   Article 12.1 of the Covenant of the League of Nations.
12   Fanning *et al.* (1998) p. 243.
13   See the very detailed account given in Kennedy (1996) pp. 18–42.

peace, security and happiness, the economic, cultural and moral well-being of the human race.[14]

Irish representatives may not have spoken too often again in the Assembly about 'the well-being of the human race', but certainly, once admitted to membership, the Irish Free State did play an active role in the affairs of the League. Its interest in the League as a way of gaining and consolidating international recognition for Irish independence remained. But the approach of Irish representatives in Geneva went well beyond that: over the remaining two decades of the active life of the League they cooperated closely with other small countries and showed a genuine interest in working to achieve the fundamental aim set out in the Preamble to the Covenant – 'to promote international cooperation and to achieve international peace and security'. The resources and personnel devoted to the permanent office maintained at the League headquarters in Geneva through the 1920s were limited, not to say tiny: this was in keeping with the parsimonious approach of the new State to foreign relations at the time. But nevertheless the Government did take membership of the League seriously: it was normal practice for senior Government Ministers to travel – overland, as they had to at the time – to attend sessions of the Assembly in Geneva each year. Once there, they took an active and positive approach to the work of the League.[15]

Membership of the League offered an opportunity – the first ever – for an independent, recognised Irish State to play a part on the international stage. So it is easy to understand why, notwithstanding the limited resources available, Irish representatives should have wanted to avail of it to the full.

In the Introduction I suggested that the attitudes and the rhetoric of a nation are formed by its particular historical experience. Some

---

14   Ronan Fanning *et al.*, *Documents on Irish Foreign Policy 1923–1926*, p. 156.

15   Dr Michael Kennedy, in Appendix 3 on pp. 267–270 of his book *Ireland and the League of Nations 1919–1946*, gives a complete list of the members of the Irish Delegation for each year from 1923, when the Irish Free State was admitted, to 1946, when the League was formally wound up.

large countries, whose peoples had a dominant role in European or world history, still retain a sense of past glories and triumphs; Irish people, on the other hand – or at least the Irish nationalist majority in the island – have tended to see themselves as a submerged people seeking to assert their identity and autonomy, and looking for international support in the struggle to do so. The realities of Irish history are, of course, more complex, but this general perception meant that a language and rhetoric of 'rights', and of international morality, came naturally to the founders of the State – as did a belief in the right of other peoples to self-determination. These ideas chimed well with the more moral approach to international relations in the post-First World War years, which, under the influence of President Woodrow Wilson, was embodied in the Covenant of the League.

Sean Lester, who succeeded Michael MacWhite in 1929 as Irish Representative to the League, became in his turn a highly respected figure in Geneva. In 1934 he was appointed to the very difficult and politically sensitive post of High Commissioner for the Free City of Danzig (now Gdansk), which was administered by the League at the time.[16] Later, he was Acting Secretary General of the League. Through the terrible years of the Second World War, as leader of a shrunken Secretariat staff in Geneva, he nursed its dying flame while Europe tore itself apart. When the League was eventually wound up in 1946 he was made Secretary General, retrospectively, with effect from September 1940.[17]

Fianna Fáil came into Government at home in 1932 and its leader, Éamon de Valera, continued the positive and active approach to

---

16   Elmer Bendiner, in his book *A Time for Angels: the Tragicomic History of the League of Nations* (p. 135), describes it as 'destined to be a small depot of political dynamite'. He refers later (p. 334) to Lester as 'the quiet but courageous Irish diplomat'. Michael Kennedy in his book *Ireland and the League of Nations 1919–1946* (p. 104) criticises the decision to replace MacWhite, 'an experienced diplomat with widespread connections' by Lester, 'a man who, on his own account, had little experience with foreign relations and foreign languages'. However, he recognises that 'That is not to fault Lester, who held the League together during World War II'.

17   Douglas Gageby, *The Last Secretary General: Sean Lester and the League of Nations*, p. 251.

membership of the League. The previous Government had presented the candidacy of the Free State for election to the League
Council in 1926, but it was not successful. It renewed its candidacy
in 1930, and on this occasion the Irish Free State, as it was still
known, was elected to serve a term as a non-permanent member of
the Council.[18] At the time of the election, the Cumann na nGaedheal
Government of William T. Cosgrave was still in power. However,
with the change of Government at home in March 1932, it fell to de
Valera, who was now President of the Executive Council and
Minister for External Affairs, to take the seat on the League Council
during the later part of Free State's term of membership. It was a
role that brought him to prominence in Geneva.

This was a fraught time for the League because of events in the
Far East. De Valera, as an important leader in the Irish struggle for
independence, had already attracted international attention more
than a decade before. Now, as the newly elected leader of an Irish
Government, taking office just ten years after a civil war, he was
again a figure of international interest when he came to Geneva to
take the Irish seat. This interest increased greatly when he delivered
a major speech to the opening session of the Assembly in September
1932. Speaking in his capacity as both President of the Council and
acting President of the Assembly, he warned that:

> the only alternative to competitive armaments is the security
> for national rights such as uncompromising adherence to the
> principles of the Covenant will afford. The avoidance of wars
> and of the burden of preparatory armaments is of such concern
> to humanity that no state should be permitted to jeopardise
> the common interest by selfish action contrary to the
> Covenant, and no State is powerful enough to stand for long
> against the League if the Governments in the League and their
> people are determined that the Covenant shall be upheld.[19]

18 The Irish Free State, with 36 votes, came third behind Guatemala (41) and Norway
    (38). It defeated Portugal, which received only 30 votes. See Kennedy (1996) p. 147.
19 Moynihan (1980) p. 221.

We have become used to this kind of language in speeches by world leaders today in the UN and elsewhere, and we may perhaps be inclined to discount it somewhat as worthy rhetoric and nothing more. But de Valera's words had a particular significance for those who heard them that day in Geneva. Japan was then in the process of overrunning Manchuria, which it subsequently annexed from China; and it had launched a naval bombardment of Shanghai. For the first time, a Great Power, a Permanent Member of the Council of the League, had attacked a fellow Member State in what appeared to be a clear breach of the Covenant. The League was facing its greatest test and, as President of the Council at the time, de Valera had to preside over its sessions during the most serious crisis it had faced since its foundation. So the question that he addressed to all Member States gathered together in the Assembly was highly significant. It was this: were the Member States of the League now willing to act, forcefully if necessary, to uphold the Covenant against an attack on its fundamental principles by a Permanent Member of its own highest Council? There could be no more serious test of the integrity of the League and of the willingness of Member States to carry through the concept of 'collective security' that it had been intended to embody.

The League faltered in its response to this crisis, unwilling or unable to uphold the fundamental principle on which it was based. It failed again to meet a similar challenge two years later when Italy, another Permanent Member of the Council, attacked and then annexed Abyssinia (now Ethiopia), a fellow Member of the League. De Valera's position on this later crisis involving Italy is of particular interest. Looked at closely, it helps to resolve the apparent paradox I touched on earlier because it shows that there was an underlying continuity of policy, or at least of logic, between his approach to the League in the 1930s, his tenacious effort to maintain Irish neutrality during the war years, and his decision to apply for Irish membership of the new collective security organisation in 1946.

It is particularly interesting that, in his speech on 25 July 1946 in the Dáil debate on UN membership from which I quoted above, de

Valera stated quite explicitly that if the League had decided on military action against Italy in 1936 after its attack on Abyssinia, it would have been Ireland's duty to play a part in that action, notwithstanding its closer cultural ties with Italy. This explicit statement by the leader of an Irish Government of willingness to join in forceful military action abroad against another country is unique in the history of the State. It is worth quoting at some length what he said on this point:

> At the time of the attack on Abyssinia, against the clear obligations of the states in the old League, there was a question of whether military action would be taken or not. It might have happened that the League at that time would have decided on military action, and if military action had been decided on – I admit it would have been difficult within the organisation – it would have been our duty to play our part in that action. That was going to be a very serious matter here, because of the fact that, in the one case, the nation against which action had to be taken was a nation which was culturally associated with ours over a long period, and the nation on whose behalf we would have had to take action was a nation which was unknown to us.
>
> That matter was going to be extremely difficult here, but, if we were to play our part as a nation, it would have been our duty to participate in that action. I do not know whether I would have been able to get a majority in the House in favour of it, and what I am trying to do now is to ensure that, whoever may be in this seat, if ever an occasion arises involving the question of the fulfilment of our obligations under that Charter [i.e. the UN Charter], if ever such a day comes, that, in advance, our people will be fortified by the knowledge that it is their duty to fulfil them and that they will not be taken by surprise in having to deal with a situation of that sort.[20]

---

20 Moynihan (1980) p. 489.

This statement in 1946, taken in conjunction with his various statements in the League in the 1930s and his speeches in 1939 when war in Europe seemed imminent, shows a continuity in de Valera's underlying policy approach over the whole of this twenty-year period.[21]

Nowadays we may think the United Nations important but we do not, for the most part, see it as central to Ireland's national security. There is a different tone to de Valera's speeches in the 1930s. As one of the founders of the Irish State, he was preoccupied throughout his life with the fundamental 'existential' questions of sovereignty and independence; and, as I explained earlier, during the 1930s he did seem to look on the League, and the concept of collective security that it embodied, as an international guarantor of the sovereign independence of all small States. As he saw it, this was a reason for Ireland, a small State still concerned about international recognition for its independence, to put its trust in the concept of collective security and to do everything possible to support the League and make it work. To uphold this principle, he would even have been ready to take the State – at that time not yet two decades old – into collective military action against Italy, a country with which, historically, Ireland had had close ties. In the latter part of the 1930s, however, it became evident to him that the collective security organisation in which he been prepared to put his trust had failed. This created a new situation. At such a time, he must have felt, each State had no alternative but to look to its own interest and to protect itself as best it could; Ireland's security interest dictated that, in the coming war, it pursue a policy of military neutrality for as long as that policy could be sustained.

---

21   This is also the view taken by Joseph Skelly in his 1996 paper 'Ireland, the Department of External Affairs and the United Nations 1946–55: a New Look' (1996). In that paper (p. 69) he says, 'Behind his mask of public indifference, de Valera strongly endorsed Ireland's entry into the United Nations. In fact, the decision to seek UN membership marked his reassertion of an Irish commitment to international organisations and involvement in international affairs temporarily interrupted by war-time neutrality.'

By 1946, however, the war was over; the clouds were clearing; and out of the rubble a new effort was being made to construct another international organisation based on the principle of collective security. This time all the major powers, including the United States, were founding members and there was a correspondingly greater prospect that it would prove lasting and effective. So, as de Valera would have seen it, there was a fundamental consistency and continuity in his decision to propose to the Dáil that it authorise the Government to apply for membership. As he put it succinctly in that speech to the Dáil in July 1946 from which I have already quoted:

> I am not conscious of any change of mind with regard to this matter of whether we should or should not join a world organisation designed to maintain peace. I have always stood for that.[22]

I have dwelt here on this underlying continuity in de Valera's approach because it seems to me to have carried through into Ireland's attitude to the UN in the late 1950s, particularly while Frank Aiken was Minister. I will deal with that in later chapters. But before I do so, there are two other questions about de Valera's decision to apply for UN membership in 1946 that seem to me worth considering briefly here.

One is why, granted all I have said, should de Valera still have delayed for nearly a year before deciding to apply for Irish membership of the new organisation?

The answer is obvious enough if one thinks of the atmosphere immediately after the war. Victors in war do not always show great tolerance for those who remained aloof while the conflict was under way; many people in Britain took a sour view of Ireland's neutral stance. Flushed with victory, if nothing else, Churchill in a victory broadcast had spoken of the possibility of having been 'forced to

---

22   See above. The quotation is from Moynihan (1980) p. 488.

come to close quarters with Mr. de Valera', though in the event Britain had 'left the de Valera Government to frolic with the German and later with the Japanese representatives to their heart's content'.[23] De Valera, prudently, had made a carefully restrained reply. For that first year after the UN was founded, de Valera must have had reason to believe that an application by Ireland to join the United Nations would not have been well received by the Allied States which were the founding members of the new organisation.

Some years ago, in an essay in the journal *Irish Studies in International Affairs*, Professor Ronan Fanning gave an interesting account of his research in the US archives on this issue.[24] He quotes 'a prescient analysis of de Valera's position' given in an internal US State Department memorandum of 29 April 1946 that noted that de Valera would 'in no event apply for membership without the advance assurance that it will be approved, for he would not dare risk a rebuff'.

Clearly it was only once he had satisfied himself that any residual hostility by Britain and the US based on Irish neutrality during the years of war had abated that de Valera arranged the Dáil debate of July 1946 and, then, with the approval of the Dáil, submitted Ireland's application for UN membership. We must assume that he was surprised to find that British and American attitudes were not the only hurdle: the application was vetoed by the Soviet Union. He can hardly have reckoned on that.

This raises yet another question: why should the Soviet Union have blocked Irish membership and maintained that position for the next nine years? The answer in part is that, as I have already explained, Ireland was not the only country to be blocked. It was caught up in an East–West stand-off. The policies of 'competitive exclusion' adopted by both the US and the Soviet Union meant that, as one writer on the UN puts it, 'the League [of Nations] problem

---

23   Arthur Mitchell and Pádraig Ó Snodaigh, *Irish Political Documents 1916–1949*, p. 239. See also Tim Pat Coogan, *De Valera: Long Fellow, Long Shadow*, p. 611.
24   Fanning (1986) pp. 35–61.

of empty chairs in the chamber had been succeeded in the United Nations by the problem of over-crowding in the vestibule.'[25] But why was Ireland in particular among those blocked by the Soviet Union? Research in the Russian archives might help to answer that question in detail. Short of that, however, we can speculate. The reasons probably included not only Ireland's neutrality in the recent war but its lack of diplomatic relations with the Soviet Union,[26] as well as the perception that, if admitted, Ireland was likely to take a 'pro-Western' line and support US positions in the Assembly.

So Ireland had to wait: it was to be nine more years before it was finally admitted to membership. This happened eventually toward the end of 1955 as part of a deal that eventually broke the logjam and brought in sixteen countries in all. So finally, on 14 December 1955 – just as the General Assembly session was drawing to a close – the Irish Consul General Jack Conway, as the nearest resident Irish representative available, walked up the aisle of the Assembly hall to take a place behind the nameplate of Ireland that the UN staff had just put in place for the occasion.

Ireland was now, formally, a Member State of the United Nations but the Assembly session was nearly over. It was only at the following session, eleven months later, that an Irish Minister for External Affairs took the Irish seat and addressed the Assembly for

---

25 See Claude (1964) p. 84: 'The Soviet Union acted to prevent the admission of non-Communist candidates unless its own protégés were simultaneously accepted; it aimed not to exclude the Western group but to secure admission of both groups. The United States, on the other hand, was determined to exclude the Soviet group even at the expense of the ambitions for membership of states acceptable to the West. While the Soviet Union was prepared to admit both groups, to get its own candidates in, the United States was willing to have both groups rejected, to keep Soviet candidates out.'

26 Formal diplomatic relations were not established between the two countries until 1973, although of course they maintained diplomatic contact through their respective Permanent Representations to the UN in New York. It is of interest that, despite the lack of formal diplomatic relations, Frank Aiken, the Minister for External Affairs, travelled to Moscow in 1968 to sign the Nuclear Non-Proliferation Treaty which he had long advocated – see Chapter 6 below.

the first time.[27] By what may have seemed a happy chance, the Minister who did so was Liam Cosgrave, the son of William T. Cosgrave, who, as President of the Executive Council of the Irish Free State, had taken the Irish seat for the first time in the Assembly of the League of Nations thirty-three years before – on 10 September 1923. Neither he nor, indeed, Frank Aiken, who succeeded him as Minister a year later, was given to overblown rhetoric. Had he been, Cosgrave might well have been tempted to echo what his father said on that earlier occasion and say that Ireland had now again

> entered into a new bond of union with her sister nations, great and small ... represented in this magnificent world concourse.

Once again, he might have added, using his father's words, Ireland had joined:

> in a solemn covenant to exercise the powers of her sovereign status in promoting the peace, security and happiness, the economic, cultural and moral well-being of the human race.[28]

So Ireland was now a Member State of the UN. Just over three years later I joined the Department of External Affairs as a very junior diplomat and was assigned to the Political and UN section of the Department.

---

27 The annual session of the General Assembly usually begins in September. It appears that in 1956, however, the opening of the regular session was deferred until November because of the Presidential election in the US. Emergency Special Sessions were convened in late October and early November in response to the virtually simultaneous crises over Suez and Hungary.

28 Fanning *et al.* (2000) p. 156.

2

Personalities of the early years

For older Irish people who take an interest in the United Nations, there is still a glow around the first five years of Ireland's membership: they tend to see the period from 1956 to 1960 as a kind of 'golden age' against which everything that followed should be measured.

There is a degree of truth in this. It happened in part because of the opportunities offered by the rather different character, composition and relative importance of the General Assembly at that time; and in part because of the *élan* that the small Irish Delegation brought to what was in effect Ireland's re-entry on the international stage after the relative isolation of the war years. But it must also be said that the crucial aspect that elevated their words and actions at the three-month annual session of the Assembly to almost mythic status was the fact that, for many years afterwards, the only account of that time publicly available was that given by the distinguished writer, historian and later politician, Conor Cruise O'Brien. As a middle-level official in the Department of External Affairs with the ear of the Minister, he was both a leading figure in the Irish Delegation and, later, a chronicler of what it achieved. So it was he who wrote the record.

As I explained in the Introduction, I joined the Department of External Affairs, as it was called then, in January 1960, early enough to be enveloped in the glow before it slowly faded over the rest of the decade; and I had the good fortune to be assigned to work in the small Political and UN section for which Conor was responsible.[1]

To paraphrase Patrick Kavanagh, that was the year of the Congo bother. It was also the year of Freddie Boland's election to the Presidency of the General Assembly; a year when important world leaders took the Assembly seriously enough to travel to New York for the early weeks of the session – Eisenhower, Harold Macmillan and Fidel Castro among many others – and the year when the sound of Nikita Khrushchev banging his shoe on the desk in the Assembly in protest at a ruling by Boland made world news. A heady time indeed for the most junior entrant, left at home to mind the section alone that autumn while his seniors left for New York to join the staff of three or four diplomats based there to make up the small Irish Delegation to the annual session of the General Assembly.

I still have warm memories of that time. I had a great sense of pride in what Ireland was doing at the UN and a sense of having been allowed to join in a small way in a great and absorbing adventure. For me, there is also a kind of projection of memory backwards even to the years before I joined the Department. In the few small rooms that the UN section occupied in Iveagh House I listened to the discussions, the jokes and the sardonic comments of my senior colleagues; I knew the files; and I read and re-read the published speeches of the Minister and the speeches that other members of the delegation had delivered in the General Assembly or its Committees in earlier years. I almost came to feel that I, too, had been part of all of that.

I think now that at the time I almost came to believe the opening words of a leading article in *The Economist* in the autumn of that year. Under the heading 'The Afro-Irish Assembly', it began 'Ireland bestrides the UN like a colossus' and went on to chronicle the role

---

1   As I explained in the Introduction, my senior colleague and mentor in the section was Bob McDonagh. We both worked to the late Paul Keating, a First Secretary, as our immediate superior; and through him to Conor, who was a Counsellor. I learned a lot from all three.

that the Irish Delegation was playing in New York. Not even *The Skibbereen Eagle* in its heyday would have gone so far.

A year later, in September 1961, I myself was sent to New York as the most junior member of the Irish Delegation to that year's session of the UN General Assembly. We arrived to a UN in crisis. On the very night we arrived, the Secretary General, Dag Hammarskjöld, was killed in an air crash on his way to the Congolese province of Katanga, to deal with the difficult and confused situation in which the UN peacekeeping force had found itself there. I will talk of this in greater detail in later chapters.

Having lived the events and themes of Ireland's earlier UN years – albeit vicariously, through the files and the speeches – I had come to expect that others would look to us for advice and leadership; and that, even if we did not quite live up to *The Economist*'s billing, our delegation would still have a central role in the work of the Assembly. The reality proved rather different. Ireland was a small Member State – respected, yes, but no colossus. Other delegations had their own ideas and interests and were well able to manage their own affairs. For me, the golden glow began to fade – very slightly. But it never quite disappeared; and looking back even today, I still see those early years of Irish UN membership as a time of heightened reality.

Over a further period of four years in the second half of the 1960s, I spent three months in New York each autumn as a member of the Irish Delegation to the annual sessions of the UN General Assembly. Frank Aiken was still Minister for External Affairs and leader of the delegation for three of those years, a respected if unusual figure in the Assembly and its Committees. By then, however, he had begun to come under criticism at home for having failed to live up to the high standard that he himself had set in the 'golden age'.

Was this fair? Was there really a substantial change of policy by Ireland and by Aiken himself at the United Nations in the latter part of the 1960s – on apartheid, on colonial issues, on disarmament, and on all the other issues on which his approach had earned great credit for Ireland in the late 1950s? Drawing on memories from the period I have referred to, and on the lore of the UN section that I absorbed when I joined it in early 1960, I think I can offer a reasonably informed view.

To start with, it is necessary to understand that the UN General Assembly in 1956 when the Irish Delegation took its seat was very different from what it is today. The Cold War was then at its height and votes in the Assembly were taken rather more seriously by the major powers than they have been at any time since. At times the Assembly became an arena for rhetorical combat between 'East' and 'West' – a contest to which both attached some importance. In a book about the UN as he observed it in those years, Conor Cruise O'Brien talked about the useful function it fulfils in providing a stage for the enactment of 'Sacred Drama'.[2] By that he meant that the organisation can help to avert bloodshed at times by serving as an arena, or rather a theatre, where countries in conflict can act out their conflicts ritually instead of engaging in real war. The UN can still exercise that function at times even today. The drama that leads to a kind of catharsis is more likely nowadays to be acted out on the smaller, more intense stage of the Security Council, but in the Cold War years of the 1950s and early 1960s it was often the General Assembly that served that function. Today, some of the more cynical critics of the whole UN structure would be inclined, wrongly, to dismiss the Assembly as little more than a temple of the winds.

The fact that a majority of the Member States at the time were grouped into two rival blocs, and the fact that the respective leaders of those blocs, the Soviet Union and the United States, tended to take the rhetorical battles in the Assembly rather seriously, gave a handful of small and medium-sized countries a real, though limited, opportunity to play a helpful role. Countries outside either alliance, such as Sweden and Tunisia, and countries that were

---

2   Conor Cruise O'Brien (text) and Felix Topolski (illustrations), *The United Nations: Sacred Drama.*

members of alliances but were prepared at times to show a degree of independence, such as Poland, Norway and Canada, could help to soften the asperities of the Cold War as reflected in General Assembly debates and resolutions. These countries did not constitute an organised group or have any general agreement to act in concert – they simply thought of themselves as 'good UN members', willing to cooperate on particular issues with a small number of other countries who were committed, like themselves, to making the system work. Ireland as a new Member State readily identified itself with this approach.

A further notable difference between then and now was the virtual absence of sub-Saharan Africa from the General Assembly. The great wave of decolonisation, driven by what Harold Macmillan, speaking in South Africa in 1960, had called 'the wind of change', had not yet gathered force. When Ireland was admitted to the UN at the end of 1955, there were far fewer countries from the developing world in the organisation than there are today. Much of Africa was still under European colonial rule. Indeed, apart from South Africa – which, although criticised for its apartheid system, had not yet become a complete pariah – only two countries of sub-Saharan Africa, Ethiopia and Liberia, were UN members. The Bandung Conference of 1955, which marked the start of a self-conscious Non-Aligned Movement under the leadership of Yugoslavia, India and Indonesia, had just taken place but the concept of 'non-alignment' was still regarded with suspicion by states committed to the respective alliances on either side of the Cold War. The 'West', led by the USA, could count with reasonable assurance on a majority, even a two-thirds majority, in the Assembly on many issues. 'Western' influence extended also to some degree to the UN Secretariat. On occasion, Dag Hammarskjöld and, in the 1960s, his successor as Secretary General, U Thant, showed an admirable degree of independence, tempered with caution. But, they also knew, as Conor Cruise O'Brien puts it, that it was almost certainly true that any Secretary General who lost the confidence of Washington would have to resign. A storm from the East can be weathered, although with difficulty; a storm from the West could probably not be weathered at all.[3]

In an Assembly such as this, Ireland as a new UN member state felt itself to be in something of a special position. It was a European state with friendly relations with its European neighbours. But its representatives at the UN, like most Irish people at home, thought of Ireland also as a submerged nation that had emerged to independence after a long struggle – in effect the first colony to shake off foreign domination in the twentieth century. When the opportunity arose they felt entitled to draw on that sense of Ireland's own history to speak out strongly against colonialism and in favour of self-determination for other suppressed peoples.

I speak of the 'sense' of Ireland's own history because – as I suggested in the Introduction – for us, as for other nations, what really matters is the narrative we construct from those aspects of our complex past that we choose to remember. There are times when the history may have to be tweaked, ever so slightly, to fit the narrative. Consider the curious case of Charles Stewart Parnell and the Afro-Asians (the term used at the UN in the 1960s to refer to what later came to be called the Third World).

In May 1960 Kwame Nkrumah, the President of Ghana, one of the first African countries to achieve independence from colonial rule, visited Dublin. Since we had few such international visitors at the time, this was an important occasion. Some weeks beforehand, Conor Cruise O'Brien sent me over to the National Library to do some research. In particular I was to find a suitable quotation from Parnell that would show that he abhorred colonialism. Sadly, I couldn't – I had to report back to Conor that Parnell just didn't seem to have said anything useful on the subject. But I did bring him back a note on a kind of programme policy that one of Parnell's

---

3   Conor Cruise O'Brien, *To Katanga and Back: A UN Case History*, p. 56.

associates, Henry Harrison MP, had proposed the Irish Parliamentary Party should follow. One of these policies was 'the cause of nationality is sacred, in Asia and in Africa as in Ireland'.

Nkrumah duly arrived and at the official dinner in his honour he made a well-received speech. To the surprise of his audience he quoted Harrison's maxim as evidence of Ireland's historic sympathy for Africa. An editorial writer in *The Irish Times* next day was impressed that an African statesman should have such a detailed knowledge of Irish history. So far, so good.

Some months later, the Minister, Frank Aiken, in a speech to the UN General Assembly again quoted Harrison's maxim – but this time as a principle proclaimed by 'the then leader of the Irish nation, Charles Stewart Parnell' which 'is still a basic principle of our political thinking in Ireland today'. A few years later, the Taoiseach, Sean Lemass, in an address to the General Assembly again attributed the quotation to Parnell.

There is, I suggest, only one conclusion to draw from all of this: if Parnell didn't say that, then he *should* have said it. And who am I anyway to say that he didn't?

Whatever about Parnell and colonialism, after the relative isolation of the war years and some experience in the early 1950s in the more limited arena offered by the Council of Europe, there was a sense of exhilaration for the Irish Delegation as they took their places in the General Assembly, and a belief that Ireland could play a useful role on the wider international stage.

Over this period Irish speeches in debates made occasional references to the partition of Ireland, and Irish delegates responded with disapproval to any suggestion that a similar measure might help to resolve problems elsewhere. In 1957, in one of his earliest speeches to General Assembly, the Minister for External Affairs, Frank Aiken, was more explicit. He spoke of his belief that:

Our own outstanding problem – the division of our country
– must eventually be solved by the practical application of the

principles of the Charter and specifically the principle of self-determination of peoples. We have never ceased to demand the application of that principle in our own, as well as in other cases, and from it we have nothing to fear. Indeed it would be useless to deny that in joining this Organisation, the hope that our action might advance the attainment of this end, was present in our minds.[4]

It may have been 'present in our minds' as he said. But the Irish Delegation made no direct attempt to raise the partition of Ireland as an issue in the Assembly. I will refer later to an exchange of memoranda in 1958 in which Conor Cruise O'Brien in the Department in Dublin proposed that the Northern Ireland issue should be raised and Freddie Boland, the Permanent Representative in New York, argued trenchantly that it would be counterproductive to do so. Boland's view carried the day and it was not until the approach to the Security Council in August 1969 that I describe in Chapters 10 and 11 that the issue got a full airing at the United Nations.

Liam Cosgrave, as Minister for External Affairs in the Inter-Party Government, led the first Irish Delegation in late 1956 at the fraught General Assembly sessions that debated the Suez crisis and the Soviet suppression of the Hungarian uprising. When that Government lost office at home and Fianna Fáil returned to power, he was succeeded by Frank Aiken, who led the delegation each year from 1957 to 1968.

A good deal has been written about the differing policy approaches of the two ministers. Under Liam Cosgrave, who was in office as Minister for only a single Assembly session, there was undoubtedly a greater emphasis on what the Taoiseach in that Inter-Party Government, John A. Costello, referred to in a memorandum

---

4 Speech by the Minister for External Affairs, Frank Aiken in the General Debate in the UN General Assembly on 20 September 1957. See the first in the series of booklets of his speeches at the UN that was published annually by the Department of External Affairs, Dublin (1957) – *Éire ag na Náisiúin Aontaithe: Ireland at the United Nations*, pp. 23–24.

to the Government on foreign policy in 1956 as '[strengthening] the Christian civilisation of which Ireland is a part'.[5] It was somewhat unusual for the Taoiseach rather than the Minister for External Affairs to submit this kind of memorandum to the Government. But as Joseph Morrison Skelly points out in his study of Irish diplomacy at the UN over this period, Costello had been deeply influenced by the welcome he received in American cities during a tour of the United States around the St Patrick's Day period in 1956. He drew very optimistic conclusions from this spring festival of Irish-America about the opportunities that Ireland's newly achieved UN membership could open up, and he wished to tell the Government about this.

Costello's approach in this memorandum 'delineated an anti-communist, western, Christian interpretation of international affairs. It placed Ireland solidly in NATO's political orbit, and left no doubt as to where the government stood *vis-à-vis* the Cold War.'[6] As Skelly describes it, this attitude continued to be reflected in the views of a 'pro-western nucleus' within the Department of External Affairs and the UN Delegation. In addition to the Taoiseach, John A. Costello, and the Minister, Liam Cosgrave, the 'nucleus' he talks about included the Permanent Representative, Ambassador Freddie Boland and a Counsellor, Eamon Kennedy, who were both based in New York, and Con Cremin, the Secretary of the Department at home. In contrast, after the Inter-Party Government left office in March 1957, 'an independent locus coalesced around Eamon de Valera, Frank Aiken ... and Conor Cruise O'Brien.'[7]

This account by Skelly draws very extensively on documents in the archives and on interviews and it must be given great credence for this reason. It fits also – broadly at least – with the account given by Conor Cruise O'Brien, first in his early work *To Katanga and*

---

5   Skelly (1997) p. 32.
6   Ibid., p. 34.
7   Ibid., pp. 19–20.

Back[8] and even more personally and assertively in his later *Memoir*,[9] to which I will refer further in a later chapter.

My own memories do not go back quite this far: I joined the Department in January 1960, three years after the Inter-Party Government left office, and, understandably, as the most junior official following UN issues at that time, I had a more limited view. I knew indeed that there were differences of approach between my seniors. But I certainly did not have a sense that there were clear-cut policy groupings or alliances – I thought of the differences more as a matter of personalities, of differing political instincts and temperaments. It is true, of course, that by then the relatively 'independent' policy outlook of Aiken was in the ascendant; I, and my senior colleagues who worked under Conor's direction in the small section dealing with UN issues, were broadly sympathetic to this approach. At that stage, the emphasis in speeches about Ireland's role at the UN, which we prepared for use by Ministers at home and abroad, was more likely to be on Ireland's capacity to exercise independence of judgement than on its role in 'strengthening … Christian civilisation', as it might well have been under Costello and Cosgrave three years before. Later still, in the 1960s, the approach again became more cautious. By then the pragmatic Sean Lemass, who had succeeded Éamon de Valera as Taoiseach, was looking towards Europe, and Conor Cruise O'Brien had left the Irish Foreign Service – with something of a bang, as I recount in a later chapter.

All this is true. But looking back on this whole period today, from the softening perspective of nearly half a century, I am more inclined to focus on the extent to which, underlying the differences that certainly existed, there was a broad continuity of approach and a persistent belief that a small country like Ireland could, and should, play a constructive role in the United Nations. Indeed, as I suggested in the previous chapter, there seems to me to have been

8   O'Brien (1962).
9   Conor Cruise O'Brien, *Memoir: My Life and Themes.*

a degree of continuity also with the decades before the Second World War when the Irish Free State, as it was then known, followed rather similar policies at the League of Nations.

In the United Nations in 1956, when Liam Cosgrave was Minister, there was undoubtedly a more explicit identification of Ireland with 'the West' than subsequently, during Frank Aiken's twelve years as leader of the delegation. But more striking now to me in retrospect are the underlying similarities over this whole period: the 'moral tone' and the common concern of successive Governments since the foundation of the State – Cumann na nGaedheal in the 1920s, Éamon de Valera's Fianna Fáil in the 1930s, and both the Inter-Party and Fianna Fáil Governments in the 1950s – that Ireland should prove itself to be 'a good international citizen' and help to make the system work.

Liam Cosgrave was Minister for External Affairs in the Inter-Party Government that held office from 1954 to 1957. He was a modest, decent man whom I came to know later in the 1970s when he was Taoiseach and I a more senior official. In November 1956 he became the first Irish Minister to address the UN General Assembly following Ireland's admission to membership. One might almost say that this was a distinction of a kind that seemed to run in the family since, as I noted earlier, his father, as President of the Executive Council (equivalent to 'Taoiseach' today), had been the first Irish Government leader to address the League of Nations after the Irish Free State was admitted to membership in 1923.

According to the account given by Conor Cruise O'Brien, it was he himself who drafted the Minister's speech. The Permanent Representative, Freddie Boland, did not like the first draft he pro-duced, so Conor rewrote it to make it conform more closely to what seemed to be required at the time. Boland approved the revised draft; the Minister, trusting Boland's judgement, accepted it without reservation.[10] The speech was well received at home, as well as by other delegations in the Assembly. But then, a general policy speech

10   O'Brien (1998) pp. 182–183.

of this kind by a visiting Foreign Minister, especially one speaking in the Assembly for the first time, is always the subject of warm congratulations from other delegations seated nearby. Some of these may even be sincere.

The Inter-Party Government lost office in early 1957. Cosgrave was succeeded by Frank Aiken. Since Aiken led the delegation for over twelve years, and a booklet containing the text of his speeches to the General Assembly was published by the Department each year, it is understandable that today it is his name that is most associated with Irish policies at the UN over those early years.

The new Minister took the UN very seriously and travelled to New York to lead the delegation every autumn. As a junior member of the delegation a little later, in 1961 and in the later 1960s over four successive General Assembly sessions, I sat behind him regularly – sometimes in the Assembly and sometimes in Committee – and I came to know him fairly well at that time. He frequently spoke Irish at the start of any conversation but usually reverted to English after five or ten minutes.

Aiken was a taciturn man; a man of great and gritty integrity, conviction and stubbornness; somewhat puritan in outlook and cautious about State expenditure; at heart an engineer with an inventive cast of mind. He had been close to Éamon de Valera since the 1920s and probably even before then. During the 1930s he had been Minister for Defence in de Valera's Government; and, as 'Minister for the Co-ordination of Defensive Measures', he had worked closely with de Valera in the crucial task of maintaining Irish neutrality during the difficult years of the Second World War. He visited Washington, DC in March 1941 to ask for arms that could be used to protect the country from invasion but his visit, and particularly his meeting with President Roosevelt at the White House, went very badly and he came home more or less empty-handed.[11] After the war, from 1945 to 1948 he was Minister for Finance. Over that whole period, de Valera himself was both Taoiseach and

11   Robert Fisk, *In Time of War*, pp. 265–267.

Minister for External Affairs. When Fianna Fáil returned to Government in the 1950s, however, de Valera appointed Aiken, still one of his closest associates, to be Minister for External Affairs – the first person apart from de Valera himself to hold that office in a Fianna Fáil government. Aiken resumed his post as Minister for External Affairs when Fianna Fáil returned to office in 1957 after several years of Inter-Party Government; he remained Minister when de Valera was succeeded as Taoiseach by Sean Lemass and later Jack Lynch. He left office when the Government was reshuffled in mid-1969 and was replaced by Dr Patrick Hillery.

Nowadays the Irish Foreign Minister, like the Foreign Ministers of other countries, would expect to visit New York for a week or two at the start of the annual session of the General Assembly and make one substantial policy statement in the 'General Debate' with which the session opens. He would then leave to deal with other business else-where – in Brussels or at home. In the 1950s and 1960s, however, before the Northern Ireland issue erupted and long before Ireland joined the EU, an Irish Foreign Minister was much less busy than his successor would be today. Aiken liked New York and the ambience of the UN. He also believed the UN to be important – indeed vital for smaller States like Ireland. As Minister, he was willing to spend long periods at the General Assembly each year – longer than any other Foreign Minister, and far longer than any Irish Foreign Minister could possibly afford to spend today. Unlike other Foreign Ministers, who usually came and went, he was prepared to take the delegation seat and speak at Committee meetings as well as at Plenary sessions of the General Assembly if one of the Assembly Committees was dealing with a subject of concern to him. This made him a curious but respected figure even to junior members of other delegations.

The fact that he had been a revolutionary in his youth, now turned elder statesman, gave him a particular stature in the Assembly. He could – and did – recall an era before Ireland's independence was recognised, when there was neither League nor UN to look to for support. On 6 October 1960, for example, speaking in the General Debate that opens each annual session of the General Assembly, he told the delegates:

> In 1913 I became a volunteer in our national revolutionary army. We had few weapons. We armed ourselves largely with the weapons we captured. We fought elections as well as guerrilla battles until we established our government, with the active support of three-fourths of our people ... We had no international forum to appeal to, no United Nations to support our struggle for freedom.

Now, however, as he explained to the Assembly, there was a vital difference – the existence of the United Nations:

> a body in which the small nations have an influence such as they have never before possessed in their history: an influence quite out of proportion to their material power and resources; an influence, moreover, which will disappear if this Organisation should fail ... Against the background of our own fight for recognition, we view with admiration – and almost with incredulity – this Organisation, where every struggling people has its vigorous champions in the Assembly.

The fact that the UN now existed meant, in Aiken's view, that the kind of armed struggle in which he himself had participated in Ireland some forty years previously should no longer be necessary. Peoples seeking self-determination could now look to a more peaceful approach, and the UN must respond:

> one of the most vital tasks of this Organisation is to try to ensure swift and orderly transition towards a new world of free nations. We must help this transition to take place without endangering peace.[12]

---

12   Department of External Affairs (1960) pp. 14–16.

Aiken's ability to refer back to his own personal experience as a guerrilla leader, and the strong anti-colonial stance of the Irish Delegation under his leadership, gave him a particular authority in the eyes of many smaller States when he counselled, as he sometimes did, against resort to 'armed struggle' by national liberation movements seeking independence.

Aiken's almost Roman character and qualities were well supported and complemented by the worldly-wise, sophisticated manner, the gravitas and the wide diplomatic experience of the Permanent Representative, Frederick H. Boland, and by the intellect, the literary talent and the activist instincts of a younger Conor Cruise O'Brien and a number of other talented young Irish diplomats of the time. The interest of the Minister in the work of the Assembly, and the fact that it became a major focus for Irish foreign policy at that time, meant also that the Department of External Affairs assigned some of the best and the brightest young and middle-level officials to serve on the delegation in New York for the three-month session of the General Assembly in autumn each year.

Boland, generally known as 'Freddie' and by his immediate contemporaries as 'Fred', was Permanent Representative – which is to say Ambassador – of Ireland to the UN in New York from 1956 until 1963. In the absence of the Minister he was head of the Irish Delegation. He was supported by a small staff of other, more junior, diplomats based, like him, at the Permanent Mission in New York; and during sessions of the General Assembly by a small number of other diplomats drawn in temporarily from the UN section of the Department in Dublin, and from Irish diplomatic and consular missions abroad.

Boland was the most distinguished Irish diplomat of his time – a weighty and urbane figure who moved with ease through the lounges and corridors of the UN building where information is traded in quiet voices and many of the most important contacts are made. I recall that, as a very junior and naïve diplomat in 1961, I, like others on the delegation, occasionally picked up a snippet of political information and reported it to him. But I was constantly surprised to find that, even if he had been working at his desk in the office, or travelling to a speaking engagement in another US city – as often happened in 1961 because of the fame he gained as President of General Assembly in 1960 – he generally knew what I wanted to tell him, and more, already.[13]

Boland had joined the Department of External Affairs in 1929. He was Assistant Secretary during the war years – a very responsible post at a time when Ireland was hard put to maintain its neutrality. I heard him in relaxed mood after dinner one evening in his apartment in New York recount some interesting anecdotes in relation to Ireland's surprisingly successful counter-espionage effort against spies sent from Germany during the war. Among other things he told us that in February 1947 he had interviewed the German spy Hermann Goertz in jail in Dublin shortly before he committed suicide to avoid being handed over to the Allies.[14] Boland became Secretary of the Department shortly after the end of the war. In 1950 he went to London as Ambassador, and served there until he was appointed to the UN post in June 1956.

Freddie, as I remember him, was a very proper diplomat; which is to say that he seemed to me to be smooth, sophisticated, polished and the soul of discretion. In his biography of Dag Hammarskjöld, Brian Urquhart, who served for decades as a senior figure in the UN Secretariat, includes Boland as one of five representatives of 'middle powers' who, he says, were:

---

13 My junior colleague in the Permanent Mission, the late Brendan Nolan, seemed to have a similarly wide range of contacts. It was always difficult, if one met him in the UN lounges, to have a sustained conversation, as he was constantly being greeted by friends and acquaintances from other delegations.

14 Eunan O'Halpin, in his book *Defending Ireland: The Irish State and Its Enemies since 1922* (p. 204), says that 'G2 [i.e. Irish Army Intelligence] reported directly on all political, subversive, or military matters having any international dimension to the two most senior officials in External Affairs, Joseph Walshe and Fred Boland, whose minister was also the taoiseach.' My memory is that Boland said the interview took place in jail the night before Goertz's suicide, but O'Halpin (p. 277) describes the incident as follows: 'in February 1947 the highly strung Goertz, under a complete misapprehension about the Allied screening to which he would be subjected, and who had an exaggerated idea of his own importance, swallowed poison and died outside the Aliens Office after being informed by the Garda that the government had no choice but to send him home.'

the type of level-headed, widely respected, able, high-minded, and practical men who could provide the support and understanding which alone made it possible to set up and maintain the complex, novel, and difficult mechanisms of UN peacekeeping operations.[15]

He was all of that – a 'sound' man, shrewd and suave with it; 'sleek-headed' enough, in the literal sense at least, to win the approval of Shakespeare's Julius Caesar. An 'insider' in the UN but also, I think it is fair to say, not one to counsel new and adventurous policies.

By the time he was posted to New York, Boland had already had considerable experience of multilateral diplomacy – that is to say of international organisations. For a time in the 1930s he had been head of the League of Nations section in the Department of External Affairs; he was a member of the Irish Delegation to the Assembly of the League in Geneva in 1932 and again in 1934, at a time when he was based in the Irish Legation in Paris.[16] The smoothness of his diplomatic style, displayed internally as well as externally, may be judged from a report he sent home from Geneva on the failure of Éamon de Valera to gain election as President of the League Assembly in 1934:

> In the circumstances, the result may be regarded as highly satisfactory. We had the next best thing to the honour of the Presidency of the Assembly, i.e. the fact of being asked not to run in order to make possible the election of the person who was ultimately elected.[17]

Boland served as Permanent Representative of Ireland to the UN for some eight years. The respect in which he was held there is

---

15 Brian Urquhart, *Hammarskjöld*, p. 257.

16 See Appendix 3, p. 267 of Kennedy (1996) for a full listing of the members of the delegation each year.

17 Letter from Frederick H. Boland in Geneva to Seán Murphy (Dublin) on 10 September 1934. See Catriona Crowe *et al.*, *Documents on Irish Foreign Policy* (Vol. IV, 1932–1936), p. 305.

evident from the fact that he was elected Chairman of one of the main Committees in 1958 and President of the General Assembly in 1960. He also occupied the Irish seat on the Security Council, on which Ireland served a one-year term in 1962. When he retired eventually in 1964 it was to take on well-earned directorships in some important Irish companies, as well as the role of Chancellor of Dublin University. The transitory nature of fame in an organisation like the UN became apparent to me however when, one day in retirement later in the 1960s, he returned to the UN and joined his successor, Con Cremin, with whom I was in discussion in the busy delegates' lounge where much quiet business is done. Sadly, no one recognised him although in his time, only six years before, he had been one of the most distinguished Presidents of the General Assembly. I took it as a useful lesson.

As I mentioned earlier, Boland was succeeded by Con Cremin, who remained as Permanent Representative until the early 1970s. Cremin was a shy man, but one who earned the respect, and even the affection, both of Ministers and of those who worked under him and were able to see past his shy exterior. He was scholarly and polyglot – he spoke many European languages, all in a strong Kerry accent – and committed and hardworking with it. I would certainly not describe him, like Boland, as smooth or 'sleek-headed', but, like Boland, his political instincts were essentially cautious and conservative. It was not that he had an agenda of his own to pursue; it was rather that his instinctive concern would have been to keep his Minister out of trouble – a useful reality check, perhaps, on some of Aiken's more creative and adventurous ideas, and one which I think Aiken himself welcomed.

I recall hearing Cremin say on one occasion that as First Secretary at the Irish Legation he had seen German forces enter Paris in 1940. Along with the Minister[18] at the Legation, Sean Murphy, he moved

---

18   'Minister' in this sense is a diplomatic rank: it means the head of a Legation. Since the Second World War, there has been an inflation of diplomatic titles. There are now few if any 'Legations' left: virtually all have been upgraded to the nominally higher status of 'Embassies', headed by Ambassadors.

to Vichy during the years of occupation and he remained there until 1943, when he was sent to wartime Berlin to take up the post of Chargé d'Affaires of the Irish Legation there. A recent book dealing with the early part of his career notes that, as bombing intensified and Allied forces advanced steadily in late 1944 and early 1945, he was authorised by the Department at home on several occasions to leave Germany and return to Ireland.[19] He moved south from Berlin, but, to his enormous credit, stayed in Germany until the town to which he had moved was occupied by American forces in late April 1945. Later he served successively as Ambassador in a number of posts – the Holy See, Paris and London. He was Secretary of the Department at home, initially under Liam Cosgrave as Minister, and later under Frank Aiken. Later still in New York, I saw him work well and harmoniously with Frank Aiken all through the second half of the 1960s, and with his successor, Dr Patrick Hillery, when Aiken left office in 1969. He earned the respect of both men. Although his innate shyness could be something of a barrier, especially for a junior official, I too remember him with affection.

If Boland and later Cremin, the two successive Permanent Representatives in New York over this decade and a half, were distinguished – as indeed they were – then Conor Cruise O'Brien has to be described as distinctive. He was a member of the visiting delegation each year from 1956 to 1960. By then he was already the author of two important books – one under a pseudonym.[20] He was also an occasional contributor on political and literary issues, again under a pseudonym, to at least two British journals of opinion, *The New Statesman* and *The Spectator* – a posture that, taking account of their limited circulation, he once described as having a foot in both graves. In his day job as a diplomat, he was head of the UN section at home and a principal adviser to the Minister; and he travelled out

---

19   Niall Keogh, *Con Cremin: Ireland's Wartime Diplomat*, pp. 88–92.
20   *Parnell and His Party*, written under his own name (Clarendon Press, Oxford, 1957); and *Maria Cross* under the pseudonym 'Donat O'Donnell' (Chatto and Windus, London, 1954).

to New York each autumn with the Minister and several other diplomatic colleagues to augment the small staff based permanently in New York for the duration of the General Assembly session.

Conor was an activist who was creative – even radical to a degree – in his approach to the role that a delegation like Ireland's might play; his elegant literary style was in evidence when he drafted speeches for the Minister or for himself. But as a writer and historian of distinction he also had an opportunity to write the record himself at a time when no other record was being written – or at least published – and his pen has helped to impart the kind of golden glow I spoke of earlier to the events in which he participated. His pen could also, be it said, inflict a sharp stab on occasion on those with whom he disagreed or of whom he disapproved. Anyone who looks back on the book he wrote in 1962 after his return from UN service in Katanga[21] will see some of the scars which that implement could inflict. Boland appears there under his own name and later, along with his wife, under a wounding acronym; Eamon Kennedy, a colleague based in the Irish Mission in New York at the time, with whose conventionally conservative approach Conor was often at odds, is depicted in less than flattering terms.

From his later book *Memoir*,[22] published in 1998, it is clear that

21 O'Brien (1962).
22 O'Brien (1998). As I emphasise here, I have always enjoyed and admired Conor, both personally and for most of what he has written, but sadly this particular book, which is a very late work, is marred – for me at least – by some elementary mistakes. For example, on p. 170, he says 'Ireland had been formally admitted to the UN in 1956 but a full Irish delegation first took its seat in the General Assembly in the Autumn of 1957.' In fact Ireland was formally admitted in late 1955 and first took its seat in 1956. This mistake leads him to displace by one year many of the dates in this and the immediately following chapter. On p. 182 he speaks of 'the General Debate which closes each session of the General Assembly'. In fact this debate takes place at the start and not the end of the session. A more serious error occurs on p. 179 where he says that 'The Charter allows a power which feels threatened by the actions of another power to act in legitimate self-defence.' If this were so, then it would legitimise a pre-emptive, or even a preventive, attack like that of the US and UK against Iraq in 2003. In fact the Charter legitimises self-defence only 'if *an armed attack occurs* against a Member of the United Nations' (emphasis added), and then only 'until the Security Council has taken measures necessary to maintain international peace and security' (Article 51).

for Conor, the old rivalry with Boland and Kennedy was still very much alive forty years on. In describing his own role in advising the new Minister Frank Aiken on the courageous change of policy in 1957 that became known as 'the China vote' – an issue I will deal with in a later chapter – he attributes the 'pro-American' policy of the delegation under Liam Cosgrave to Boland, whose 'policy was to follow the American line in all matters of importance', and to Kennedy, who was Boland's deputy at the Permanent Mission in New York. Both, he says, 'believed sincerely in the policy of un-flinching support to the Leader of the Free World' but were also moved by a desire to ensure that they would have American support in their own efforts to gain election to offices in the Assembly: Boland in 1960 to the Presidency of the Assembly, and Kennedy in 1958 to the post of Rapporteur of the Fourth Committee. He goes on to describe his own position at that time:

> I heartily approved the assumption by Ireland of a more independent position. But I was also aware, in a less dis-interested way, that the new Irish line, if sustained, would make quite a big difference to my own life, and be to the immediate benefit of my influence and my career ... I was thus turning from a rather wan and peripheral figure in the Irish delegation to a person at the centre of things. And I found this, in itself, congenial.
>
> I could also sense plenty of trouble ahead in relations with the Permanent Mission ... But I liked the prospect of trouble better than the deathly Pax Americana which had prevailed in 1957.[23]

I have to say again that I greatly admired Conor Cruise O'Brien, who was responsible for the Political and United Nations section to which I was assigned when I joined the Department in January 1960. I still do, even though I could not easily agree with some of the

---

23   O'Brien (1998) pp. 187–188.

shifting positions that he adopted later in a long, varied and distinguished career that took him through many turns from 'anti-partition' pamphlets in the 1950s to membership of a minority Unionist party in Northern Ireland. Certainly at the period I am talking about here my own views would have been far closer to his than to those of his two colleagues in New York. To me their general approach seemed conventional and conservative while Conor's was refreshing. Furthermore, I had my own disagreements with Eamon Kennedy many years later, when he was Permanent Representative at the UN and I, as 'Political Director' at home, was responsible for policy advice to the Minister on our UN voting positions. So I know what Conor meant. But I have to say also that I think that he carried the old rivalry and his combative style much too far when he questioned Boland's and Kennedy's fundamental integrity, as he did when he suggested in his *Memoir* published in 1998 that they took a pro-American position in order to further 'their career prospects within the UN'. Boland died many years before the book appeared, and Kennedy was seriously ill when it was published, so neither could have responded to this caustic criticism.

Conor himself is now gone too – in death greatly honoured as a writer, a historian, a journalist, an academic and a critic; remembered for his role in Irish politics in the 1970s; and recognised belatedly, even by those who disagreed profoundly at the time, for the courage of his prophetic warnings to Irish nationalism at a time of turmoil and violence in Northern Ireland.

It is difficult at this remove to distinguish clearly in Aiken's speeches between what Aiken wrote himself and what other members of the Irish Delegation, especially Boland and O'Brien, may have drafted for him. But even if his officials did much of the drafting at that time, the voice was authentically Aiken's own. Indeed the tone, and the emphasis on the organisation as the guarantor of the independence of small and vulnerable Member States, is reminiscent at times of de Valera's speeches to the League in the 1930s. Some of this, of course, may have come from Boland, who, like Aiken himself, would have had a clear memory of the hopes placed in the League of Nations in the inter-war years. For both men, the memory of the failure of the League in the 1930s must still have been strong: after all, it was little more than twenty years before. Certainly Boland would have had a large hand in the drafting of the speech that the Minister delivered in the General Debate in the opening weeks of each annual session of the General Assembly. As I remember it he usually returned to Dublin from New York each summer to consult on the draft with his colleagues in Dublin and with the Minister – no doubt also to take a holiday at home. The extent of active Irish foreign policy interests at the time was limited, and this speech by the Minister, in a debate that allowed each speaker to range widely over the world scene, was in many ways the major Irish foreign policy event of the year.

These speeches, and indeed virtually all of Aiken's speeches in other debates, avoided polemics about the Cold War. Instead there were frequent thoughtful reflections on the position and role of 'Great Powers' and the importance of the UN to smaller States concerned about their security. The speeches are all clearly written, and indeed trenchant at times; they bear re-reading today. No doubt other members of the delegation, and particularly Conor Cruise O'Brien, can claim some credit for this, especially in the earlier period. Speaking in the General Assembly on one occasion in October 1959, Aiken rebutted charges by the Soviet representative that Ireland was a 'tool of imperialism' by citing a reference to Michael Davitt in the *Soviet Encyclopaedia* as 'a staunch fighter against colonial oppression'.[24] At the time Conor was studying Russian. I rather doubt if Aiken was. As time went on, however, especially in the later 1960s, Aiken, in a reversal of the usual practice, was more and more inclined to draft his own speeches and then offer them to his officials for comment.

The major issues that preoccupied the delegation at the time can be traced through the booklets containing Aiken's collected

---

24 Department of External Affairs (1959) p. 37.

speeches at the General Assembly that were issued by the Department each year from 1957 until the late 1960s.[25] These speeches by the Minister were not, of course, the only statements of position by Ireland over these years: other members of the delegation spoke regularly in one or other of the Assembly's main Committees, as indeed I did myself, and their speeches are available in the UN records. But the collected speeches of the Minister provide a good summary guide to the concerns of the Irish Delegation at the time and the positions they took on various issues. Topics dealt with in these booklets include: many aspects of disarmament; the representation of China in the UN; the situation in Tibet; the situation in the Congo; the need for support for the independence of the Secretary General; the Middle East; the financing of peacekeeping; and the Irish draft resolution calling for the negotiation of a treaty to prevent the spread of nuclear weapons. On all these issues the Irish Delegation under Aiken took what might fairly be called a constructive, and at times a creative, approach.

Detailed studies of Irish policy at the UN over the first decade and a half of membership, which draw on archive material, are now beginning to appear;[26] Conor Cruise O'Brien, in his book about his experiences as UN representative in Katanga in 1961, gave his own view of the activities of the Irish Delegation to the General Assembly in the early part of this period.[27] So I will limit myself in this book to an account of some selected issues. In most of these cases, I can draw on personal memories.

---

25 The booklets, which appeared each year from 1957 onwards, were published by Browne and Nolan Ltd for the Department of External Affairs. The last volume in my possession is that for 1967. I think that the practice of publishing the collected speeches of the Minister in this format may have petered out some time in the following years.

26 Skelly (1997); Michael Kennedy and Joseph Morrison Skelly (eds), *Irish Foreign Policy 1919–1966: From Independence to Internationalism*; and Michael Kennedy and Deirdre McMahon (eds), *Obligations and Responsibilities: Ireland and the United Nations, 1955–2005*.

27 O'Brien (1962).

The episode that looms largest for me now, all of forty-seven years later, is our involvement in UN peacekeeping in the Congo over a four-year period from 1960 onwards. This was Ireland's first commitment to a major UN peacekeeping operation, and before the operation ended in 1964 the Irish Defence Forces, for the first time in their history, had suffered losses in combat abroad. In sending this force to the Congo, the UN itself stepped into very deep waters; indeed, in view of subsequent events, one might even say into the heart of darkness. It is a story that warrants a separate chapter – or even two.

3

Into the Congo

Spell a word of nine letters: l-a-n-d-s-w-e-r-k. If my memory is correct it was a Saturday night in 1960 or 1961. I was a very junior official in the Department of External Affairs and I had been called into Iveagh House to decode an urgent message from Ireland's UN mission in New York. At the time we used an old-fashioned code book for coded messages of a relatively low level of security, and of course the code book, which was a kind of dictionary of words alongside their code equivalents, had no entry for 'landswerk'. So, in decoding, I had to spell out this strange word one letter at a time.

The message, when decoded, proved to be a request from the Irish contingent with the UN force in the Congo: they were asking for a number of the Swedish armoured cars that were then in service with the Irish Defence Forces to be shipped out to them from Dublin. Communication systems at the time were not good. As a result the message had to be sent by a very indirect route – from the Congo, through UN headquarters in New York, then to the Irish Mission to the UN and so on to External Affairs in Dublin for transmission to the Department of Defence.

Thinking about this long-ago incident reminds me that Ireland's involvement in UN peacekeeping operations spans the whole of my own diplomatic career, and more; back indeed to 1958 – only three years after Ireland took its seat for the first time in the UN General Assembly on 14 December 1955. Over the period since then, tens of thousands of members of the Irish Defence Forces have served in trouble spots in all corners of the world; and Ireland's record of participation in peacekeeping over half a century is a matter of justified pride for Irish people.

Unlike the more robust concept of enforcement action, UN peacekeeping is not mentioned explicitly in the UN Charter: it is a creative development based on the general principles of Chapter 6, which allow the Security Council to make recommendations in regard to the 'Pacific Settlement of Disputes'.

UN peacekeeping can be said to have started in 1948 when UNTSO – a corps of unarmed military observers drawn from other Member States – was placed along ceasefire lines to help maintain a truce between Israel and its Arab neighbours. A similar observer group was interposed between Indian and Pakistani forces in 1949. Peacekeeping, in the more usual sense of a small, lightly-armed military force – a symbolic line of 'blue helmets' interposed with their consent between warring parties – dates back to the Suez crisis of 1956.

At that time, after Israel had gone to war against Egypt, two European powers, the UK and France, in secret collusion with Israel, intervened and attacked Egypt. Their overt purpose was to separate the original combatants, Israel and Egypt. In reality they wanted to re-establish control over the Suez Canal, which had been nationalised by Egypt's President Nasser a short time before. Their attack on Egypt was inept and their action was widely condemned. After a week of fighting, Egypt and Israel agreed to a ceasefire and the UK and France came under very strong international pressure, not least from US President Eisenhower and Secretary of State John Foster Dulles, to end their attack and withdraw. The UN Secretary General, Dag Hammarskjöld, with the support of Lester Pearson of Canada and others, devised a proposal for a UN peacekeeping force and the General Assembly agreed to send a UN Emergency Force of some 6,000 – known for short as UNEF I – to the Sinai to take up position between the Egyptian and Israeli forces. Its arrival in the area allowed the UK and France to withdraw their forces, without too much loss of face, from what by then had become a disastrous situation for them.

This first full UN peacekeeping force became a model for other such forces over the years. As it happened it was established in 1956 just as an Irish Delegation attended a full session of the General Assembly for the first time.

Two years later, in 1958, Ireland dipped its own toe in the water: at the request of the UN it sent unarmed officers of the Defence Forces to serve for several months as members of the UN Observer Group in Lebanon (UNOGIL). Eventually some fifty Irish officers were involved. This group of unarmed observers was not quite comparable to UNEF, which was an organised military force, but it marked the first involvement of members of the Irish Defence Forces in a UN peacekeeping operation of any kind, or indeed in any kind of international service abroad.

In 1960 Ireland went much further: for the first time in its history it contributed an armed military contingent to a full-scale peacekeeping force – the UN operation in the Congo, which came to be known as ONUC, an acronym based on its title in French. This operation lasted four years and, before it concluded, it came close to bringing about the break-up of the UN. It also cost the lives of a number of members of the Irish Defence Forces. A great deal has already been written about the operation as a whole and about Ireland's participation in it. In writing about it here, I will draw largely on personal memories from the period just after I joined the Department of External Affairs.

The Congo, a massive territory in the centre of Africa, with many diverse ethnic groups, achieved independence on 30 June 1960. The omens for the new State were not good. It began what soon became a precipitate slide into chaos and virtual dissolution as a viable state.

In the 'Scramble for Africa' the participants at the Berlin Conference of 1884–85 had 'awarded' the Congo Free State to King Leopold II of Belgium. Under his personal rule for nearly a quarter of a century there had been appalling abuses and use of forced labour to increase rubber exports. After these gross human rights abuses were exposed, largely through the work of Sir Roger Casement, an Irishman in the British consular service, international pressure forced Leopold to relinquish personal control and the vast territory became a colony of the Belgian State in 1908. The half-century of Belgian colonial rule that followed left the country ill-prepared for independence: it had no more than a handful of educated administrators for a territory the size of Western Europe, and, so it is said, some 17 university graduates in all. As its constitution the new State had only the *Loi Fondamentale*, which was simply an Act passed by the Belgian Parliament when it agreed to grant the territory its independence; and it had a poorly trained national army. This was the so-called Force Publique, which became the ANC – the Armée Nationale Congolaise. It began to mutiny in early July within days of independence. Its soldiers were not at all appeased by a remarkable decision of the new Congolese Government to promote every member of the army simultaneously by one rank, so that all the privates became corporals overnight, all the corporals sergeants, all the captains majors, and so on.

In granting independence, Belgium had retained bases in the Congo. Now, in a situation of growing chaos, it deployed its troops from these bases in what was said to be a protective role – directed largely to the protection of Europeans still in the region. Within days, the mineral-rich province of Katanga in eastern Congo, backed by European mining companies and Belgian, French and British interests, seceded and declared itself an independent State under the leadership of Moise Tshombe, the provincial Prime Minister.

On 10 July, ten days after it had become independent, the new Congo State issued the first of several appeals for help: Lumumba, the Prime Minister, asked the UN for help in training the army. Three days later he and Kasavubu, the President, appealed jointly to the UN for help against 'external aggression'. There were also somewhat disjointed appeals for help from members of the Congolese Government to both the US and the Soviet Union.

In those years the tide of decolonisation in Africa, which was to rise to a flood later in the 1960s, was still only beginning to flow. There was a widespread feeling, at the UN and elsewhere, that the newly independent Government should be supported and that Cold War rivalries should not be imported into central Africa. Furthermore, since the deployment of UNEF during the Suez crisis of 1956, the idea that the UN could play a useful role in peace-keeping had taken hold. So on 13 July 1960 Dag Hammarskjöld availed of Article 99 of the Charter to request an urgent meeting of the Security Council. This was the first ever use of this Article which allows the Secretary General, on his own initiative, to raise with the Security Council any issue that he believes to be a threat to international peace and security. It was not used again until 1979.[1]

Hammarskjöld, in consultation with African delegates led by Tunisia, which had a seat on the Security Council at the time, drafted a resolution for adoption by the Council. The text began by calling on Belgium to withdraw its troops. It went on to authorise him as Secretary General to provide the Congolese Government 'with such military assistance as may be needed, until, through the efforts of the Congolese government with the technical assistance of the United Nations, the national security forces may be able in the opinion of the government, to meet fully their tasks'.[2] The text is worth quoting here because its ambiguities were to make it a matter of contention later. Hammarskjöld also proposed to the Council a set of basic principles to govern the operation of the proposed force: its command would remain with the UN; its deployment was to be temporary; it would not become party to internal conflicts; and it was to use force only in self-defence. On his recommendation, the

---

1   See Madeleine G. Kalb, *The Congo Cables*, p. 12 and footnote 33 on p. 398.
2   Adopted as Security Council resolution S/4387 of 14 July 1960 (now listed as Resolution 143). The full text of the resolution is given by O'Brien (1962) Appendix I, p. 331. An extract is quoted also in John Terence O'Neill and Nicholas Rees, *United Nations Peacekeeping in the Post-Cold War Era*, p. 50. See also summary in Kalb (1982) pp. 12, 13.

Security Council passed the resolution in the early morning hours of 14 July.

There was a surprising degree of unity in the Security Council across the Cold War divide at this early stage – a unity that was made easier because of the ambiguities in the text. The US, where President Eisenhower was still in office, voted in favour. So too did the Soviet Union: it saw support for a territory emerging from colonialism as something that would win it popularity with what were then called 'Afro-Asian' States. The three other Permanent Members of the Council, each with the right of veto, abstained. The Chinese seat at the UN was still in the hands of the Nationalist Government, which generally agreed with US policies but took a rather passive, hands-off attitude on this kind of issue. Britain and France were more dubious. Both countries sympathised with Belgium, the former colonial power; both, like Belgium, had interests in mining companies, such as the Union Miniére, which operated in the Katanga area; and both still had colonies of their own in Africa. Northern Rhodesia (now Zambia), next door to Katanga, was still a British colony, as indeed were Southern Rhodesia (now Zimbabwe) and Nyasaland (now Malawi). So these two Permanent Members also abstained in the Council vote. But at least they did not use their vetoes to block it and, to that extent, they too acquiesced in the setting up of the UN Force.

Hammarskjöld moved quickly to implement the resolution by asking a variety of non-aligned countries to provide contingents for the UN force. He drew mainly on independent African countries in order to show that this was primarily an African responsibility. This would also head off possible accusations later from the Soviet Union that the whole operation was no more than imperialism in disguise. In order to reassure the Belgians, he also wanted some European contingents but he knew that in order to avoid problems with the Soviet Union they would have to be drawn from non-NATO countries. So he approached his own country, Sweden, and Ireland.

The request arrived in Dublin through the Irish Mission to the UN in New York in the early days of July 1960, just six months after I had joined the Department of External Affairs. I remember helping colleagues in the Political and UN section, under the direction of Conor Cruise O'Brien, to put together material for a memorandum to the Government. This was the formal submission in which the Minister for External Affairs, Frank Aiken, with the agreement of the Minister for Defence, recommended to the Government that it should agree to the UN request. On 19 July the Government decided to do so.

This was a historic decision: it meant that, for the first time ever, units of the Irish Defence Forces, bearing arms, would serve abroad. As we look back today at Ireland's participation over the years in many different UN peacekeeping forces around the world, it is easy to forget just how strange and novel it was for the Ireland of 1960 to decide to send a contingent of soldiers, all of them volunteers, to join the new UN Force in the Congo.

Ireland has never had compulsory military service. The Irish Defence Forces were small and poorly equipped, and I think I am right in saying that they still used some First World War weapons at the time. They enjoyed good standing at home but they had never served overseas – indeed, Irish law did not permit such service outside the jurisdiction of our own State. And the Congo was a faraway country of which we knew little and with which we had no obvious connection. Why then did the Government decide to send first one battalion, and then two – at one time perhaps one-ninth of our armed forces in all – to serve in that distant country in Africa?

Under Article 25 of the Charter UN Member States agree to accept and carry out the decisions of the Security Council. But a decision authorising a peacekeeping force like that which the Council had adopted on this occasion does not impose an obligation on any particular Member State to contribute a contingent. The main reason for the positive recommendation was undoubtedly a belief that Ireland, when asked to support the UN in a practical way, should live up to what it had been saying for four years now in the General Assembly.[3]

Irish Governments have always believed that small States, in particular, have need of an effective international organisation to limit conflict and promote the rule of law in international life. I explained in an earlier chapter that this had been a theme of the Irish Delegations to the League of Nations in the 1920s and 1930s and one that had been repeated over the years since Ireland had been admitted to the UN.

Frank Aiken had now been Minister for three years. He had made some thoughtful speeches in the General Assembly in favour of decolonisation in Africa and elsewhere; and he had argued that, since there was now an organisation such as the UN to support their case, it was no longer necessary for national liberation movements to resort to the use of armed force, as he himself had felt obliged to do in Ireland in an earlier era when no such organisation existed. He had also argued in the Assembly for the gradual development of what he called 'areas of law'; and, more controversially, he had offered a plan for phased withdrawal along lines of longitude by US and Soviet forces that were confronting each other in Central Europe. Furthermore, he had proposed and advocated what was still a novel, and indeed controversial, idea at the time – the negotiation of a treaty to prevent the further spread of nuclear weapons. This proposal, which I will describe in a later chapter, eventually came to fruition with the signature of the Nuclear Non-Proliferation Treaty in 1968.

This was all admirable in its way. But now, unexpectedly, in mid-1960, came a test of whether Ireland was ready to live up to the rhetoric of its Minister and his delegation. Was it prepared to give practical evidence of its support for these ideas and principles by responding to the request of the UN Secretary General to send a contingent of Irish soldiers into Africa? Aiken and the Department believed that it had a moral obligation to do so.

---

3   Skelly (1997) p. 269.

There were other reasons too. The Irish Permanent Representative (that is, Ambassador) to the UN in New York, Freddie Boland, was at the time running a hotly contested campaign against two opponents for election as President of the UN General Assembly: he won the election two months later.[4] Undoubtedly, there was a belief that a positive response to the request from the Secretary General would help his campaign by showing that Ireland was a 'good UN member'. The Defence Forces too, whose officers had tasted UN service in the Lebanon two years before, probably saw the possibility of service abroad in a good cause as a help to morale and to recruitment.

It is possible that there was also one other, less tangible, reason why the Government responded favourably to the UN request. This was the fact that a positive response would mean providing help in its difficulties to the Congo in particular. Frank Aiken, like some other older members of the Government, had been active as a young man in the Irish independence struggle in the early part of the century. He had joined the Volunteers as early as 1913.[5] Undoubtedly he would have remembered Roger Casement, whose name in Irish minds of that generation was indelibly associated with his heroic exploits in reporting atrocities in King Leopold's Congo Free State and against the Putumayo Indians in Peru, and with a later doomed effort to import arms to Ireland from Germany in the *Aud* in 1916. Indeed, although he was only a teenager at the time, Aiken, like other members of the old guard, might even have known Casement personally. Perhaps he saw the decision to respond to the request to send Irish troops to help the UN in the Congo as a fitting closing of the circle that Casement's work there had opened half a century before.

---

4   The General Assembly elects an individual each year to preside over its sessions. The post, which is a prestigious one, is generally rotated among regional groups and is often filled by agreement among members of the group. In 1960, however, in addition to Boland, there were two other candidates from Europe – Jiri Nosek of Czechoslovakia and Thor Thors of Iceland – and Boland had had to run a vigorous campaign. He was successful and was elected to the post when the Assembly opened in mid-September.

5   See previous chapter.

The decision by the Government to respond positively to Hammarskjöld's request was taken quickly and the Defence Forces began to assemble a contingent to join the newly established UN Force in the Congo. Before they could leave, however, it was necessary to amend the Defence Acts, which, at the time, made no provision for service abroad of an armed contingent of the Irish Defence Forces. The participation of Irish officers in the Observer Group in Lebanon two years previously had created no such difficulties because all those who participated were unarmed volunteers, but now the law would have to be changed. This was dealt with quickly: legislation was rushed through the Dáil, and the Defence Forces quickly put together a battalion to serve with the UN, all of them volunteers.

I think back with sympathy to those heroic members of the first Irish military contingent to serve overseas on a UN mission, in a country about which they could have known very little at the time. They were transported out to the Congo from Dublin in huge US military aircraft in late July and early August 1960. Their equipment was, to say the least, rather outdated – bolt-action Lee-Enfield rifles, I think, of First World War vintage – and their communications equipment was poor. Their uniforms were those they would have worn in Ireland: the 'bull's wool' of which they were made was more suited to the rigours of the Irish winter than to the steamy heat of an equatorial climate. Then, and long afterwards, their ranking system was deliberately kept low so that, for example, a captain in the Irish army might well be the equivalent of a major or perhaps even a lieutenant colonel in other contingents. Nevertheless they went out with enthusiasm and *élan* to serve in a country that was soon to prove itself to be indeed the 'heart of darkness'.

In early September, a few months into Congolese independence, its Government, torn like the country itself by tribal loyalties, began to come apart. President Kasavubu, leader of the Bakongo people of the lower Congo region, dismissed the Prime Minister, Patrice Lumumba. He countered by dismissing Kasavubu. While this was happening, Colonel Desiré Mobutu, the army Chief of Staff, led a coup – at least in the sense that he proclaimed that he had 'neutral-ised all political leaders' and set up a Commission in their place. In a later period, almost certainly with the help of the CIA, he made himself dictator and, notoriously, misruled and plundered the Congo for a generation. At this early stage, however, he seemed to be acting in tacit cooperation with Kasavubu.

Who was in the right? Which of the two leaders – Prime Minister or President – was legally entitled to dismiss the other? In other times a small country like Ireland would take little notice of such political dilemmas in a distant, French-speaking, African country. Generally speaking, when Ireland sends a contingent to serve with a UN force it refrains, on principle, from trying to give it continuing political direction. It sees that as, properly, a matter for the UN chain of command – though not all countries are so correct in these matters.

Here, however, there was no question of intervening in the established chain of command. A battalion of Irish soldiers had been assigned to a UN force with a mandate to assist the Congolese Government; and that Government now seemed to be breaking up. The Irish Government could not but follow what was happening with interest and concern. Irish representatives in New York, like those of other troop-contributing countries, were already attending regular meetings of the 'Congo Advisory Committee' that the Secretary General, Dag Hammarskjöld, had set up to advise him on the conduct of the operation. Frank Aiken, the Minister for External Affairs, was preparing to go to New York to lead the Irish Delegation to the General Assembly and he might want to attend some of these meetings. He would also want to speak in the General Assembly about the Congo situation, which was the most difficult issue facing the UN at the time. What should he say – in particular, what line should he take on the reciprocal dismissals by each other of President and Prime Minister?

I, with the wisdom of just nine months in the Department, was given the task of looking into this question to prepare a briefing of some kind for my senior colleagues and, ultimately, for the Minister. I remember working laboriously through the French text of the *Loi Fondamentale*, the Act of the Belgian Parliament passed in May 1960, which was the only constitution the Congo had at the time. I analysed its provisions Article by Article, and tried to puzzle out an answer. I eventually prepared a paper that went up the line in early October to the Secretary of the Department, Con Cremin.

What view did I take? My own sympathies, like those of many in Ireland, would have been with Lumumba. Months later, he was to be captured and done to death by his enemies in controversial circumstances that made him a hero thereafter to anti-colonialists. But I had to be careful and judicious in the memorandum that I prepared. Looking back now on an old, yellowing carbon copy that I retained, I see that I was clear at least in saying that the situation was confused – 'The one certainty now seems to be that all parties have … contravened the fundamental law to a greater or lesser degree.' I see that I was also dubious about the right of the President, Kasavubu, to dismiss the Prime Minister, Lumumba, without parliamentary approval, especially since the Parliament had subsequently voted confidence in Lumumba in a way that seemed to renew his authority; and I see that I concluded, somewhat more firmly, that 'Lumumba can … derive no support from the Fundamental Law for his various declarations purporting to dismiss the Chief of State and to assume full powers for himself.' Certainly a well-balanced analysis – a judicious mixture of the one hand and the other! But I did come to a conclusion: it seemed that on a strict interpretation of the power granted to each under the *Loi Fondamentale*, Kasavubu was still legally Head of State, and Lumumba, probably but less certainly, was still legally Prime Minister. A Daniel indeed come to judgement, you may say.

If the political situation on the ground in the Congo was confused, the response of the UN General Assembly to these events was equally so at the outset. Procedurally, two issues arose: there was to be a debate in the Assembly on 'The situation in the Republic of the Congo', and there would now also be a question of credentials – who was legally entitled to speak for the Congo? The Assembly decided to postpone the first of these, the main debate on the Congo situation, until a Conciliation Commission that it had agreed to send to the Congo had reported back. In the meantime, however, the US pressed the Assembly strongly to adopt a report of the Credentials Committee that would have the effect of seating the Kasavubu representatives. Ireland, like other troop-contributing countries, wanted this issue deferred but the US had its way and the Assembly voted to accept the report.

Did my paper of October reach the Minister and influence what he said a month later in New York? At this remove, I cannot be sure. But a glance back now at his speech in November in the General Assembly shows a Solomon-like wisdom in his approach: he simply avoided a judgement and gave the best of reasons for doing so:

> Any solution of the Congolese difficulties must be a Congolese solution. We should continue to avoid taking sides in the internal political controversies of the Congolese people and leave to them the task, difficult though it may be, of evolving political institutions appropriate to their needs.[6]

In the end, the Assembly voted by a narrow margin to recognise the Kasavubu faction and allow it to take the Congolese seat. Ireland, having failed to achieve the postponement of the decision that it and other troop-contributors had wanted, decided to abstain in the vote.

I should explain that, at this stage, Conor Cruise O'Brien and other senior officials who dealt with UN-related issues in the Department were in New York: they had travelled there as usual with the Minister, Frank Aiken, to attend the three-month annual session of the General Assembly. The Department was very small at the time and I was left to mind the UN section – a cabin boy, one

6   Speech of 21 November 1960, Department of External Affairs (1960) p. 36.

might say, left to deal with the captain. I found myself called down frequently to the splendid office of the Secretary of the Department, Con Cremin, in order to report directly to him about issues raised by the Delegation in New York.

That November, the great adventure of Ireland's venture into the heart of Africa on behalf of the UN turned to tragedy. An Irish patrol in Kivu province in the eastern Congo ran into an ambush at Niemba, and nine Irish soldiers were killed by Baluba tribesmen armed with primitive weapons. These were the first soldiers of the Irish State to die abroad on active international service. Their bodies were brought home for burial. Like thousands of others, I went down to O'Connell Street to see the funeral cortège pass. Standing on the pavement I listened to the sombre music of the Dead March – a sharp and poignant counterpoint to the cheerful, spirited music to which they and their companions had marched out and into Africa some months before.

Ireland was sobered by the tragedy: this was no longer a great adventure; these deaths were real. But if the innocent idealism of the initial decision to join the UN force was tempered by the stark reality of Niemba, it was not diminished. I do not recall that there was any serious proposal at the time that the Government should withdraw the Irish contingent – as has happened more recently with larger countries that suffered similar losses in support of UN operations in Africa. Rather, there was a kind of sad pride in the fact that Irish peacekeepers had given their lives for an international ideal, and a belief that continuing the commitment would give meaning to their sacrifice.

Over the following months, the UN was drawn deeply into the quagmire that rapidly developed in the Congo. Indeed, in the following years, the organisation almost broke apart under the stresses set up by the task of nation-building in a country that was really at that stage no more than a colonial assemblage of disparate tribal regions; a country where post-colonial interference by European powers was a major factor; and a country that was eyed by both sides in the Cold War as a region of possible strategic value.

In the early stages of the peacekeeping operation, on 22 July and 9 August 1960, the Security Council adopted two other resolutions on the Congo,[7] but the apparent unity of purpose of those early Council meetings between the US and the Soviet Union did not last long. It had been a tenuous unity at best, and the ambiguities of the mandate and the complexities of an ethnically diverse colony launched unprepared into a precarious independence soon led to dissension among the major powers, whose support for such an operation was essential. The Soviet Union, in particular, grew deeply suspicious of the direction of the operation by the Secretary General, Dag Hammarskjöld, and it withdrew its support completely from him.

This meant that within months of the setting up of the operation, it had suddenly become difficult, because of the danger of a Soviet veto, to get further supporting resolutions through the Security Council. So, on 17 September 1960 the legally controversial 'Uniting for Peace' procedure devised at the time of the Korean War was invoked. This allows an issue to be passed to the General Assembly if the Council is unable to act because of a veto. The procedure is based on the theory that, while the Charter clearly states that 'the primary responsibility for the maintenance of international peace and security' lies with the eleven-Member Council (as it then was), the Assembly, where all Member States are represented, must be presumed to have a residual power to act when the Council cannot do so. So, over the opposition of the Soviet Union and of Poland, which was a Council member at the time, the Assembly was summoned to meet in an emergency special session.

On 20 September, the Assembly adopted a resolution supporting the earlier Security Council resolutions and requesting the Secretary General to 'continue to take vigorous action in accordance with [those resolutions], to assist the Congolese Government in the

---

7　Resolutions S/4405 and S/4426. These are now listed as Resolutions 145 and 146 respectively.

restoration of law and order and to safeguard its unity, territorial integrity and independence'.[8] This further alienated the Soviet Union, which saw the use of the Assembly – where African and other 'Afro-Asian' Member States still supported the UN operation – as no more than a device to get around the veto it could exercise in the Security Council. It was angry, too, at Hammarskjöld's approach to the direction of the UN force. Earlier, it had accused him of acting in the interest of 'Western capitalism'. Now it withdrew its cooperation completely.

That year, 1960, saw a remarkable gathering of world leaders for the annual session of the General Assembly in September. They included, among many others, US President Eisenhower, who was in the last months of his final term as President, Nikita Khrushchev of the Soviet Union, Fidel Castro of Cuba, Tito of Yugoslavia, Kwame Nkrumah of Ghana, who was still at that time a hero of the anti-colonial movement, President Nasser of Egypt and Harold Macmillan, the British Prime Minister. For a few weeks, the world's news media focused their attention on a meeting of the UN General Assembly to a greater degree than ever before or since.

In his address to the Assembly Eisenhower strongly supported Hammarskjöld and his Congo policy. He did not mention the Soviet Union by name but he spoke of a flagrant attack by 'a few nations' on the Secretary General as 'nothing less than an attack upon the United Nations itself'.[9] At the time this was a serious charge in the eyes of the US. But the world has changed: in more recent times some US Presidents have been less inclined to defend the UN. Khrushchev, however, was not deterred by Eisenhower's strong words. Addressing the Assembly on the following day, he renewed the attack on Hammarskjöld: the pro-Western 'bias' of the Secretary General, he said, was 'particularly glaring' in relation to the Congo – he had 'virtually adopted the position of the colonialists'.

---

8 General Assembly resolution 1474 (ES-IV). For the full text of this and other resolutions up to 24 November 1961, see O'Brien (1962) Appendix I, pp. 331–339.
9 Kalb (1982) p. 110.

Khrushchev then launched a bombshell: no single individual, he said, could be a neutral, impartial Secretary General. The post should be abolished and replaced by a 'troika' – a three-person executive, drawn from 'East', 'West' and the Non-Aligned Movement.

The proposal astonished the Assembly, which saw it as a most serious development for the future of the UN. Hammarskjöld was its second Secretary General ever. His predecessor, Trygve Lie, had also fallen foul of the Soviet Union in his time. Would every Secretary General have to suffer the same fate? Would there indeed ever *be* another individual Secretary General if the Soviet Union were to take this position? Frank Aiken, speaking for Ireland in the same debate two weeks later, described Khrushchev's proposal as 'tantamount to the disruption of this Organisation'. Khrushchev's proposal found little favour with the Non-Aligned Movement. As U Thant, the Burmese Permanent Representative who attended a Conference of Heads of State of Non-Aligned Countries in Belgrade (and who was later to become Secretary General himself) put it in his memoirs:

> many delegates who attended the conference felt that the troika concept was against the letter and spirit of the Charter of the United Nations, and if put into practice, would have rendered the whole United Nations system ineffective and impotent.[10]

Ireland had an unusually prominent position at this session of the General Assembly. Freddie Boland, the Irish Permanent Representative to the UN, a diplomat with experience of the pre-war League of Nations, had been elected to the prestigious post of President of the Assembly at the opening of the session in September. He had his hands full in chairing meetings of world leaders so little used to being called to order. But the greatest test of his suavity and diplomatic skill came when Khrushchev, sitting in

10   U Thant, *View from the UN*, p. 4.

the Soviet Union seat in the Assembly, took exception to a speech by Harold Macmillan and began to bang on the desk with his shoe as Boland tried – largely in vain – to call him to order.

This was indeed a startling event for us in Dublin. Here was the leader of a nuclear-armed superpower, a very volatile figure indeed, being called to order by an Irish civil servant, albeit a very distinguished one. I remember vividly the opening words of Khrushchev's riposte to Boland, which I have since heard played over on radio many times, in the voice of the interpreter: 'We live on earth, not by the grace of God, and not by your grace, Sir, but by the might and strength of our great Soviet People.' Ominous words indeed when addressed to an Irish diplomat by the erratic leader of one of the two superpowers with the capacity to destroy the world.

It is easy to understand that this event caused great apprehension in Dublin. The apprehension was so great that the reports of the episode in the Irish newspapers at the time were not thought to be sufficient. The British papers were not yet available in Dublin next morning, and, in an era of less rapid communication than today, there was a lack of detailed information for the Government about what exactly had happened to give rise to this tirade against Boland. The Taoiseach, Sean Lemass, was naturally greatly concerned. As what I might call the boy minding the shop in the UN section in the absence of my betters in New York, I had a call from the Secretary, Con Cremin, asking me to get further information urgently for the Taoiseach. For reasons that I cannot now clearly recall, the best way to do this seemed to be to ask the Irish Embassy in London to send us everything they could from the British press, which had reported extensively on the incident because Harold Macmillan had been the main object of Khrushchev's protest. This was long before the era of the fax, let alone the internet. So the teleprinter – a permanent telex line between the Irish Embassy in London and the Department in Dublin – chattered away all that morning as the Embassy sent us long transcriptions of the stories in the main British newspapers. I assembled them as fast as I could so that they might be sent over urgently to Merrion Street in the hope that they would appease a somewhat impatient – and worried – Lemass.

Freddie Boland, happily, survived Khrushchev's anger and went on to preside for many more days over the proceedings of the General Assembly. In a later episode on another day, his gavel broke as he called a speaker to order. As a result of all of this he became something of a hero to the public in the United States and received many replacement gavels from well-wishers. As time went on the two separate episodes were conflated, and the received opinion today is that Boland broke his gavel in a heroic attempt to restrain Khrushchev's intemperate shoe-banging display. *Si non e vero* …

As the UN was drawn further and further into the Congo, so too was Ireland. Already in late July 1960, Hammarskjöld had asked for more Irish troops and in August the Government responded by sending a second battalion. So, for a time, we had two battalions serving simultaneously with the UN force. In January 1961, an Irish General, Sean McKeown, was chosen to command the whole UN peacekeeping force of some 20,000. Two months later, in March 1961, Hammarskjöld asked the Irish Government to release Conor Cruise O'Brien for service with the UN Secretariat, first as his representative in Katanga and later in New York. The Government, already deeply involved in the Congo, refused the request at first but agreed with some reluctance when it was renewed at the end of May.[11]

By then the UN operation in the Congo had become something very different from peacekeeping in the classic sense of a 'thin line of blue helmets' interposed by consent between belligerents who have ceased to fight. The wily Moise Tshombe maintained Katanga's secession with a great deal of outside help, particularly from Belgium and possibly too from the UK and France; and another Congolese politician, Antoine Gizenga, had declared a provisional government of his own in Stanleyville. UN involvement had started

11   O'Brien (1962) pp. 40–41.

with a limited – and ambiguous – mandate from the Security Council. It was now turning into an effort to cope with nation-building in a country the size of Western Europe that had dissolved into chaos and tribal loyalties; where there were rival governments; and where the wealthiest province had seceded with covert – and often open – help from outside. It was a task for which the UN at the time did not have the resources, the experience or the necessary support from the major powers. On the contrary, at times it faced active opposition from the Soviet Union and, throughout, a lack of support at the very least from France and the UK.

As the months passed and the situation in the Congo deteriorated with the death of Lumumba, there was a high degree of what today is called 'mission creep'. John F. Kennedy had by now replaced Eisenhower as US President and his UN representative, Adlai Stevenson, was active in trying to promote a solution through the United Nations. On 21 February 1961 the Security Council adopted a new and stronger resolution. This urged the UN to 'take immediately all appropriate measures to prevent the occurrence of civil war in the Congo, including … the use of force, if necessary, in the last resort'. It also urged 'that measures be taken for the immediate evacuation of all Belgian and other foreign military and paramilitary personnel and political advisers not under UN command, and mercenaries'.[12] In addition it called for the convening of the Congolese parliament, which had been adjourned by Kasavubu in the previous October; the reorganisation of Congolese armed units; and an investigation into Lumumba's death. This resolution was adopted by nine votes to nil with two abstentions. Of the five Permanent Members with veto rights, the UK as well as the US and China voted in favour: France and the Soviet Union abstained.

This was a new and rather sweeping mandate from the UN body with authority to take such decisions – although it is of interest to

---

12 Resolution 161 of 21 February 1961. Full text in O'Brien (1962) Appendix I, pp. 336–338. A summary of the text of the Security Council resolution of 21 February 1961 is given in *Yearbook of the United Nations: Special Edition: UN Fiftieth Anniversary 1945–1995*, p. 34.

note that at no point in the resolution did the Council explicitly invoke its authority under Chapter 7 of the Charter to take forceful action to maintain international peace and security, as one would expect it to do in a similar situation today. The exact extent of this new mandate was still ambiguous in some ways. It did however seem to many people to give the UN Force the task of preventing the secession of Katanga and removing foreign mercenary forces from that province; and the UN Force was authorised to use force in carrying out this mission. This was a very considerable extension and blurring of the mandate of what many had understood at the outset to be a peacekeeping force carrying arms to be used only in self-defence.

Two months later, in April 1961, the General Assembly adopted a resolution expressing the conviction that the central factor in the grave situation in the Congo was the continuing presence of Belgian and other foreign military and paramilitary personnel, political advisers and mercenaries, in total disregard of repeated resolutions of the United Nations.[13]

At the end of May 1961, Conor Cruise O'Brien was seconded from the Irish Foreign Service to the UN Secretariat and in June he took up the post of representative of the Secretary General in Katanga. Over the following months he tried to carry out the Security Council resolution of the previous February by persuading Tshombe's foreign military and political advisers to leave the scene. In early August, however, there were still several hundred Belgian officers in Katanga as well as several hundred foreign 'mercenaries'. These soldiers of fortune came from South Africa and Rhodesia as well as from Belgium, Britain and other European countries. They also included a number of French officers who had fought in the war in Algeria and now saw themselves as fighting for a similar cause in Katanga.[14] They were nicknamed *les affreux* – which could be loosely translated as 'the terrors' or 'the frightful ones' – and they

---

13 Res 1599 (XV).
14 See Urquhart (1973) p. 551 and Kalb (1982) pp. 288–289.

lived up amply to that name when they led Katangese 'gendarmes' on 'pacification' missions in rebel areas in the northern part of the province.

On 1 August 1961, after unsuccessful efforts by the UN to promote negotiations between Tshombe and Congolese political leaders, Kasavubu, who was still formally President of the Congo, appointed Cyril Adoula to head a new Congolese Government. Hammarskjöld, the UN Secretary General, at this point shared O'Brien's view of the urgent need to get the mercenaries out of Katanga. On his advice, Adoula, as Prime Minister and Minister of Defence of the Congo, issued a formal order expelling 'all non-Congolese officers and mercenaries serving in the Katanga forces who have not entered into a contractual engagement with the Central Government of the Republic of the Congo'. The order was signed also by Kasavubu as President and by two other Ministers. It referred explicitly to the Security Council resolution of 21 February and, in effect, was a request to the UN to help in carrying the Council's decision.[15]

On 28 August 1961, in 'Operation Rumpunch', UN forces in Katanga at Conor Cruise O'Brien's direction rounded up scores of foreign officers for deportation. He suspended further arrests when Tshombe agreed to cooperate with the UN and the Belgian consul promised to arrange the repatriation of the remaining Belgian officers. At this stage the USA was publicly supportive of the UN position but it did not want to see Tshombe's position completely destroyed: it felt that it was still possible, through peaceful negotiation, to persuade him to cooperate with the UN and the Congolese Government. Harold Macmillan, the British Prime Minister, also had concerns about the possibility of chaos in the Congo: as he wrote subsequently in his autobiography, 'we wanted a united Congo but not a Communist Congo'.[16]

Hammarskjöld, for his part, appears to have been hesitant about

---

15 For the text of the order in English see O'Brien (1962) Appendix 2, Annex 1, pp. 345–346.
16 Harold Macmillan, *Pointing the Way: 1959–1961*, p. 444, as quoted in Kalb (1982) p. 290.

further forceful action. He had been under attack from the Soviet Union over nearly a year now – ever since Khrushchev, in a speech to the General Assembly on 23 September 1960, accused him of 'virtually adopting the position of the colonialists'. And at this stage, Khrushchev's call for the replacement of the post of Secretary General by a 'troika' still stood.[17]

Hammarskjöld's main support against the sustained assault of the Soviet Union had come from smaller non-aligned Member States and particularly from African States. The secession of Katanga, with the support of some Western States, was however a continuing offence to them; and Hammarskjöld undoubtedly wanted to be able to show a success in dealing with that issue since the UN General Assembly was about to open in New York. But he would also have been aware that it would be argued that although the Security Council resolution of 21 February had spoken of the use of force in the last resort if necessary to prevent civil war, it had not explicitly authorised the use of force to end the secession of Katanga. He had to take account too of the views of major Western powers on this point. The view of the United States was particularly important: it had generally backed him but he had to be wary of being seen to be embraced too closely by it or being identified too much with its Cold War concerns.

On 11 September, in Elisabethville, the Katangese capital (now Lubumbashi), Khiary – the Tunisian head of UN Civilian Operations in the Congo – handed O'Brien warrants from the Congolese authorities for the arrest of five Katangese Ministers, including Tshombe, who was to be arrested only as a last resort. He then returned to the Congolese capital, Leopoldville (now Kinshasa), saying as he left, according to the account given later by O'Brien, *surtout pas de demi-mesures* – 'above all, no half-measures'.[18] Following this, on 13 September, in 'Operation Morthor' the UN force under O'Brien's direction took further forceful action against the

---

17   See Kalb (1982) p. 111.
18   O'Brien (1962) p. 246.

Katangese forces and the mercenaries who led them. This time, however, they met with strong resistance and fighting broke out at the radio station and the post office in Elizabethville.[19] Tshombe escaped and fled to Northern Rhodesia next door. The UN force had no air support so the Katangese forces were able to dominate the skies with the few small military aircraft available to them. At the time they were reported to have three Fouga Magister jet trainers although it emerged later that they may have had only a single plane available. But one plane, however small, beats no plane. Since the Fouga was the only armed aircraft in the skies of Katanga it could strafe at will with its machine gun and it caused enormous trouble to the UN force as fighting continued over the following days.

Western powers, including the US, were now becoming seriously concerned at the turn of events in Katanga. Hammarskjöld too was worried. He was already on his way from New York to Leopoldville, the Congolese capital, when it became clear that the UN operation was running into serious difficulties. A company from the Irish contingent that had been sent – ill-advisedly perhaps – to a town called Jadotville some distance from Elizabethville, at the request of Europeans living there, had been besieged. It was surrounded by Katangese forces and cut off from supplies and, even more seriously, from water.

At this point, Tshombe from across the border in Northern Rhodesia sent a message offering to talk to Conor Cruise O'Brien. Against O'Brien's advice, Hammarskjöld decided to take up the invitation himself by flying to meet Tshombe in Northern Rhodesia to see if he could deal with the situation through negotiation. Furthermore, he decided not to take O'Brien, his representative in Katanga, with him.

On the night flight from Leopoldville, the Congolese capital, to Ndola in Northern Rhodesia to meet Tshombe, Hammarskjöld's plane took a roundabout route to avoid attack by the Katangese Fouga Magister that had already shot it up a few days previously.

19   Kalb (1982) p. 292.

Some minor damage had been done but this was now repaired. The plane maintained radio silence for most of the flight. Shortly after midnight, as it approached the airport at Ndola, it contacted the control tower. Thereafter there was silence. After waiting some time, Lord Alport, the British High Commissioner in Northern Rhodesia who had come to the airport with some others to greet Hammarskjöld, assumed that the plane had diverted elsewhere. So they went home and the airport closed down for the night. A search began, belatedly, on the following day and eventually the wreckage of the plane was spotted from the air, some nine miles from Ndola airport. The six-man crew and nine of the ten others aboard, including Dag Hammarskjöld and Sergeant Francis Eivers, an Irish security officer, had been killed in the crash. One badly burned survivor, Sergeant Harold Julien, an American-born UN Security officer, was still alive. He was briefly lucid at times but unable to explain what had happened. He died in hospital five days later.

I have a vivid personal memory of these events, which happened just as I was on my way to New York with three more senior colleagues to join the Irish Delegation to the forthcoming session of the UN General Assembly. The Assembly was to open on the third Tuesday in September. On the previous Sunday, 17 September, we set out from Dublin on the Aer Lingus flight: the Minister, Frank Aiken – who, as usual, would lead the Delegation – was to join us later.

I remember two lesser things from that Sunday morning as we took our seats in the plane. One was the large front-page headline in the *Sunday Independent*: 'Irish win at Jadotville'. It sounded like a reference to an international rugby match but it was in fact a story about the Irish company beleaguered at Jadotville in Katanga. Unfortunately the news was to prove premature. The Irish soldiers did not 'win': instead, cut off from supplies and from water, with an uncertain mandate and obsolescent equipment, and anxious to achieve a peaceful outcome, they agreed to surrender to the Katangese forces. The other, a more personal and more amusing episode, was the arrival of a press photographer, as we understood it, to take a photo of the four of us, the members of the Irish UN Delegation. At the request of the hostess, we left our seats on the plane, straightened our ties, and lined up to face him on the tarmac. Our self-importance was somewhat deflated when he took the precaution of checking who we were before he took the photograph. No, we were not the winners of the Frigidaire slogan contest from Manchester on our way to claim the prize of a holiday in New York; we were merely the Irish Delegation to the UN General Assembly – or part of it. Altogether a less noteworthy group. Somewhat crestfallen, we slunk back to our seats on the plane to await take-off.

On the following morning, in the San Carlos Hotel in New York, we awoke to what was truly startling news not just for us but for the world: Dag Hammarskjöld, the Secretary General was dead; the UN was rudderless: and what was already a crisis had become a disaster.

4

Back from Katanga

What was to be done? The situation on the morning after Hammarskjöld's death was absolutely unprecedented. The UN had suffered an enormous personal loss in the death of a charismatic leader, albeit one who had been under siege in some respects over the past year. Under his direction, the UN had become deeply involved in what was now a chaotic situation in the Congo. In Katanga, the UN force had suffered losses and was in serious difficulties. But now Hammarskjöld was gone. The Secretariat was leaderless – the Secretary General had been its only elected official – and it looked indeed as if he might prove to have been the last individual ever to hold that office. Over the previous year, the Soviet Union had gone from attacking him personally to demanding the complete abolition of the post of Secretary General and its replacement by a 'troika', a three-person executive, which would be wholly ineffectual. As one Permanent Member of the Security Council, the Soviet Union was not in a position to make its view prevail – but it was certainly in a position, by using its veto, to block anything of which it did not approve. So it seemed doubtful that there could ever be another Secretary General. And the General Assembly was to open on the following day.

As I remember it, Ambassador Freddie Boland, the Irish Permanent Representative, was a guest on many TV and radio programmes on that Monday. Since he had been the President of the General Assembly for the previous year, he was due to take the chair for the last time at the opening meeting of the new General Assembly next day and to vacate it as soon as the Assembly had elected a President to replace him for the forthcoming session. This would probably be Mongi Slim of Tunisia, a highly respected figure at the UN. In this emergency, could Slim take over the post of Secretary General and combine that with his role as President of the General Assembly for the next year? It did not seem feasible even if he were to leave the task of presiding over the Assembly to his Vice-Presidents. In any case, he was not well regarded by the Soviet Union, which still stuck by the troika proposal that Khrushchev had made at the previous session despite lack of support for it from Afro-Asian Member States. Other possibilities were Ambassador Ralph Enkell of Finland and C.V. Narahsimhan of India, a senior official in the Secretariat who had been Chef de Cabinet to Hammarskjöld.

Boland was a central figure in this time of crisis and he was deeply engaged in consultations with other delegations about how to resolve it. Some commentators suggested on TV that, in view of the fact that as outgoing President of the General Assembly he was the only remaining elected officer of the organisation, he should declare that he was taking up the mantle of the late Secretary General. Wisely, he declined to be part of what might have been seen as a mild form of *coup d'état* – in this case, perhaps, it should be called *coup d'organisation*. At a meeting of the Irish Delegation the next day, however, Boland himself told us privately that the US Permanent Representative, Adlai Stevenson, and his deputy, Yost, had urged him strongly to be prepared to accept appointment to the post of Secretary General. He had turned down the suggestion and he was adamant that he would not accept the post. The Taoiseach and the Minister, he told us, would undoubtedly feel that Ireland was already too deeply committed and that we should not take on any further obligations at the UN.

Was this really the case? If the post of Secretary General had actually been offered to Boland, would the Government at home have wanted him to turn it down? It is true that at that time the Department was generally disinclined to seek high international office for its officials – Aiken had a cautious, indeed almost puritan approach in such matters – and it was certainly true that Ireland was already deeply involved at the UN just five years after it had joined. Indeed, the past year had been something of an *annus mirabilis* for Ireland as a Member State: Boland himself was just finishing a fraught year as President of the General Assembly – the session over which he had presided had been one of the most notable in the history of the organisation; General MacKeown was the Force Commander in the Congo; and Conor Cruise O'Brien was still filling what had become a kind of pro-consular role as UN representative in Katanga. But if there had really been a serious prospect of the appointment of an Irish diplomat as Secretary General of the UN, I doubt if either Lemass or Aiken would have turned it down.

Thinking about it now, it seems to me more likely that Boland, a man of long international experience stretching back to the League of Nations, was shrewd enough to know that such an offer was really not on, notwithstanding the encouragement given to him by Adlai Stevenson. One obstacle would be the likelihood of a veto by the Soviet Union: at that time Ireland did not have diplomatic relations with Moscow; that came thirteen years later. In any case, at this point the Soviet Delegation still held to Khrushchev's demand for a 'troika' rather than a single Secretary General. Furthermore, the first two Secretaries General of the organisation had come from small European countries: both, after a time, had incurred the antagonism of the Soviet Union. Given this background, Boland would have calculated that only a candidate from one of what were then called the 'Afro-Asian' Member States would have sufficient support to be able – just possibly – to get past the Soviet opposition to the idea of a single Secretary General.

Boland did, however, play a major part over the following months, along with a few other Permanent Representatives, in the effort to preserve the office of Secretary General and secure agreement on a replacement for Hammarskjöld. This small group – essentially Boland, Slim of Tunisia, Nielsen of Norway and U Thant of Burma – consulted widely with other Delegations. It was particularly important to gain the agreement – or at least the acquiescence – of the five Permanent Members of the Security Council, each of which would have a veto over any appointment. The group of self-appointed 'facilitators' succeeded eventually in getting general agreement to the appointment of one of their own number, U Thant of Burma. At this stage, however, the Soviet Union would accept him only as 'Acting Secretary General' – a title that was not used in any other case before or since. It took another year before it accepted his appointment to a full term of office as Secretary General.

As I look back now on a stray manuscript note that I made after that first internal meeting of the Irish Delegation on the evening of Tuesday, 19 September, I find further evidence of both Boland's shrewdness of judgement and his central role in these events. 'The most likely candidate,' I noted, 'will be U Thant of Burma, of whom the Ambassador [i.e. Boland] spoke highly.' This prediction of Boland's was made to us one day after news of Hammarskjöld's death reached New York and some six weeks before Thant's appointment as Acting Secretary General was eventually agreed.

On the previous day, Monday, Boland had asked each of the four of us who had flown out from Dublin to join the delegation to try our hand at drafting what he should say in opening the General Assembly session on the following afternoon. He needed something that would measure up to the gravity of the occasion. So we worked together in one large room, each of us, like a schoolboy, covering up his homework from the others as we laboured to find rhetoric to match the occasion. He collected our efforts and thanked us for our work. But when he opened the Assembly next day, he confined himself to some three or four sentences of his own. As I recollect it, the gist of what he said was that the Assembly was meeting in the shadow of a great tragedy and that there was nothing to do but adjourn until the following morning.[1] In the delegation seats we looked at one another, realising that he had set us the exercise on the previous day largely in order to keep us occupied – one might say to keep us out of mischief.

In the meantime, Conor Cruise O'Brien was still at his post as UN representative in Katanga although there were already rumours in New York that, in view of the difficulties that had arisen in Katanga, he would be recalled to a post in the Secretariat in New York. I noted at the time that our colleagues in the Irish Permanent Mission in New York thought that the Secretariat had 'behaved in a hopelessly inefficient and ill-informed way' over the preceding few weeks. Since the Secretariat was now in effect 'headless', it did not seem to me at the time to be very likely that anyone in it would have the power to recall such a prominent senior official from his post.

Half a century on the question remains: did Conor exceed his authority and go far beyond what the Security Council, the Secretary General, UN Headquarters in New York and local headquarters in the capital, Leopoldville (now Kinshasa) had intended? Hammarskjöld's biographer, Sir Brian Urquhart, a very distinguished and long-standing senior official of the Secretariat who had been friendly with Conor until these events occurred (and who was sent to replace Conor when he was recalled from Katanga),

---

1   Since writing the above I have checked back on a copy of *United Nations Review*, Vol. 8, No. 10, for October 1961 which I still have. It was the first issue of the journal after Hammarskjöld's death in September. It shows that my memory is broadly correct, but not wholly accurate. On page 6 it reports Ambassador Boland's words of 19 September to the General Assembly as follows: '…the General Assembly meets today in the shadow of an immense tragedy, in the midst of deep and heartfelt mourning which extends far beyond the walls of this chamber to millions of men and women throughout the world. This is not the moment to speak of the loss which we have sustained or to recount the high qualities and the virtues which gave those who have died so firm a hold on our respect and admiration. There will be opportunities for that. For the moment I would simply propose that, as a tribute to the memory of the late Secretary General and of the devoted officers who died with him, and as a mark of our profound condolence with their families and relatives, we should stand and observe a minute of silence, after which this meeting should be adjourned …'

seems to think that he did. He contends that Hammarskjöld's aim was to settle the problem of Katangese secession by bringing Moise Tshombe, the Katangese leader, and Cyril Adoula (who was by then the Prime Minister of the Congo) together; and he seems to suggest that the fact that UN forces had become engaged in combat in Katanga showed that Conor and/or Khiary and other UN personnel involved had either failed to understand or were acting contrary to this policy. In his biography of Hammarskjöld, albeit in a footnote, Urquhart dismisses a view that he attributes to Conor that Hammarskjöld's willingness to meet with Tshombe amounted to virtual surrender. He goes on:

> This verdict ignores both the fact that Hammarskjöld regarded the Katanga fighting as an incidental interruption of his primary objective, which was to bring Adoula and Tshombe together, and that all over Katanga, as well as in the press of much of the world, the UN was on the defensive. Seen in this broader perspective, his instructions to O'Brien appear rather as a firm and realistic attempt to get the UN, and especially O'Brien and the UN Katanga command, out of an impossible situation into which they had fallen through military and other forms of incompetence. Hammarskjöld's approach to Tshombe was designed to end the fighting, to restore the effort of August 28 to expel the mercenaries with Tshombe's cooperation, and to pursue urgently his original objective of bringing Tshombe together with the central government to settle the problem of secession peacefully.[2]

Urquhart's view of these events was strongly contested by Conor, and it led to a rupture of their previously friendly relations.[3] In his

---

2 Urquhart (1973) p. 581.

3 That it was strenuously contested by Conor I know personally from asking him about it years before his death: his response was a sweeping generalisation to the effect that all political memoirs lie. If true, that would cast considerable doubt on his own account – and indeed on my own recollections in this present volume

own autobiography, published years after his Hammarskjöld biography, Urquhart is more inclined to excuse Conor because of the near impossibility of the task he had been given:

> I knew Conor and liked him very much, but thought him an improbable choice for this ghastly job. He was a brilliant and creative man, but not necessarily suited to the task of superintendent in a lunatic asylum.[4]

Not the most politically correct image to evoke, one would have to say.

Is it true that the forceful action by the UN in Katanga in mid-September 1961 that was to have such fateful consequences was, for whatever reason, contrary to the more peaceful approach that Hammarskjöld had wanted the UN to pursue? Or was it rather that Hammarskjöld, in deep difficulties as Secretary General because the UN under his leadership had become stuck in a quagmire in the Congo, under severe criticism by the Soviet Union and facing the growing impatience of non-aligned states at the failure to end the secession of Katanga, did really want a more robust approach towards the implementation of the mandate of the Security Council? So, wanting something to be done but hesitating, Hamlet-like, to act resolutely himself, had he consciously chosen as UN representative in Katanga someone who, he believed, would be temperamentally more likely to take an activist approach? A question that I cannot answer definitively here: it merits a book. As it happens, Conor has written one about his time as UN representative in Katanga. More than forty years on, it is still a good read.

In that book he suggests that when Hammarskjöld and the UN Secretariat looked for an Irish official, they were offered a choice between his colleague at the Permanent Mission, Eamon Kennedy and himself – the one conventional, conservative, reliable and 'safe'; the other more notable for 'originality'. 'If he [Hammarskjöld]

---

4   Brian Urquhart, *A Life in Peace and War*, p. 174.

did not pick the "safer" man, it is because he wanted the less "safe" one.' Towards the end of the book, Conor summarises the Hammarskjöld-as-Hamlet thesis very well in two sentences:

> The policy which Hammarskjöld was pledged to apply – and which, knowing what he was doing, he picked me to apply – implied revolutionary change in Katanga ... But, when it came to the point Hammarskjöld shrank back.[5]

So was Hammarskjöld's 'native hue of resolution sicklied o'er with the pale cast of thought'? Did he really hope for robust and resolute action by his subordinates to resolve the tangle in Katanga? The 1982 account by Madeleine G. Kalb – who has studied the exchanges of cables between New York and the Congo closely – would suggest that whether or not this was so, senior UN officials in the Congo, including Conor, Linner and Khiary (who gave instructions to Conor) had some reason to suppose that he did. As she puts it:

> The exchange of messages between New York and Leopoldville [the Congolese capital] cited by Urquhart was fairly ambiguous and it is not unreasonable to suppose that Linner and Khiary felt that they would be more faithful to their chief's true intentions if they read between the lines of his instructions rather than following them to the letter. Cordier [another very senior UN official] had taken this approach in September 1960 and had never been disowned by Hammarskjöld; Linner had exceeded his instructions regarding Parliament as recently as July and had won Hammarskjöld's praise. This kind of creative insubordination would have been fine if the September 13 operation had been successful. Since it was not, the Secretary-General and his top aides found themselves in an embarrassing position.[6]

---

5   O'Brien (1962) p. 305.
6   Kalb (1982) p. 293.

But if it is impossible to know now just what was in Hammarskjöld's mind, it is fair to point, as some commentators have done since, to the extraordinary character of the Security Council resolution of 21 February 1961 which was the legal basis for the forceful action that the UN, under Conor's direction, had taken in Katanga in the following August and September. I will quote from just one of these books – the account given in a study of UN peacekeeping by the late Sir Anthony Parsons, who served later as Permanent Representative of the UK to the UN, and whom I got to know well and admire when I knew him, twenty years later, as a colleague on the Security Council:

> This resolution had no parallel in UN history. The Council had authorized a 'non-threatening' peacekeeping force, neither mandated nor equipped to fight a campaign, to adopt an enforcement role without first determining that a threat to international peace and security existed, i.e. without a formal move to Chapter VII of the Charter, still less the adoption as a first expedient of non-military coercive measures such as economic sanctions. It also left the command and control of such an enforcement operation in the virtually unfettered hands of the Secretary-General, a procedure anathema to Charter purists such as the Soviet Union.
>
> This hybrid was the best the Council could do in the dense labyrinth of the Congo.[7]

Hammarskjöld as Hamlet? It is plausible and it fits well with all we know of his temperament. We will never know for certain now.

The crash at Ndola on the night of 17 September 1961 left the UN bereft of its Secretary General. The events that led up to that tragedy had also left the organisation lost in the Congo labyrinth. What, you may ask, happened next? After Hammarskjöld's death the UN in the Congo negotiated an uneasy ceasefire with Tshombe's forces,

---

7   Parsons (1995) p. 87.

which the Katangese side later broke repeatedly. The UN by now had also begun to run into serious financial difficulties. A number of Member States, including the Soviet Union, France and Belgium, were refusing to pay their share of the costs of the Congo operation, which were already running at some $10 million per month.[8]

The US by now was seriously alarmed about the whole situation, and the continuing secession of Katanga remained a sore point for African countries. There was a widespread fear at the time about what would happen if the colonial boundaries in Africa, however illogical, were to be open to revision when colonial territories became independent States. The US was also increasingly concerned that if the secession were not ended soon, the Soviet Union would gain greatly in Africa at its expense and the new Congolese Government might turn to the Soviets for support. So, despite the strong reservations of the UK and France, the Kennedy Administration in Washington was now ready to take a strong line on Katanga. It agreed to provide four transport planes for use by the UN within the Congo. It also offered to provide a small number of fighter aircraft if no other country was prepared to do so.[9] This proved unnecessary in the event, since Ethiopia, India and Sweden all supplied jet fighters to the UN force in late September and early October 1961. The passage of the four Ethiopian jets through what was then still the British colony of Uganda was delayed for a time because of what were euphemistically described by the UK as 'technical difficulties', but the planes did eventually reach Katanga.

After two months of behind the scenes negotiation in which Boland played a considerable part, the Soviet Union backed down on its demand for a 'troika' and U Thant was appointed Acting Secretary General on 3 November 1961. On 24 November, the Security Council adopted a new resolution on the Katanga situation. In a key paragraph, this authorised the Secretary General:

---

8   Kalb (1982) p. 308.
9   Ibid., p. 303.

to take vigorous action, including the use of the requisite measure of force, if necessary, for the immediate apprehension, detention pending legal action and/or deportation of foreign military and paramilitary personnel and advisers not under the United Nations Command and mercenaries as laid down in paragraph 2 of Security Council resolution 161A of 21 February 1961.[10]

It also declared that all secessionist activities against the Republic of the Congo were illegal and demanded that they cease. The resolution was adopted by nine votes to nil with two abstentions – France and the UK.[11] The US tried to amend and broaden the resolution to refer to other areas of the Congo beyond Katanga that were also in revolt, but when its amendments were defeated, Adlai Stevenson, after consultation with Washington, voted in favour.[12]

Armed with this resolution and with jet fighters and fighter bombers, and now with much more active US support, the UN in Katanga took vigorous action in early December 1961 after some of its officials were beaten up. Even the UK, where the Macmillan Government had initially stalled, now agreed to meet an Indian request for bombs for the Canberra aircraft that India had sent to help in Katanga.

The UN forcefully established its control after a period of fighting and Tshombe agreed to respect the authority of the central Congolese Government. However, he stopped short of formally ending Katanga's secession. After talks during the following year, 1962, petered out, the Katangese *gendarmerie* began to harass the UN again towards the end of the year. This time, the UN response was forceful and decisive. In January 1963, Tshombe, under serious pressure, eventually ended the secession of the province and

10   Document (S/5002), adopted as resolution 169 (1961).
11   The Security Council had a membership of eleven at the time. It is now fifteen.
12   Kalb (1982) p. 311.

accepted the authority of the central Government in a Plan of National Reconciliation. By February 1963 the new Secretary General, U Thant, was able to report very positively to the Security Council on the fulfilment of the mandate it had given and he began to phase out the UN force. It was withdrawn completely at the end of June 1964. Over the four years of its existence it had lost nearly 250 dead, including a number of Irish troops who died at Niemba, at the 'battle of the tunnel' in Elisabethville and elsewhere.

And Conor? His book recounts how he stayed on in Katanga for several months in the autumn of 1961, despite hints, which he attributes largely to pressure by the Macmillan Government in the UK, that he should resign or steal quietly away to another UN post in New York. In late November 1961 U Thant recalled him to New York for 'consultations'. Conor later offered an unforgettable description of these 'consultations' that is still worth recalling nearly half a century later:

> the body, the physical remains of the administratively defunct O'Brien, was still shuffling zombie-like up and down the long corridor of the 38th floor, being 'consulted', rather as the Chinese consult their dead ancestors.[13]

On 29 November 1961 there was a serious incident in Elizabethville in which senior UN officials were beaten up by Katangese forces and Conor's then colleague and future wife, Máire Mhac an tSaoi, who had gone there to visit him, was subjected to harassment. The next day, following a contact from Dr Ralph Bunche, UN Under Secretary, the Minister for External Affairs, Frank Aiken, who was in New York asked Conor to come to see him. What followed is best described in Conor's own account of what Aiken said:

> Mr. Thant, he said, had been in touch with him, through Dr. Bunche, about Máire's presence in Elisabethville. Mr. Thant

---

13   O'Brien (1962) p. 319.

had asked him to recall me to the Irish Foreign Service. Mr. Thant had indicated that, if Mr. Aiken did not do so, he, Mr. Thant, would call for my resignation. The reason given was that I had now shown myself to be so indiscreet as to be unsuitable for further service with the United Nations.[14]

Conor goes on to give his own view: 'indiscretion is a function of public attention and public attention, in my case, was a function of politics.' The politics in this case emerged from the confluence of the subtle hostility of British policy conveyed to the UN by the British Ambassador, Sir Patrick Dean, and the open hostility of a part of the British press, led by Lord Beaverbrook, which was happy to splash mud on the United Nations. So 'The thing to do now was to extricate myself with all speed, and with the honours of war, from the Dean-Beaverbrook convergence.'[15] O'Brien told Aiken, who had quite an affection for him and was quite upset at all that had happened, that he had better do as the UN had requested and recall him to the Irish Foreign Service.

I still have, yellowed with age and folded into my copy of Conor's book on Katanga, a copy of the UN Press Release issued on 1 December 1961. It is worth quoting even now, as a model of the kind of foolish, face-saving, spin of which Conor himself, had he not been preoccupied with the stress of the actual events, would undoubtedly have taken a scathing view.

Acting Secretary-General U Thant received on Thursday, 30 November, a request from Frank Aiken, the Irish Minister for External Affairs, for the return, as soon as possible, of the services of Dr. Conor Cruise O'Brien, who was seconded by the Irish Government to the United Nations on a temporary basis last July.

---

14   Ibid., p. 326.
15   Ibid., p. 327.

Mr. Aiken explained that he was obliged to make this request since his Department had suffered a number of losses of top-ranking personnel because of death and retirement, and required strengthening without delay.

In these circumstances, and in view of Dr. O'Brien's own wishes, the Acting Secretary General felt bound to accede to Mr. Aiken's request. Dr. O'Brien plans to leave the service of the United Nations on 8 December.

In conveying his agreement to Mr. Aiken, U Thant expressed appreciation of Dr. O'Brien's able services, indicating that he had served the United Nations with devotion and courage in one of its most difficult posts.[16]

It may have sounded plausible to the casual reader to say that the small Irish Foreign Service 'required strengthening without delay'. That was undoubtedly true at the time. But its apparent plausibility as a reason for Conor's recall vanished completely when Conor decided that he should also quit the Irish Foreign Service on the following day. So in the event his contribution towards the 'strengthening 'of his home Department, the ostensible reason for his recall, lasted exactly one day: he resigned from the Department on Saturday 2 December. Shortly afterwards, Máire also resigned. She left Katanga and joined him in New York. Together, they threw a party the following week that I attended with my colleagues from the delegation just before we returned to Dublin for Christmas. They were married in New York in January 1962.

I return again to the question I raised earlier: did Conor act rashly in September 1961? Did he exceed his mandate? The account of his side of the story that he gives in his book *To Katanga and Back* is both plausible and elegant, and still worth reading half a century later. I will offer only one supplementary comment, based on subsequent events. If Conor acted rashly and exceeded his mandate

---

16 United Nations Press Services, Office of Public Information. Press Release SG/1079, CO/170 of 1 December 1961.

in 1961, then why did the UN act even more vigorously – at the end of 1961, in 1962 and in 1963, two years after he had left to write his book? Lives were lost in those subsequent actions, including a number of Irish lives; the mercenaries were forcibly removed; and Katangese secession was brought to an end by force. If Hammarskjöld can be seen as Hamlet, then this Hamlet too had died in what seemed at the time to be the last act of the play. But in this case there was to be an epilogue. The forceful action that this Hammarskjöld/Hamlet had hesitated to order was eventually taken after his death by U Thant, the Acting Secretary General, a somewhat unlikely Fortinbras.

I can add two further personal anecdotes.

Some weeks after the crash in which Dag Hammarskjöld died, a draft resolution setting up a UN inquiry into his death was introduced in the General Assembly, where I, as the junior member of the delegation, was minding the Irish seat, while my seniors and betters were occupied in the various specialized Committees. At the delegation meeting that morning, the Ambassador, Freddie Boland – the leader of the delegation in the absence of the Minister, Frank Aiken – looked at the text of the draft. 'We should certainly vote against that,' he instructed. 'There will be enough other investigations.' At the time Sweden and what was then Southern Rhodesia were about to set up inquiries.

Later I sat in the Assembly hall behind Ireland's name-plate and listened to speaker after speaker refer positively to the draft resolution. I grew uneasy but there was no opportunity to contact the Ambassador again. So I awaited the vote. A roll-call vote was asked for – this was some time before modern electronic voting was introduced. As was customary, the name of the first delegation to vote was drawn from a hat. It was Ireland. So I would have to declare Ireland's position without knowing precisely what any other Member State would do. I had clear instructions to vote against. I voted for.

As it happened it was fortunate that I did so, because the vote in favour of setting up the UN inquiry was unanimous. Had I done otherwise that day, Ireland's solitary vote opposing an inquiry would have certainly have made headlines – the more so because of our deep involvement in the Congo and because Conor Cruise O'Brien, a central figure in the events that preceded Hammarskjöld's death, was still at that time the Secretary General's representative in Katanga. I don't recall that Freddie Boland was in the least put out at the fact that I had ignored his instructions – or indeed that he made any comment later. And no, I did not make an early and ignominious exit from the Diplomatic Service for my temerity in disobeying his direct instructions. It is perhaps more likely that I would have done so if I had done what I was told.

Was the untimely death of Dag Hammarskjöld and his colleagues on that plane really an accident? Did the UN plane, fearful perhaps of being attacked as it came in to land, fly too low and hit the tree-tops? Was it pilot error? Or was it due to something more sinister – sabotage or an attack by another aircraft? Perhaps the Katangese Fouga Magister that had damaged it some days before had returned to the attack? Certainly there were a number of people in that part of Africa at that time who would have wished Hammarskjöld dead, and the organisation he represented damaged.

Two separate official inquiries took place over the following months but neither could reach a definitive conclusion. In February 1962, the Federal Rhodesian Commission of Inquiry concluded that the crash was probably due to 'pilot error'. The UN Commission set up by the vote in the General Assembly reported three months later, in May 1962. It reviewed a wide range of possible causes. 'Pilot error,' it said, was indeed a possibility but 'The Commission, while it cannot exclude this possibility, has found no indication that this was the probable cause of the crash.' Sabotage, also, 'cannot be excluded'; and it noted that 'there are many possible methods of sabotage.' On these events I came across something that Lord Palmerston is reported as having said in 1830. Plenipotentiaries, in his view, were only of use if they disobeyed their instructions. 'A clerk or messenger would do, if it is only strictly necessary to follow them.'[17]

My second memory comes from the years after these events, when I was posted to serve in the Irish Embassy in Brussels. There, I quickly came to understand that Belgians had seen Conor as the arch-villain of the whole Katanga affair. I retained for many years the front cover of the weekly magazine *Pourquoi Pas*, the Belgian equivalent of *Time* or *Newsweek*, which showed him in lurid colours as Mephistopheles, with stubby horns on his head, over the caption *Le Roi des connards* which, I suppose, would translate as 'King of the Idiots' or 'what a schmuck!'.

A short time before I left the Embassy in Brussels to take up a new posting in Washington – probably in early 1964 – I met a hardbitten Belgian who had a finger missing. He had served in the Spanish Civil War and later as a mercenary in Katanga. He told me that many of the other mercenaries were Belgians who had fought in the Korean War and, now in poorly paid jobs at home, were avid for further action.

He and his wife boasted to me that Europeans serving with Tshombe's forces, with the help of an accomplice in the Belgian administration, had managed to divert three Fouga Magister aircraft that Belgium ordered from Germany and have them sent instead to Katanga, where they were based at Kolwezi. However, two of the aircraft developed problems and by August/September 1961 the mercenaries with the Katangese forces had only one serviceable aircraft. But they fooled the UN into thinking that they still had three by flying successive sorties from a small grass airfield near the

17 An hour-long documentary film on these events, which I think was of Swedish origin and which was made in 2001, was shown on the Irish-language TV station TG4 on 28 January 2009. It reported that four African charcoal-burners working in the forest had witnessed the crash, nine miles from Ndola airport. They testified afterwards that they had seen a second plane. One of the four spoke to camera, in English, about what he had seen. He was clear and articulate and his story sounded convincing. According to the film, however, the testimony of these Africans was given little credence and the view of some white Rhodesian police officers that there had been no second plane was preferred.

capital Elisabethville and giving the single plane a quick coat of paint and a new recognition number after each flight! He showed me a flying helmet and implied strongly that he himself had flown the aircraft. He also spoke with some contempt of the fighting qualities of the Katangese gendarmerie: he claimed that the two hundred Katangese who surrounded the Irish contingent at Jadotville had been passive and unwilling to fight. So, like the romantic hero Beau Geste defending a Foreign Legion desert fort, he and six or seven mercenary colleagues leading the Katangese had run around the perimeter and fired a machine gun burst here and there. In this way, the 134 Irish under siege had been fooled into thinking that they were surrounded by a much larger force of mercenaries. True? Possibly, possibly not. But in the Congo and Katanga of that time, who can say?

Overall, was the four-year UN operation in the Congo a success? Yes, to the limited extent that it preserved the fragile unity of the Congo and prevented the break-up that would have followed if the secession of Katanga had succeeded. But that unfortunate country had to live through more than another quarter-century of the depredations of Mobutu, who, with the covert support of the CIA, took over as dictator, renamed it Zaire and diverted billions of dollars of its mineral revenues to his personal accounts and those of his family in European banks. In more recent times, and even today, the eastern Congo has suffered greatly from tribal warfare, an influx of Hutu refugees from Rwanda and invasion by Rwandan forces and those of neighbouring States, lured there in some cases it seems by a wish to exploit the mineral wealth of the region. Reports talk of deaths in the millions – possibly the greatest death-toll in any war over the past half-century.

And the UN itself? The whole experience left it scarred and weary and brought it close to collapse. It lost an esteemed Secretary General; and his successor, U Thant, was obliged to serve his first year in an 'Acting' capacity only, because the Soviet Union, following Khrushchev's 'troika' proposal, would not agree to a full appointment. More serious still, however, was the flat refusal by the Soviet Union, France and a number of other countries to meet their assessed share of the costs of the Congo operation.

This led to a financial crisis that was almost terminal for the organisation. It led, too, to the farcical General Assembly session of 1964–65, which met under the shadow of the Article in the Charter that provides that a Member State more than two years in arrears in payment of its contributions is to be deprived of its vote.[18] The Soviet Union, by refusing to pay its assessed contributions towards the Congo operation, had reached that position by then. France would soon do so. If the Assembly were to vote on any issue – even to the extent of electing Chairmen for Committees – it would have been obliged to apply the Charter provision and deprive two Permanent Members of the Security Council of their vote.

The confrontation was sharpened by the fact that the US Delegation was under pressure to take a strong line: the House of Representatives, by a unanimous vote a few months previously, had called on President Johnson to ensure that the rule about loss of voting rights would be applied. This opened up an 'appalling vista': France and the Soviet Union, angered by losing their votes, might walk out of the organisation, followed by other countries of Eastern Europe. So the UN, like the League of Nations before it, could well have collapsed after just twenty years.

What was to be done? The simple answer was – nothing. The Assembly, by tacit agreement, was reduced to masterly inactivity. It did not dare to vote or to break into Committees, since it would have had to vote to elect Chairmen for those Committees. So it decided to proceed only by 'consensus'. In effect, it could do no more than debate, and that for the two months or so that the session lasted. As the Secretary General put it delicately, following con-sultations with various delegations, 'there is an understanding to the effect that issues other than those that can be disposed of without objection will not be raised.'

---

18   UN Charter Article 19.

Only one representative tried to step out of line by calling for a vote, as he was legally entitled to do. That was Budo of Albania, a nice enough man personally, representing what at the time, and for long after, was one of the most isolated and benighted countries in the world. On 16 February 1965, two days before end of the session, he stood at the rostrum and had the temerity to ask for a vote. There was consternation in the hall: small, poor and isolated it might be, but Albania might yet bring down the UN. Fortunately the day was saved by a most unlikely figure: Baroody, who represented Saudi Arabia for many years, though not himself a native of that country. He had the habit of wandering from Committee to Committee, and into the Security Council at times, like Homer's Thersites, 'wagging his unbridled tongue – a man of many words and those unseemly'. On this occasion, for once, he said nothing. Instead he left his seat in the hall, walked up to the podium, put his arm around Budo and led him unprotesting away.

Nevertheless, Budo maintained his position and, at a later point, sought a roll-call vote on his proposal that the Assembly revert to its normal procedures. The President, Quaison-Sackey of Ghana, ruled against him. Budo challenged this ruling and the Assembly rejected his challenge by 97 votes to 2. Only Mauritania supported his request. So Budo succeeded to the extent of forcing the Assembly to vote – its only vote over the two months that the Session lasted. A vote? But surely this meant applying the rule and depriving those who were delinquent about payment of their contributions of their voting rights? Not quite. When needs must, and there is a general wish to do so, a rule – even one set in stone in the Charter – can be flexibly applied. The US, the leading 'hardliner' on applying the rule about loss of vote strictly, took the position that this had been a procedural vote, not one on an issue of substance and so the Charter Article about punishing delinquents did not have to be invoked. The Assembly breathed a sigh of relief and went on to another day of normal non-business, before adjourning until the following autumn.

This crisis over how to pay for UN peacekeeping, and the threat that it seemed to pose to the very existence of the UN, deeply affected the Irish Minister for External Affairs, Frank Aiken. Aiken was by now an unusual and yet a respected figure in the General Assembly. He was a man of deep conviction, who believed very strongly in the United Nations and saw an effective UN, with a capacity for peacekeeping, as vital for all small nations; he had stoutly defended Hammarskjöld when he came under severe attack for his conduct of the Congo operation. Aiken's personal standing in the Assembly had grown because of the success of his campaign on the issue of nuclear non-proliferation. As I recount in Chapter 6, the resolution that he had eventually steered to a unanimous decision in 1961 was generally credited with inspiring the negotiations then under way on a Nuclear Non-Proliferation Treaty. He now turned his attention actively to the financing of UN peacekeeping and began to campaign vigorously on that issue.

For several years, this was Ireland's main foreign policy initiative at the UN.[19] Aiken's argument was that peacekeeping finances had to be put on a sound basis – otherwise major countries would enjoy a double veto. First, they could use their veto in the Security Council to block the establishment of a UN force. But even if they did not do that, and they allowed a UN force to be set up, they could still exercise a second veto in practice by declining to pay their assessed contributions towards its maintenance.

Aiken was convinced that this was wrong and that it would prevent the UN from developing an effective peacekeeping capacity – something that in his view, as we have seen, was particularly important for smaller Member States. There was also an Irish financial issue involved, since the UN had agreed to refund to countries that contributed peacekeeping contingents the extra costs that they incurred, over and above the normal upkeep of their

---

19   Con Cremin, who was Ireland's UN Ambassador from 1964 to 1974, gave an account of this in an essay entitled 'United Nations Peace-Keeping Operations: an Irish Initiative 1961–1968'. See Cremin (1984).

forces, and Ireland was now owed a good deal of money. In the mid-1960s, therefore, Aiken asked formally to have an item entitled 'The Authorisation and Financing of Future Peacekeeping Operations' placed on the agenda of the General Assembly. Over the following three or four years, the delegation, and Aiken personally as its leader, campaigned strongly on the issue and worked hard to mobilise support for the draft resolutions that it presented at each successive session of the Assembly.

To start with, the Irish Delegation was able to rally five or six small countries as co-sponsors for this approach. As I recall it, each year in the late 1960s, such diplomatic muscle as we could muster in the UN General Assembly was put behind the effort to gain votes, and if possible additional co-sponsors, for this initiative. I and other members of the Delegation were sent out individually into the highways and by-ways of the UN to work the corridors and lobby for support. No member of a small delegation was safe from being pressed to a coffee or a drink or a discussion in a soft armchair in a dark corner of one of the delegates' lounges while he or she heard our arguments. At delegation meetings each morning, we reported our success, or lack of it, to the Minister: a promise of a vote in favour earned a commendation; a commitment to join as a co-sponsor of the Irish draft resolution was a major achievement.

My memory is that Aiken's approach was strongly supported by countries such as Ceylon, Ghana, Ivory Coast, Liberia, Nepal, Somalia, Costa Rica and the Philippines, all of which eventually became co-sponsors of the Irish draft resolution. It is sad to think that, since then, some of these countries have themselves suffered serious internal conflicts that have led the UN to engage in peacekeeping efforts on their territory. Aiken's valiant campaign deserved to succeed. But in the climate of the times it did not, and support gradually fell away over the following years to a degree that left him fighting with decreasing hope of success for a cause already lost from an early stage.

However, despite the failure at that time to agree on a fully secure system of compulsory assessment to meet the costs, UN peace-keeping did continue – though sometimes on a hand-to-mouth basis. It had its successes – in the Sinai, in Cyprus, in Lebanon and many other places – and some notable failures, in Srebrenica and Rwanda.

In more recent times, the scope of UN peacekeeping has widened greatly. Today a typical peacekeeping operation may have a robust mandate from the Security Council, and it will frequently be part of a broader peacebuilding effort by the UN that will also include other components covering areas such as civilian policing and police training, humanitarian work, human rights, legal training, election monitoring and so on. At present there are up to 85,000 people engaged in UN peacekeeping, in this broader sense, in various trouble-spots around the world.

The UN has long since come through the trauma that followed its involvement in the Congo in the 1960s, when it was drawn in for the first time to the effort to rescue a 'failed state'. But it did learn valuable lessons from the experience – among them a measure of caution about making too deep a commitment, with limited resources and capacity, to that kind of effort. To that extent there is still a lingering memory in the UN corridors of the quagmire of the Congo in which, at one time, the organisation came close to foundering.

5

The China Vote

At the very end of his book about his Katanga adventure, Conor Cruise O'Brien recalls the reply of the venerable Trinity scholar Dr Luce, when he said that he was writing a book about the Congo – 'Is there a book in that, do you think?' Conor's book, and many others since, proved that there was. Even by Dr Luce's austere standard, one would have to say that there are many books in the other events and issues in which Ireland was involved at the UN over the first fifteen years of our membership. I will limit myself here, however, to a selective account of what seem to me the more interesting episodes from that period, for most of which Frank Aiken was Minister for External Affairs.

Much the most contentious issue that arose for the Irish Delegation during the early Aiken years was the vote in favour of a proposal to discuss the representation of China in the General Assembly. The seismic tremor that it caused had occurred more than two years before, but when I joined the Department in January 1960 occasional after-shocks were still being felt.

'The Republic of China' was a founding Member of the United Nations. Indeed, it is one of only five Member States mentioned by name in the UN Charter, where it is listed as one of the five Permanent Members of the Security Council, along with the US, the UK, France and the USSR. Its representatives took part in the preliminary talks in Dumbarton Oaks in 1944 when the major Allied powers negotiated the first draft of the Charter; and, in 1945, it was one of the four 'sponsoring powers' of the San Francisco Conference where the UN was established.

At that time, the 'Nationalist Government' headed by Chang Kai Shek was recognised internationally as the legitimate government of China. During the war against Japan, his forces had cooperated to some extent with Chinese Communist forces in order to fight a common enemy. But after the war ended in 1945, this uneasy co-operation came to an end and civil war resumed in China. By 1949, the Communist forces under the leadership of Mao Tse Tung had defeated the Nationalist armies, taken control in Beijing, and proclaimed a state described as 'The People's Republic of China'. Chang Kai Shek and his Government fled to the offshore island of Taiwan. There they suppressed local opposition and established themselves in power. Although they controlled only Taiwan and some small neighbouring islands, they maintained a claim, then and for many years afterwards, to be the legitimate Government of all of China. There was now a stalemate in the civil war: the Nationalist Chinese forces continued to receive strong support, both political and military, from the United States, and, largely because of this, the forces of the new Communist Government were not in a position to attack the last remaining Nationalist stronghold in Taiwan.

Mao's People's Republic, having consolidated its control of the mainland, claimed the right to represent China in the United Nations and strongly disputed the right of the Nationalists in Taiwan to speak for all of China. Neither of the two sides, however, would accept that there were now 'two Chinas'. Both strongly insisted that there was only one, and both were adamant that it included Taiwan as well as the mainland. The question was who was to speak for it, and who would occupy China's seats in the General Assembly and in the Security Council respectively. This was a matter for each of these two major UN organs to decide for itself. In 1950, however, the Security Council, under strong pressure from the United States, rejected a proposal to discuss the issue and the Soviet Union walked out from the Council in protest.

In June of that year, North Korean forces invaded South Korea. In the absence of the Soviet Union, which was still in a pique about the refusal to debate the question of China's seat, the Council adopted resolutions calling on North Korea to withdraw and recommending that Member States help South Korea to repel the attack. In early July the Council went further: it recommended that Member States supplying military forces to help South Korea should assign their forces to 'a unified command under the United States of America'; and it authorised this 'unified command' to use the United Nations flag.[1] In the early stages of the Korean war, the US-led 'United Nations' forces successfully repulsed the North Koreans but as they drove forward close to its border, China was drawn into the war on the North Korean side. The 'UN' forces were forced back down the peninsula but after an amphibious landing at Inchon they fought their way back up again. The fighting continued until a truce was declared in 1953. An uneasy peace line was then established across the Korean peninsula close to the 38th Parallel. The so-called 'Demilitarised Zone' or DMZ between the two Koreas along this line remains a place of great tension even to the present day.

US opposition to the claim of the People's Republic to represent China in the UN was greatly reinforced by these events. It could hold the line in regard to the seat in the Security Council but it was by no means certain that it could command the necessary votes to block a decision to seat the People's Republic in the General Assembly. Some countries such as the UK, which normally followed a US lead, would part from it on this particular issue because they maintained diplomatic relations with the People's Republic in Beijing rather than with the Nationalist Government in Taiwan. So, from 1950 onwards, US policy was to keep the issue from arising in the General Assembly. It put strong pressure on other countries to support this approach and it was able to assemble a majority year

---

1   Document S/1588 adopted on 7 July 1950 as resolution 84 (1950). As well as the US, some twenty-one other UN Member States responded by supplying forces.

after year in the 1950s to vote down a proposal to place the question on the Assembly agenda for discussion.

The first time an Irish Delegation had to face a decision on how to vote on the question was at the Assembly session of 1956. Liam Cosgrave, the Minister for External Affairs in the Coalition Government, who led the delegation that year, told the Assembly that Ireland would support the US position. He argued that it would be inappropriate to discuss the seating of the People's Republic because its actions had violated the Charter and also because a fellow Communist State, the Soviet Union, had invaded Hungary some weeks before. In explaining Ireland's vote, however, he acknowledged that, eventually, the international community would have

> to decide whether we are going to leave the de facto government of over 500 million people without representation in the United Nations, or whether we should compromise on the matter.

This seemed like a hint of future change. However, in his book on *Irish Diplomacy at the United Nations* Dr Joseph Skelly reports that Liam Cosgrave told him in 1992 that this was certainly not his intention – indeed he implied to Skelly that even then, thirty-eight years later, his view of China had not greatly changed.[2]

The issue came up again at the next Assembly session in September 1957. By now there had been a change of Government in Ireland. Fianna Fáil was in office and Frank Aiken was Minister for External Affairs. As leader of the Irish Delegation he spoke at a meeting of the General Assembly on 23 September to explain the vote he was about to cast. He condemned China's 'aggressive policies'. But he also argued that the aim should be 'to win

---

2 Skelly (1997) pp. 61–62. In a footnote on p. 62, Skelly reports on a personal interview that he had with Liam Cosgrave on 11 April 1992: 'Cosgrave said: "Of course you should never say 'never'", but that is what he had in mind. He added that in the light of the fact that the Chinese government has not changed in many respects, perhaps Ireland's policy was the right one.'

acceptance for the principles of the Charter in China and to secure self-determination for the people of Korea'. Progress towards these ends could best be made 'by having a full and open discussion of the question of the representation of China' in the Assembly. He then went on, contrary to the US approach, to vote in favour of a proposal by India to put the issue on the agenda for discussion. This proposal was defeated by 29 votes to 43 with nine abstentions.[3]

In a book entitled *Memoir: My Life and Themes* which was published in 1998, and which I have mentioned in an earlier chapter, Conor Cruise O'Brien ascribes Aiken's decision to vote for discussion of the China question to his own advice, during a discussion shortly after the Minister assumed office. Aiken, he says, told him that he wanted to follow a more independent line at the General Assembly than his predecessor. In response:

> I told the Minister that if any delegation at the General Assembly wished to be accepted as following an independent line, the test was the annual vote on the representation of China.

He went on to explain the details of the issue to the Minister:

> much of it he knew, or at least sensed, already but I was able to fill in a lot of details, and what I said made sense to him. In the end he simply said: 'Very well, we shall vote against the compromise, and in favour of a straight vote on the question of which delegation should represent China in the Assembly.'[4]

---

3   A table in the annual report of the Irish Delegation on the Twentieth General Assembly (1965) (a document internal to the Department) shows that the Assembly voted by 47 in favour, 27 against and seven abstentions to accept the recommendation of its General Committee, the effect of which would be to keep the issue off the Assembly agenda. The figures I have used in the text above are those for the vote on a proposed Indian amendment that would have reversed the report of the General Committee on this point and put the question on the agenda of the Assembly. See Department of External Affairs (1957) p. 28.

4   O'Brien (1998) pp. 186–187.

Certainly Aiken had a very high regard for Conor Cruise O'Brien – though he was still only a middle-level official at the time – and it may well be that it was indeed O'Brien's advice that determined Aiken's decision. But Aiken was a Minister of long experience with memories stretching back to de Valera's role in the League of Nations and his own participation in the War of Independence. I would not be at all sure that the stubbornly independent integrity of Aiken's own character would not have brought him to the same decision even if Conor had not given the advice he did.[5]

In a much earlier book, *To Katanga and Back,* Conor gives what we can now see, fifty years later, as an amusing account of the reaction of one eminent American to this new and radical position of the Irish Delegation. The US Delegation had been told in advance what Ireland proposed to do. Shortly afterwards:

> the Irish Consul General in New York received a telephone message from the Archbishop of New York, Francis Cardinal Spellman. His Eminence wished to know whether it was true that Mr. Aiken was 'going to vote for Red China' … His Eminence wanted to make his own position clear. 'Tell Aiken', he told the Consul-General, 'that if he votes for Red China, we'll raise the Devil.'[6]

Amusing, yes, at this remove to think that a leading Churchman exercised such influence in the nether regions. But far from amusing for those involved at the time. It would be too much to say, in the conventional phrase, that 'all Hell broke loose', but the Cardinal's

---

5   So far as I am aware Conor did not give this account of how Aiken reached his decision in any of his previous books. While I have always valued his writings, I pointed out in a footnote in an earlier chapter that *Memoir: My Life and Themes,* the particular book in which he recounts this story, is a very late work and sadly, one that contains a number of inaccuracies. This leads me to wonder if Conor may perhaps have overstated the extent to which Aiken's decision to take a radical position on the China issue was entirely due to his, Conor's, advice. I do not doubt either the advice that Conor gave nor that that advice would have been important to Aiken, but I still think it possible that Aiken might have come to a similar decision himself in any case.

6   O'Brien (1962) p. 23.

powerful friend did indeed emerge on stage, and rather quickly, accompanied by several lesser demons who plagued Aiken and the Irish Delegation with whips and scorpions over the next few years. One that wielded these instruments to some effect was Spellman's own diocesan paper, the *Catholic News*. Another, sharper and even more persistent in its attack, was the paper of the neighbouring Catholic diocese across the river from Manhattan, *The Brooklyn Tablet*. I had not yet joined the Department of External Affairs when this assault first began, but when I joined in January 1960 I read all the files of clippings on the issue that the UN section had accumulated over the previous two years. Even at that stage the attacks still erupted intermittently and there were occasional new clippings to be added to the bundle already on file.

The vote also had repercussions at home in Ireland. The Roman Catholic hierarchy criticised the Minister strongly for his position.[7] They were joined in this by some priests of the Maynooth Mission to China, more commonly known as the Columban Fathers. This was understandable perhaps, as theirs was a missionary society whose priests in China had been expelled or imprisoned by the Communist government. Dr Michael Browne, Bishop of Galway, the most active polemicist among the hierarchy – sometimes known, aptly enough, from the episcopal style he used in signing his name, as 'cross Michael' – was particularly vociferous. The weekly Catholic newspapers in Ireland – *The Irish Catholic* and *The Standard* – not to be outdone by their American counterparts, echoed and amplified the criticisms from across the Atlantic; and the main Opposition party, Fine Gael, understandably enough, profited by the occasion and joined with gusto in attacking the Minister for his policy.

In face of this storm of criticism, Aiken maintained his position and continued over the following years to vote in favour of

---

7   On p. 191 of a book from which I have already quoted, Conor Cruise O'Brien (1998) plays down greatly the reactions of both American Catholics and the Irish Roman Catholic hierarchy at home ('a damp squib', 'faint rumblings from individual churchmen'). I can only say that my own memory of the time, and my memory of the files we kept in the UN section, is rather different.

discussion of the question of the representation of China in the General Assembly of the United Nations. Anyone who knew him, and what I have described earlier as his gritty integrity, conviction and stubbornness, would have expected no less. But behind that strong outer perimeter, it seems evident to me now that the sustained attack on his position had some effect.

There was some indication of this as early as 1959. In explaining Ireland's vote for the first time in 1957, he had spoken of 'acceptance for the principles of the Charter by China' and 'self-determination for the people of Korea' as aims on which progress could be made by open discussion of the question of Chinese representation in the Assembly. By 1959 these points, with some additions, had become for him issues to be *negotiated* with China before any decision on Chinese representation was taken. In a speech to the Assembly on 21 September 1959, he noted that the question of seating the People's Republic was not before the Assembly and that it was an issue on which the Irish Government had not yet taken a position. He went on:

> If a proposal were before the Assembly at this moment to accept the Peiping [i.e. Beijing] Government as representing China, my delegation would advocate that, before any substantive decision were taken, a United Nations effort should be made through negotiation to secure from the Peiping Government an undertaking to refrain from using force against any of their neighbours, to give religious freedom to the Chinese people and to allow the people of all Korea to decide their destiny in an internationally supervised election.[8]

The issues that Aiken was suggesting should be negotiated with China – religious freedom in China, the reunification of Korea and a commitment by China not to use force against its neighbours – were matters on which Chinese pride was unlikely to allow it to give

---

8   Department of External Affairs (1957) p. 6.

commitments, at least explicitly and publicly, in return for a seat that it considered itself entitled to occupy, in an organisation with which it had been formally at war only six years before. But what Aiken said is subtly phrased. It introduces the idea of conditions but stops short of saying that acceptance of these conditions by the People's Republic should be an absolute precondition. Rather the UN ought to make an *effort* to secure the suggested undertaking. There was an echo in Aiken's approach here, perhaps, of the position taken by Éamon de Valera on the admission of the Soviet Union to the League of Nations in 1934. De Valera on that occasion spoke and voted in favour of the admission of the Soviet Union to membership of the League while urging it strongly to guarantee 'the rights of liberty of conscience and freedom of worship'.[9]

Much more significant than these subtle nuances in an Assembly speech, however, was the Irish initiative in 1959 on the question of Tibet. It may have been undertaken on its own merits but it also had an important, and not altogether incidental, effect in reassuring critics of 'the China vote' in Ireland and in the US.

Over the centuries, Tibet, because of its inaccessibility, had been able to maintain a degree of independence that fluctuated according to the strength or weakness of China, its large and powerful neighbour to the north and east. In 1950, the year after Mao's People's Republic had established itself in Beijing, Chinese forces invaded Tibet. Over the following years, they established control there, displacing what they considered to be a backward, feudal regime. As China extended its control it encouraged Han Chinese settlers to migrate into the territory. Sporadic Tibetan resistance through the 1950s developed into a more organised rebellion in 1959. This was suppressed by China with some brutality and Tibet's political/religious leader, the Dalai Lama, sought asylum in India, where he has since lived in exile. China consolidated its hold on the territory and today it considers Tibet to be one of five 'autonomous regions' of China. The majority of the population are now Han

9   See Moynihan (1980) p. 260.

Chinese; sporadic indirect contacts and efforts at a negotiated settlement between the Dalai Lama and the Chinese Government have
had no substantial result although they still continue from time to
time.

In 1959, as Joseph Skelly recounts in his book on *Irish Diplomacy
at the United Nations 1945–1965*,[10] Freddie Boland, the Irish
Permanent Representative at the UN in New York, while admitting
that the precise legal status of Tibet *vis-à-vis* China was uncertain,
recommended to Aiken and to the Department of External Affairs
in Dublin that the Minister should make a public statement, 'in a
speech in his constituency or elsewhere', condemning China's attack
on Tibet. This suggestion was taken up at home; Conor Cruise
O'Brien was asked to draft a speech that was delivered by Aiken in
Dundalk on 12 April 1959.[11] In it, he roundly condemned China's
'unprovoked aggression' against Tibet which, he said, had 'shocked
the conscience of the world'.[12] Boland ensured that the text was
circulated widely in New York.

At the General Assembly session that autumn, Aiken spoke in his
General Debate speech of 'the brutal crushing of Tibetan autonomy,
[and] the expulsion of the religious leaders of the Tibetan people'.
He followed this by joining with what was then the Federation of
Malaya (now Malaysia) in asking to have a new item, 'The Question
of Tibet', added to the agenda for debate.[13] When the issue came up
for discussion in the Assembly he contended that Tibet had 'always
been acknowledged to be a distinct and separate entity'. Some

---

10   Skelly (1997) p. 172. Skelly gives a full account of the Tibet initiative on pp. 171–187
     of his book.
11   Conor Cruise O'Brien (1998, p. 194) describes Aiken's position as follows: 'Aiken
     could see quite clearly, of course that he was being offered a way in from the cold
     of American displeasure over the China vote. But he didn't shrink from the way in,
     any more than he had flinched from the cold ... Aiken wanted to do his best for the
     Tibetans, as Dev had done for the Abyssinians, and was not deterred, but pleased,
     by the thought that he was also thereby doing himself some political good and
     confounding his adversaries.'
12   Skelly (1997, pp. 174–5) quotes the text as reported in *The Irish Times* of 13 April
     1959.
13   Department of External Affairs (1959) pp. 4–5 and 21–52.

delegations, he said, had argued that the issue should not be debated in the absence from the Assembly of representatives of the People's Republic. Aiken responded that Ireland favoured discussion of Chinese representation, and he noted that, as his co-sponsor the Federation of Malaya had pointed out, the People's Republic was a party to the Bandung Declaration of 1955, which included a pledge by all those involved to abide by the principles and purposes of the United Nations.[14]

The resolution on Tibet submitted jointly by Ireland and Malaya was a moderate one. A preambular paragraph spoke of 'the distinctive cultural and religious heritage of the people of Tibet and … the autonomy which they have traditionally enjoyed'. But the resolution did not press the issue of Tibetan independence – had it done so it would have been less likely to win broad support. Its main operative paragraph was limited to a call for 'respect for the fundamental human rights of the Tibetan people and for their distinctive cultural and religious life'. The Assembly adopted the resolution on 21 October 1959 by 45 votes to nine, with 26 abstentions.[15]

The People's Republic ignored the call of the Assembly. Two years later, in 1961, when I was myself a member of the UN Delegation, Ireland and the Federation of Malaya – joined now by two new co-sponsors, El Salvador and Thailand – put forward another resolution on Tibet. Much of the text was on similar lines to that adopted two years before, but there was a significant addition: one of the operative paragraphs referred to the right of the Tibetan people to self-determination. It read as follows:

---

14   The Conference held at Bandung in Indonesia in April 1955 is generally regarded as the beginning of an active, self-conscious Non-Aligned Movement, committed to 'positive neutralism'. Nehru and Sukarno were important figures at the Conference. Some 29 countries attended. Many were from Asia; Tito's Yugoslavia and Nasser's Egypt were also prominent. The Conference set out 'five principles of co-existence': mutual respect for territorial integrity and sovereignty; non-aggression; non-interference in each other's internal affairs; equality and mutual benefits; and peaceful coexistence.

15   Department of External Affairs (1959) p. 52.

Solemnly renews its call for the cessation of practices which deprive the Tibetan people of their fundamental human rights and freedoms, including their right to self-determination …

In his speeches up to then Aiken had been generally ambivalent about the exact degree of autonomy that Tibet enjoyed historically; in addressing the Assembly in 1959 he noted that the Irish Delegation 'cannot claim to speak with authority on the complex question of the history of the international status of Tibet'.[16] In 1960 he went so far as to say that the claim of the People's Republic to sovereignty over Tibet, and its claim that 'anything that happens in Tibet is a purely Chinese affair … has a certain logic',[17] but it was a logic that would debar the Assembly from debating other issues on its agenda such as Algeria or human rights in South Africa. The case he had made in those earlier years in favour of a UN resolution had focused, for the most part, on the need for China to respect the human rights of the Tibetan people; and, he argued, the Assembly, had 'clearly recognized on many occasions that the provisions of the Charter regarding human rights override any objection on grounds of domestic jurisdiction'.[18] (This would have been a doubtful proposition for many delegations at the time and a large number would reject it even today.) The 1961 resolution, however, went well beyond this – it introduced for the first time the new idea that the people of Tibet had a right to self-determination. Nevertheless, despite Aiken's more cautious approach in earlier speeches, Ireland was again an active co-sponsor of the resolution.

Notwithstanding this 'hardening' of the text, the resolution was adopted again by the Assembly. This time the vote was 56 votes in favour to 11 against, with 29 abstentions. Two things had happened since 1959 that may help to account for this vote: the membership of the UN had grown; and in 1960, the Assembly had adopted a

---

16 Ibid., p. 39.
17 Department of External Affairs (1960) p. 25.
18 Department of External Affairs (1961) p. 30.

(A partial view of) the vote in UN Security Council on 14 December 1955 to recommend to the General Assembly that Ireland and fifteen other countries be admitted to membership of the UN

The Irish Consul-General in New York, Jack Conway, takes the Irish seat in the UN General Assembly on 14 December 1955, the day Ireland became a member of the UN

The first Irish Permanent Representative appointed to the UN, Ambassador Fredrick Boland, presents his credentials to the UN Secretary General, Dag Hammarskjöld, in 1956

The first Irish Delegation ever to the UN General Assembly in November 1956. The Minister for External Affairs, Liam Cosgrave TD, is sitting behind the name-plate. Immediately to his right is Eamon Kennedy; next is Ambassador Freddie Boland; next to him, leaning over, is Paul Keating (all three from the Irish Mission to the UN); then (seated) Conor Cruise O'Brien; and, wearing hat, Sheila Murphy (both from the Department of External Affairs)

The Minister for External Affairs, Frank Aiken, talking to the Permanent Representative of Burma, U Thant, on 8 October 1958. U Thant later became Secretary General of the UN

The Irish Minister for External Affairs, Frank Aiken, and Ambassador Freddie Boland in the UN General Assembly in 1958. Conor Cruise O'Brien is on the right of the picture, and there is a partial view of Paul Keating behind

Meeting of the First (Political and Security) Committee of the UN General Assembly on 8 October 1958. Frank Aiken occupies Ireland's seat. Behind him (hand to face) is Conor Cruise O'Brien and behind him, half hidden, is Bob McDonagh, another member of the Delegation who was a Third Secretary at the time and years later became, successively, Secretary (General) of the Department of Foreign Affairs, Ambassador to Italy and Permanent Representative to the UN. The Israeli seat, to Aiken's right, is occupied by the Israeli Foreign Minister, Abba Eban (who seems to be speaking)

Ambassador Frederick Boland of Ireland presides over the UN General Assembly (1960). The Canadian Prime Minister, John Diefenbaker, addresses the Assembly on 26 September. On the podium to Boland's right is UN Secretary General Dag Hammarskjöld; to his left is Andrew Cordier, Under Secretary General

Frank Aiken sitting in Ireland's seat in the UN Security Council during the Cuban missile crisis debates in October/ November 1962. To his left is Ambassador Freddie Boland. Behind, between two heads is Jack Molloy, who was at the time Assistant Secretary in the Department of External Affairs. The huddled figure on Boland's other side is Sean Morrissey, the Legal Adviser in the Department of External Affairs. Also in the photo are UN Secretary General U Thant (hand to mouth) and, to his left, holding pencil, Ambassador Zorin of the Soviet Union

Frank Aiken addresses the UN Security Council on 24 October 1962 during the Cuban missile crisis. Immediately behind him is Tadhg O'Sullivan (Counsellor at the Irish Mission); Ambassador Freddie Boland (side-face) is to his left. The figure half seen between them and behind is Jack Molloy (Assistant Secretary), and the person beside him with arms folded is Sean Morrissey, Legal Adviser in the Department of External Affairs. To Aiken's right is Ambassador Alex Quaison-Sackey of Ghana, who became President of the General Assembly in 1965

Ambassador Roger Seydoux (left), Permanent Representative of France to the UN, conversing with Frank Aiken, Minister for External Affairs of Ireland, during the Security Council's deliberations on the Cuban Missile Crisis, October 1962

William O'Connor (Private 1st Class), about to depart for the Congo, says farewell to his wife and infant son (July 1960)

In the course of his farewell visit to the Ethiopian contingent on 5 March 1962, Lieut. General Sean McKeown, the Irish Commander of the UN peacekeeping force in the Congo (ONUC), inspects the Band of the Armée Nationale Congolaise, which participated in the parade

Private Tony Hindley, an Irish peacekeeping soldier attached to the UN peacekeeping force in Cyprus (UNFICYP), escorts a Greek woman across the bridge in Ayios Theodoros from the Turkish to the Greek sector on 27 March 1964

The author, Noel Dorr (far right), at a meeting of the Special Political Committee of the General Assembly in 1967

The Minister for External Affairs, Frank Aiken, sits in the Irish seat in the Special Political Committee in 1967 during a debate on the financing of UN peacekeeping missions. The author, Noel Dorr, is seated behind the Minister

US President
Richard Nixon
addresses the UN
General Assembly in
September 1969. The
Irish Delegation, led
by the Minister for
External Affairs, Dr
Patrick Hillery, is
five rows from the
front near the centre
of the assembled
delegates

The Irish Foreign Minister, Dr Patrick Hillery, addresses the UN Security Council on 20 August 1969 in regard to Ireland's request for a UN peacekeeping force for Northern Ireland. Seated immediately behind him are the Permanent Representative, Ambassador Con Cremin (legs crossed), and, to his left, Patrick Power (Counsellor at the Irish Permanent Mission to the UN). Behind them again are Declan Connolly (also of the Irish Mission, writing) and Padraic MacKernan (half-hidden). Other figures of possible interest are the Permanent Representative of Finland, Ambassador Max Jakobson (with earphone, facing towards Dr Hillery) and, at the edge of the picture, Ambassador Berard of France (white hair, looking at a document)

The UK Permanent Representative, Lord Caradon (left), in discussion with his Irish counterpart, Ambassador Con Cremin, in the UN Security Council on 20 August 1969 (before Dr Patrick Hillery's address to the Security Council)

landmark 'Declaration on Granting Independence to Colonial Countries and Peoples'. This may have influenced some delegations to be more open to a text referring to self-determination for Tibetans.

Aiken's initiatives in the Assembly on behalf of Tibet brought him into relatively frequent contact over the following years with the Dalai Lama and with his brother Thondup, who dealt on his behalf with delegations in New York. In these contacts, Aiken advised the Dalai Lama that it would be a mistake to raise the issue again in the Assembly unless there was a reasonable assurance of at least the same level of support as had been achieved in 1961.

The question of Tibet did not come up again until the autumn of 1965 when, at the request of the Philippines Delegation, it was added to the agenda of the Assembly at a late stage by a vote of 41 to 26 with 46 abstentions. Supporters of the Tibetan case were disappointed at the apparent fall-off in support shown by this procedural vote and Aiken had serious misgivings about pursuing the substantive issue. Nevertheless, he joined with six other Member States – El Salvador, Malaysia, Malta, Nicaragua, Philippines and Thailand – in co-sponsoring a resolution that was eventually adopted by the Assembly by 43 votes to 26 with 22 abstentions. This time, the idea of self-determination for the Tibetan people was not included in the text. The debate was sparsely attended and the Irish Delegation felt that the fall-off in support and the increase in negative votes for what was, in one respect at least, a weaker text than that of 1961 fully justified the cautious pessimism it had expressed privately to its co-sponsors before the vote.[19]

By this stage the effort to press the question of Tibet was petering out. Frank Aiken and the Irish Delegation had played a leading part in raising and pursuing the issue. But there was little more that could be done at the UN, and it seems unlikely now that Tibet will ever recover to any significant degree the autonomy that its isolation

---

19   In this account I have drawn on the annual internal Reports of the Irish Delegation on the General Assembly sessions of 1965, 1966 and 1967 (parts of which I wrote myself in the two latter years).

had enabled it to maintain through history under successive reincarnations of its political–religious leader, the Dalai Lama.

The issue of Tibet and that of the representation of China in the UN were related – which is why I have dwelt on the Tibet issue here. It is clear enough from Skelly's account that Boland's recommendation in 1959 for a strong public statement by the Minister condemning China's attack on Tibet's autonomy played a large part in engaging Aiken and the Irish Delegation with the issue over the following seven years. Certainly, there is no doubting the sincerity of Frank Aiken's concern for the fate of the Tibetan people and, once he took up the issue, he showed genuine conviction in the way he pursued it over the following years. But, as Boland had foreseen in 1959, Ireland's active role also served another purpose. As Skelly puts it: 'he also hoped to provoke an Irish censure of China to temper the negative reaction in the west to the delegation's China vote. That is why he stressed that Aiken should deliver the message. If the spokesman of Ireland's China policy condemned the invasion of Tibet it would send an unmistakable signal to the west as to where Ireland really stood.'[20] Aiken had withstood a great deal of pressure – and considerable abuse – in voting as he did from 1957 onwards for a discussion of Chinese representation. But it is likely that behind that stoic and unchanging outward façade, he may have felt some private relief about the extent to which Ireland's active policy on Tibet had helped him, and the Irish Delegation, to tack back so as to come a little closer to the mainstream of 'Western' thinking in the Assembly.

In 1961, four years after Ireland first voted for discussion of the China issue, the situation in the Assembly changed in a way that further eased the pressure on Aiken and the delegation. Until then, the US had worked each year to rally other delegations to vote down any proposal that would lead to consideration of the question by the Assembly. By 1961, however, a number of newly independent States had been admitted to membership and the composition of

20   Skelly (1997) p. 173.

the Assembly was beginning to change. The US came to believe that it would no longer be able to command a majority against discussion of the issue. So it took a new approach. It did not oppose inscription of the question on the agenda: instead it focused its effort from 1961 onwards on an Article in the Charter that provides that 'Decisions of the General Assembly on important questions shall be made by a two-thirds majority of the members present and voting.'[21]

Was a decision on the representation of China that would allow the People's Republic Delegation to replace that of the Nationalist Government in Taiwan an 'important question' in this sense or not? The question could be argued either way. In ordinary discourse, everyone could see that it was of course an issue of great importance: it would involve not only the seating of the People's Republic Delegation in the Chinese seat but the exclusion of the Nationalist Chinese Delegation that had previously held that seat – which, in ordinary parlance if not in UN procedural terms, amounted to the expulsion of Taiwan. In a parliamentary sense, on the other hand, it could be argued that this was merely a procedural issue, since everyone accepted that China was already a full Member of the UN: it was simply a matter of whose credentials were to be recognised and which delegation was to occupy China's seat. This, it could be argued, as a procedural issue, could be decided by a simple majority in the Assembly.

In addressing the Assembly on the issue towards the end of the 1961 session, Aiken took a very reasoned and balanced approach. He spoke of the importance of the 'universality' of the UN; and he recognised that a case could be made for representation of the Government that was in effective control of the vast majority of the Chinese people. This would not necessarily imply approval of its policies or its governmental system. But the aim should be 'not simply to pronounce ... on the rival claims' of the two Governments, 'but to do our best to ensure that the differences between

---

21   Article 18.2.

them should be settled by peaceful procedure'. In particular, he concluded, 'the Assembly should not at this moment take any decision which might be regarded as providing a pretext for the use of force between Peiping [i.e. Beijing] and Taiwan.'[22]

The speech was admirable. What mattered, however – as always on such issues – was the vote. When it came to it, the Irish Delegation took a pragmatic and, arguably, a 'common-sense' approach, which also, conveniently enough, brought it on to the side of the US on the issue: it voted in favour of the proposition that any proposal to change the representation of China was an 'important' one that required a two-thirds majority for adoption.

That year the Assembly supported the US position by a vote of 48 to 36 with 20 abstentions. Aiken and the Irish Delegation were now 'off the hook': they could continue, as they had done every year since 1957, to support discussion of the representation of China in the Assembly, while voting, whenever the issue came up, that that was an 'important question', a decision which would require a two-thirds majority. Cardinal Spellman and *The Brooklyn Tablet* might still have an occasional comment, but they could hardly object. The issue, formally speaking at least, was now a procedural one.

In addressing the General Assembly in 1964, however, Aiken introduced a novel idea: he focused on the rights of the indigenous people of Taiwan. First, he acknowledged that the constitutional position within the United Nations would be strengthened if the five nuclear powers occupied the five permanent seats on the Security Council. For that reason, he acknowledged that it might be desirable to have the People's Republic of China, which was now the fifth nuclear power, occupy one of the permanent seats on the Council. But, he went on,

it would, in my opinion, be intolerable that this should be done by denying Taiwan and its twelve million people a right

---

22   Speech to the General Assembly by Frank Aiken on 11 December 1961. The text is available in Department of External Affairs (1961) pp. 22–28.

to membership of the United Nations. For I am sure that the people of Taiwan wish to govern themselves, as they did before being occupied by China, and later, Japan.[23]

Aiken spelled out this idea further in a speech at the following session on 30 September 1965. He recalled his earlier suggestion

> that it would be well if the ancient nation of Taiwan were admitted in its own right to the Assembly, and that subsequently the Peking Government took the China seat in the Security Council, provided that they accepted to be bound by the principles of the Charter and were warned that they would be open to criticism if they did not desist from imperialist expansion in Tibet, India and elsewhere.[24]

Speaking again on the issue a year later, on 28 November 1966, he said that he would welcome the People's Republic of China in the United Nations as representing the ancient nation of China. But he would regard it as a grave breach of the principles of the Charter to admit Peking at the price of denying to the people of Formosa (i.e. Taiwan) their right to self-determination and the right to be represented in the UN as a sovereign, independent State. The Chinese had as little right to pretend that the nation of Formosa (that is to say Taiwan) was an integral part of China, he said, as the British had to claim part of Ireland.

'One China', 'two Chinas', 'which China?' – these were the terms in which the issues had been argued out for a decade and a half. But no one until then, so far as I know, had spoken in the General Assembly, as Aiken had now done, of 'the ancient nation of Taiwan' or the right of 'the people of Formosa' to self-determination. In

---

23 Speech in the General Debate at the 19th session of the Assembly, 8 December 1964. I have taken the quotation from an extract of the speech which is quoted in the Department of External Affairs (internal) *Report on the Twentieth General Assembly of the United Nations 1965*, p. 27.

24 Speech in the General Debate at the 20th session of the Assembly, 30 September 1965. Ibid.

doing so, he was referring not to the two million or so Nationalist Chinese under Chang Kai Shek, who had taken refuge in the island in 1949 while still claiming to be the legitimate Government of all of China, but to the eight to twelve million indigenous inhabitants of the island whom the Nationalist Chinese forces had repressed with considerable brutality and loss of life.

The idea was Aiken's own.[25] Some of us at the time might have thought of it as 'far-out' – or perhaps as a rationalisation of what, ultimately, would in effect be a pro-US vote against seating the People's Republic Delegation in the Assembly. But looking back now, it seems to me to be quite characteristic of Frank Aiken: unexpected, courageous, slightly off-centre or even quirky in its way, but rooted in a deep conviction about the right to self-determination that had its origins in his own deep involvement in the Irish struggle for independence that began long before when he joined a Volunteer company in 1913 at the age of fifteen.

Novel it may have been, but no one else at the UN, so far as I know, picked up the idea and it was lost in the general polemic about the filling of the Chinese seat. The argument continued each year until 1971, two years after Aiken had left office as Minister for External Affairs and been replaced by Dr Patrick Hillery. Support for the US position of blocking the seating of the People's Republic by voting that such a decision would require a two-thirds majority was eroded as the years passed. Eventually in 1971, as Henry Kissinger was opening up contacts with Beijing for a subsequent visit by President Nixon, the US could no longer hold the line in the UN. On 25 October 1971 the vote in the Assembly on the preliminary procedural question about the kind of majority

---

25 I have no evidence for this but it strikes me as just possible that he had read and was influenced by a long essay entitled *The China Impasse: A Formosan View* by Li Thian-hok (described as 'a Formosan student of Far Eastern affairs') which appeared in the April 1958 number of the influential journal *Foreign Affairs: An American Quarterly Review* (Vol. 36, No. 3). The article (p. 8) notes 'Two distinct features [which] run through the modern history of Formosa. One is the continuous struggle for liberty against unwanted intruders; the other is the long periods of separation from China.'

required for a decision went against the US position – greatly to its chagrin and that of its Permanent Representative at the time, George Bush Sr. The result was a decision by the Assembly to decide the substantive issue by a simple majority. The Assembly then voted to allow the People's Republic to take the Chinese seat. Although no more than a simple majority was needed, the proposal was actually adopted by a majority of more than two-thirds (76 votes to 35 with 17 abstentions). I was not dealing with UN issues at the time but I followed the outcome with interest. At this stage the issue was one of substance, no longer obscured behind veils of procedure: Ireland voted in favour and thereby formed part of the over-whelming majority which decided that the People's Republic should take the Chinese seat in the General Assembly.

Some delegates and indeed some Permanent Representatives danced in the aisles in celebration when the result of the vote was announced. But some paid later for their temerity. A decade after these events, I sat in the Irish seat in the Security Council through sixteen abortive votes over a two-month period as we tried to agree on a new Secretary General. The voting was by secret ballot. But it was an open secret that, each time, China vetoed Kurt Waldheim and the US vetoed the African candidate, Salim Salim, who was by then Foreign Minister of Tanzania and whom I got to know well later. Salim, who was at the time his country's Permanent Representative in New York, was one of those who was reputed to have danced in the aisles in 1971. If he did, he paid heavily ten years later for his dance of joy.

6

Stopping the Spread of Nuclear Weapons

If 'the China vote' was the most contentious issue for Ireland during its first decade and a half of UN membership, the issue for which the delegation deserves greatest credit was certainly the 'nuclear non-proliferation initiative' – that is to say, Frank Aiken's courageous effort from 1958 onwards to promote the idea of a treaty to curb the spread of nuclear weapons. This was one of those rare initiatives, like the idea of a conference on the Law of the Sea pursued in the mid-1960s by Malta, which, if taken up and pressed with persistence, skill and determination by a small Member State, can eventually open up a wholly new area for international negotiation and, eventually, international cooperation.

Aiken raised the issue for the first time in 1958 when he spoke in the General Debate that takes place at the start of each Assembly session. Later in that session, in the course of the more detailed debate on disarmament in the First Committee, he submitted a draft resolution. This proposed that the Assembly establish a committee that would study the dangers inherent in the further spread of nuclear weapons and make recommendations to the General Assembly session in the following year.

At that stage, the general climate was none too favourable and some important countries that later endorsed the concept of preventing the spread of nuclear weapons were far from sympathetic to Aiken's initiative.

The initial US reaction was that the proposal was unacceptable. The UK and some other NATO members took a similar view. The US at the time was considering placing tactical nuclear weapons in some NATO countries, while keeping them under its own control. Furthermore, the general view of NATO countries, and particularly of the US, was that arms agreements of any kind must be subject to effective control and they did not see how it would be possible to ensure that the Soviet Union, for example, would not pass nuclear weapons secretly to other countries such as China. The Soviet Union, on the other hand, was somewhat more open – it seemed, initially at least, to have a real concern about the further spread of nuclear weapons. Some other countries were concerned about anything that would freeze the inequality between nuclear 'haves' and 'have nots'. There was also a widespread belief that it was preferable to keep negotiations on arms control measures within existing disarmament bodies rather than set up a special committee to make proposals on stopping the spread of nuclear weapons, as the Irish resolution proposed.[1]

It is understandable that, in this first draft resolution, Aiken thought it better to look for a special committee to focus solely on the non-proliferation issue. The broader question of 'disarmament' has been the subject of debate in various commissions and international conferences since the early part of the twentieth century – and even before. But it has always been difficult to get the nations of the world to agree to serious and substantial disarmament measures.

A glance back to the beginning of the twentieth century will show how intractable the problem has always been and how little had been achieved by the late 1950s.

The Peace Conference held at The Hague in 1899 grew out of a proposal by the Czar of Russia that referred in its very first sentence

---

1   In this summary of initial reactions, in addition to my own memories, I have drawn
     to some extent on two other accounts: (a) Skelly (1997) pp. 252–253 and (b) Evgeny
     M. Chossudovsky, 'The origins of the treaty on the non-proliferation of nuclear
     weapons: Ireland's initiative in the United Nations (1958–61)'.

to 'a possible reduction of the excessive armaments which weigh upon all nations' as the ideal towards which the endeavours of all Governments should be directed.[2] Unfortunately the Conference achieved little in this respect although it did agree to prohibit, for a period of five years, the launching of projectiles and explosives from balloons. Not, it has to be said ruefully, an agreement that had any great impact on the world during the century that followed.[3]

After the First World War, the slaughter in the trenches was blamed in part on arms sales by 'merchants of death'; this, along with the new moral tone introduced into international affairs by US President Woodrow Wilson, led to a new focus on disarmament in the post-war years. This found expression in the Covenant of the League of Nations, which committed the Member States to recognising that 'the maintenance of peace requires the reduction of national armaments to the lowest point consistent with national safety and the enforcement by common action of international obligations.'[4]

Opinions differed then, as always, on what arms are 'defensive' and what 'offensive', as well as on the level of armaments needed to ensure 'national safety'. Nevertheless, major powers did take some limited steps towards disarmament over the following decade: they agreed under the Washington Treaty of 1922, for example, to limit the size and number of their battleships. Ten years later, a large-scale Disarmament Conference opened in Geneva after five years of detailed preparation. By then, however, the rise of Hitler and Mussolini and the militaristic policies of Japan had led to a deterioration of the international situation and the Conference got nowhere: it adjourned in June 1934 and never reconvened. By the late 1930s important countries such as Britain and the US were turning their minds to rearmament, as Hitler's aggressive policies in Europe seemed to be leading the world inexorably to war.

---

2   'Rescript of the Russian Emperor' of 24 August 1898. See James Brown-Scott, *Texts of the Peace Conference at the Hague, 1899 and 1907*, p. 1.

3   For the text of the Declaration on this question see Brown-Scott (1908) p. 79.

4   Article 8.1 of the Covenant of the League of Nations.

The UN Charter, agreed towards the close of the Second World War, picked up again the question of general arms reduction. It spoke of the 'maintenance of international peace and security with the least diversion for armaments of the world's human and economic resources'. The Security Council was to be responsible 'for formulating … plans for the establishment of a system for the regulation of armaments'.[5] The Charter also allowed the General Assembly to discuss 'the principles governing disarmament and regulation of armaments' and make recommendations to Member States and to the Security Council.[6] But the world had changed fundamentally since the 1920s and early 1930s because the US had developed nuclear weapons and used them on two occasions in the closing months of the Second World War.

This led to a focus in the immediate post-war years on how to deal with these devastating new weapons. The General Assembly set up an Atomic Energy Commission in 1946 and the United States, the sole nuclear power at the time, put forward a far-sighted plan to put the sources of atomic energy under international control. This was rejected by the Soviet Union. Later, as the Cold War intensified, proposals by the Soviet Union were rejected in turn by the West.

In 1947, the Security Council set up a Commission for Conventional Armaments to parallel the Atomic Energy Commission. But negotiations between 'East' and 'West' achieved little – largely because of mutual distrust and fundamental disagreement on whether disarmament measures or measures to relax tension and create greater security should come first. In the early 1950s, the General Assembly replaced these two separate Commissions by a single Disarmament Commission; in 1957 it dissolved this again; and in 1958 it set up a new Disarmament Commission of which all 81 UN Member States were to be members. Since this was, to say the least, an unwieldy body for serious disarmament negotiations, the major NATO and Warsaw Pact countries set up a separate Ten-

---

5   Article 26 of the UN Charter.
6   Article 11.1 of the UN Charter.

Nation Committee that was initially outside the UN framework. A link with the UN was established when the Committee was approved by the Disarmament Commission in 1959 and the new Committee began work eventually in 1960.[7]

What I have said so far will, no doubt, seem like a tedious recital of the many twists and turns of disarmament negotiations through the first part of the twentieth century. But it may also help to convey something of the atmosphere at the time Aiken first introduced his proposal about limiting the spread of nuclear weapons. The so-called arms race was accelerating and not only the US but also other important countries – the Soviet Union, the UK, France and the People's Republic of China – were testing and developing nuclear weapons. Substantial disarmament measures seemed a distant dream.

Later, in the second half of the twentieth century, several important arms control treaties in relation to nuclear weapons were negotiated, but even today there is still little substantial progress towards the aim set out in the UN Charter – 'the least diversion for armaments of the world's human and economic resources'. This is not for want of ambitious proposals.

In 1959, for example, just a year after Aiken first raised the non-proliferation issue, Khrushchev, the Soviet leader, made a proposal in the Assembly for 'General and Complete Disarmament'. This would require that all the world's military forces be disbanded permanently within four years. Thereafter, countries would retain only limited forces for internal police work. It sounded wonderful but, granted that the Soviet Union was already a superpower, it was widely seen at the time as a somewhat cynical propaganda gesture. Nevertheless, this grandiose scheme seemed to trump all other proposals; and 'General and Complete Disarmament under effective international control', became, in principle at least, the ultimate aim of virtually all subsequent disarmament discussions and of two

---

7   In this account I have drawn largely on Alf Ross, *The United Nations: Peace and Progress*, pp. 282–291.

successive 'Disarmament Decades' during the 1970s and the 1980s. It is still an improbable dream – an ideal we would all wish to see realised, just as we hope that one day the lion will lie down with the lamb – and sadly, just about as likely.

In contrast, what was important about Aiken's approach in the late 1950s was that he set himself a limited aim: not to achieve large-scale disarmament, although that was something he would certainly have wanted, but to prevent the immediate situation from becoming worse. He looked for an agreement under which countries with nuclear weapons would agree not to give them to non-nuclear powers, and those other countries in turn would agree not to acquire or manufacture them.

This was a modest enough idea compared to Khrushchev's utopian proposal; and Aiken was realistic in the way he approached it. As he explained to the First Committee a year later:

> I may say quite candidly that our approach to the problem of disarmament and the associated problem of the spread of nuclear weapons is based on the assumption that the nuclear powers must act in their own enlightened self-interest: that, until their security is fully assured to their own satisfaction by an international force, they will not voluntarily part with any of the powers which the monopoly of these weapons gives them. What we ask is that they should hold the keys of the stores and assume the responsibility before their own people and before humanity for seeing that nuclear weapons are not spread throughout the world until a cut-off of all production can be achieved and existing stocks devoted to peaceful uses.[8]

Aiken did not achieve immediate success with his first proposal in 1958. But he and his closest immediate advisers at the time, Boland and O'Brien, were wise enough not to force the issue at that stage.

---

8   Department of External Affairs (1959) p. 68.

Instead, when the debate had ended, he asked that the First Committee should vote only on a single paragraph in the preamble to his draft resolution – a paragraph that recognised the dangers inherent in the spread of nuclear weapons. The Committee approved this paragraph by 37 votes to 0 with 44 abstentions. The Soviet Union and its allies in the Warsaw Pact voted in favour; the US and its allies in NATO all abstained. Aiken then withdrew the resolution, believing it more prudent to fight another day and on another battlefield.

He returned to the issue a year later, in 1959. First he asked to have a new item – 'Prevention of the Wider Dissemination of Nuclear Weapons' – placed on the agenda of the Assembly. Then, in a speech in the General Debate towards the start of the session, he linked his proposal for an agreement to limit the spread of nuclear weapons with a further proposal for what he called 'areas of law'.

This was an idea that he mentioned in many speeches around this time. He proposed that in certain parts of the world, particularly those areas where the 'entangled interests of the two great power groups' made war more likely, a group of nations would commit themselves to abide by the Charter and uphold the rule of law in return for corresponding guarantees from the other Member States. In particular, within such an area those countries that did not already have nuclear weapons would guarantee not to acquire them, or indeed any other weapons of mass destruction. In return, the major nuclear powers, together with other UN Member States, would bind themselves to defend the area from attack by means of a standing United Nations force. This approach would be particularly appropriate in Central Europe, where, he suggested,

the security of the great powers, the peace of Europe and the peace of the world, would all be better and more effectively served if [US and Soviet] troops were drawn back until they were 1,000 miles or more apart, and if the area … became an area of law, without foreign troops, and with a restriction on armaments.[9]

Aiken's proposal for 'areas of law' was an imaginative one, and his idea of linking it to a step-by-step withdrawal in Central Europe more imaginative still. It had echoes of a rather different plan put forward in 1957 by Adam Rapacki, the Polish Foreign Minister, for withdrawal and 'de-nuclearisation' of the region. But it met with little success. (I remember one of my senior colleagues a little later telling me, somewhat irreverently, that 'all we need to make Irish foreign policy these days is an atlas, a ruler and a pencil.') Aiken's ideas about the urgency of stopping the spread of nuclear weapons, on the other hand, were beginning to gain ground even among those who were sceptical initially.

Later in the 1959 session of the Assembly, he put forward a new draft resolution. This time he took account of the general wish to keep arms control negotiations within existing frameworks. So he did not propose, as he had done in 1958, that a special study committee should be set up: instead the text would have the General Assembly 'suggest' to the new Ten Nation Disarmament Committee that was to meet shortly in Geneva that it should consider 'appropriate means' to avert the dangers inherent in the further spread of nuclear weapons. Among those 'means' should be 'the feasibility of an international agreement subject to inspection and control'.[10]

In his speech introducing the resolution in the disarmament debate in the First Committee, Aiken noted that scientists at that time believed that 'the production of a few Hiroshima-style atom bombs is well within the reach of ten or more countries ... [and] what is within the reach of ten states now is likely to be within the reach of an indefinite number of additional states in the future.'

He could see that there would be questions about which countries were to be regarded as 'the nuclear powers'. His answer

9   Speech of 23 September 1959. Ibid., p. 18.
10   For the full text of the resolution see ibid., p. 77.

was that it was 'all the powers producing nuclear weapons at the time when the suggested agreements are ready for signature, whatever the number may be at that date'; and, he continued, 'the longer the agreements are delayed, the greater is the danger of an increase in the number of nuclear powers.' He was even far-sighted enough to foresee something that has become a matter of serious concern today. Eventually, he said, nuclear weapons might not even be confined to States. 'Revolutionary organisations and groups can come into possession of such weapons by various means, and they are ever more likely to do so according as these weapons become more numerous, more easily transportable and part of standard military equipment.'[11]

This new Irish draft resolution was approved by the General Assembly on 20 November 1959 by a vote of 68 to 0 with 12 abstentions.[12] Oddly enough, 'East' and 'West' had changed positions since the previous year: the US and other NATO countries, except for France, now voted for the resolution, while the Soviet Union and its Warsaw Pact allies had changed to abstention.

A year later, at the 1960 session of the Assembly, Aiken put forward a new draft resolution and four other countries joined as co-sponsors – Ghana, Japan, Mexico and Morocco. The text was more specific than in 1959: it called on 'all Governments to make every effort to achieve permanent agreement on the prevention of the dissemination of [nuclear] weapons'.[13] It also called on States to take temporary and voluntary measures, pending the negotiation of such an agreement: nuclear powers should refrain from transferring nuclear weapons to countries that did not already have them, and non-nuclear powers should refrain from manufacturing them. The

11   This and previous quotations are taken from the Minister's speech of 13 November 1959 in the First Committee. For the text, see ibid., pp. 60–70.
12   The resolution was adopted in the First Committee on 16 November 1959 by 66 votes to 0 with 13 abstentions. It was approved at a plenary meeting of the Assembly four days later by a vote of 68 to 0 with 12 abstentions (Spain, which had abstained in the Committee vote, and Paraguay which had been absent, both voted in favour).
13   For the text of the resolution see Department of External Affairs (1960) pp. 65–66.

Assembly adopted this new resolution on 20 December 1960 by 68 votes to 0 with 26 abstentions.

Over this whole period, Aiken continued to lobby at every opportunity, even outside the immediate framework of the UN, to gain support for the idea of a non-proliferation treaty. I recall that some time in early 1961 I was asked to draft an article on the non-proliferation issue, which, after vetting by a more senior colleague, would be submitted to the Minister. I cannot claim that what I did was wholly original: since I was quite junior in the Department, and new to the issue, I must have picked up some ideas from the Minister's own speeches to the General Assembly. Nevertheless, I was pleased with myself when the text appeared as an article over the Minister's name later that year in the prestigious American publication *The Bulletin of Atomic Scientists.*[14]

Aiken's quiet and stubborn persistence was finally rewarded a year later. On 30 November 1961 he submitted a new draft resolution to the First Committee. The text was quite short. In its main operative paragraph the resolution called

> upon all States, and in particular upon the States at present possessing nuclear weapons, to use their best endeavours to secure the conclusion of an international agreement containing provisions under which the nuclear States would undertake to refrain from relinquishing control of nuclear weapons and from transmitting the information necessary for their manufacture to States not possessing them and States not possessing nuclear weapons would undertake not to manufacture or otherwise acquire control of such weapons.[15]

This time Ireland was the sole sponsor.

---

14 Skelly, in the Bibliography to his book *Irish Diplomacy at the United Nations 1945–1965*, p. 301 refers to an essay by Frank Aiken entitled 'Can We Limit the Nuclear Club?' which appeared in the *Bulletin of the Atomic Scientist* [sic] Vol. 17, No. 7 for September 1961. That must be the article in question.

15 For full text of the resolution see Chossudovsky (1990) p. 135. See also Skelly (1997) p. 263.

Some months earlier, in late September, the US representative, Adlai Stevenson, and his Soviet opposite number, Valentin Zorin, had issued a joint statement of principles to govern disarmament negotiations. A week later each of the two, separately, circulated more specific proposals on behalf of his country. Aiken picked up on these proposals and when he introduced his draft resolution on non-proliferation on 30 November he spoke of what he called 'the wisdom of these two great nuclear Powers': this was to be seen in the fact that the measures suggested in both papers for preventing the further spread of nuclear weapons seemed to him to be identical. As evidence of this, he arranged that the text of his speech as circulated would set out the relevant passages from the two separate proposals side by side. The congruence between them, he said, 'gives fresh encouragement to all who had not lost hope during our long-frustrated search for a first step towards stable peace'.[16]

The omens now at last were favourable for his proposal and the debate that followed was correspondingly short. The Committee approved the Irish draft resolution on 30 November. Four days later, on 4 December 1961, it was adopted unanimously by the UN General Assembly.

In the esoteric language of UN procedures there is a significant difference between a resolution adopted by 'consensus' and one adopted by 'unanimity'. The former leaves scope for reservations and qualifications by individual delegations – the latter means just what it says. So the unanimity of the General Assembly was the best possible outcome to Aiken's four years of patient effort and the careful diplomatic groundwork by his senior officials. I was glad to be present in the Assembly hall for this historic vote. I knew that I had come late to the issue and I was by far the most junior member of the delegation that year. But as I remembered the September issue of the *Bulletin of Atomic Scientists* and my efforts as the Minister's 'ghost-writer', I could feel that I had had some small share in the achievement.

16   Department of External Affairs (1961) pp. 15–16.

That clear and unanimous expression of the will of the UN General Assembly in December 1961 was only a first step – albeit a very important one – towards an actual treaty. Seven years later, after a lengthy and difficult negotiation between the major powers, the Nuclear Non-Proliferation Treaty, which 'the Irish Resolution' had called for, was signed.

Ireland's role in first raising the issue ten year earlier and gaining unanimous international support for it was, by then, widely recognised. The Treaty was opened for signature simultaneously in three capitals – London, Moscow and Washington – on 1 July 1968. Frank Aiken, as Minister for External Affairs, went to Moscow at the invitation of the Soviet Government, to sign it there on behalf of Ireland, even though Ireland had no diplomatic relations with the Soviet Union at that time. In a speech at the signing ceremony he said that, notwithstanding criticisms on other issues, the gratitude of the smaller countries was due to the Great Powers for negotiating the Treaty. At a dinner on the following day he presented Ireland's formal instrument of ratification to the Soviet Foreign Minister, Andrei Gromyko. As a result, Ireland became the first country to ratify the new Treaty – just as it had been the first to raise the issue in the United Nations ten years before.[17] The Treaty came into force on 5 March 1970.

In the years since then, the Nuclear Non-Proliferation Treaty, known for short as the NPT, has served as a bulwark against the spread of nuclear weapons and it has now been signed and ratified by more countries than any other agreement in the field of arms control or disarmament. It is reviewed at conferences convened every five years. At the Review Conference of 1995, it was agreed to extend it indefinitely.

Nowadays, however, nearly forty years after it first came into force, the Treaty is under increasing pressure. Many of the other signatories believe that the main nuclear powers have failed to live up to the commitment they undertook in the treaty to negotiate in

---

17   See the account given in Chossudovsky (1990) pp. 129–130 (and footnote 37).

good faith on effective measures for nuclear disarmament.

Although the Cold War is long over, Russia and the United States between them retain thousands of nuclear weapons, about half of them operationally deployed. Britain, France and China show no sign of reducing their more modest nuclear stockpiles substantially – indeed Britain plans to modernise its nuclear deterrent over the next decade or so. India and Pakistan are now nuclear powers. It is widely known that Israel, though it will not admit it, has long had nuclear weapons. Even North Korea, one of the poorest countries in the world, has conducted a nuclear test, and there is a serious question mark over Iran's intentions. There are now at least eight acknowledged nuclear powers, and there is a danger that other countries with the necessary capacity may soon be tempted to join them. More ominous still is the possibility that the necessary technology may pass beyond the control of organised governments and even, perhaps, come into the hands of international terrorist groups. In recent years it has been revealed that a ring, led by a Pakistani scientist, has been trading internationally in nuclear materials and 'know how'. There may be other such cases. The question now is whether the barrier that Frank Aiken was the first to propose more than fifty years ago will hold much longer.

One hopeful sign as I write is the interest and concern that US President Obama is showing in the issue. In an unprecedented step in September 2009 he took the US seat as chair of the UN Security Council and shepherded through, by unanimity, a resolution on the nuclear non-proliferation issue. In the first operative paragraph this resolution emphasised that

> a situation of non-compliance with non-proliferation obligations shall be brought to the attention of the Security Council, which will determine if that situation constitutes a threat to international peace and security.[18]

---

18   Resolution 1887 (2009).

This concern is welcome but it remains to be seen how far the Security Council, and its permanent members in particular, will be willing to carry it through in practice in specific cases.

Since 1947, the *Bulletin of Atomic Scientists* published at the University of Chicago has shown a symbolic clock-face on the cover of each issue. The minute hand of the clock was closer to, or farther from, midnight according to the editors' assessment of the current dangers that nuclear weapons pose to the world as a whole. When Aiken's article appeared in September 1961, the time was seven minutes to the hour. In 1991 after the end of the Cold War it went back ten minutes. As I write, the time on the clock is five to twelve. It is still ticking.

7

A Year on the Security Council

Ireland has been elected three times to membership of the UN Security Council. On two occasions it won the seat in a hard-fought election campaign and served a full two-year term – in 1981–1982 and 2001–2002 respectively. In contrast, when Ireland first took a seat on the Council in 1962 it was almost by default: it split a term with Liberia and served on the Council for only a single year.

Writing a number of years ago about that term of membership in 1962, I described it as 'now almost forgotten'.[1] Perhaps that was a bit unfair – or at least too personal a view. Some months into the year 1962, I was transferred from the UN section of the Department and moved abroad, to a different area of work in Brussels. I was not directly involved in UN issues again until the mid-1960s, a few years later. This, and the much more vivid memories I retain of Ireland's two-year term on the Security Council in 1981–82 in which I was involved myself, may have helped to make 1962 seem less note-worthy to me in retrospect. I should have remembered two important issues at least from that year that came before the Council – Kashmir and the Cuban missile crisis. One was a dispute largely limited to two neighbouring countries, but one that had already been the cause of several wars; the other the world's most dangerous confrontation since the Second World War, if not in all of history. I will deal with both of these issues in the present chapter.

The Security Council today has a total membership of fifteen. Five are Permanent Members; the other ten are elected by the

---

1   See Noel Dorr, 'Ireland at the United Nations', p. 118.

General Assembly to serve for two-year terms. The election usually takes place in the autumn, when the Assembly, by secret ballot, votes to choose States to fill the seats of the outgoing members for the two-year term beginning in the following January. A two-thirds majority is needed for election.

In 1962, however, before the Charter was amended in 1965, the Council had a membership of only eleven: in addition to the five Permanent Members there were six elected members at that time. There was also at that time a so-called 'gentleman's agreement' that governed the allocation of the elective seats between the different regional groups of States. The agreement dated from 1946, when there were very few 'Afro-Asian' States in the Assembly, and it did not allocate any seats to Asia or to Africa. As the membership of the United Nations grew from the mid-1950s onwards, however, this agreement came under pressure. The pressure increased greatly from 1960 onwards after the admission to UN membership of a large number of newly independent African States. The general position of the Irish Delegation to the General Assembly at this time was to support limited reform of the Security Council and a more equitable distribution of seats.

In a paper published some years ago,[2] Dr Michael Kennedy, using documents of the time from the archives, gave an interesting and very detailed account of how Ireland came to be a reluctant candidate for election to the Council for 1962. I draw in part on this below and add some comments of my own.

The 'Western European Group' had agreed in 1960, with some misgivings, that Portugal should be its candidate. The 'gentleman's agreement' was coming under pressure by then, and this was not exactly the best choice for a regional group concerned to hold its allocated seat against possible competition from other regions. Portugal was a dictatorship under Salazar; it was also widely

---

2   Michael Kennedy, '"Persuade an alternative candidate to stand": why Ireland was elected to the United Nations Security Council in 1961', in Kennedy and McMahon (2005) Chapter 6, pp. 154–181.

criticised for its determination to hold on to its colonies – Angola and Mozambique in Africa and Goa and Macau in Asia. The Indian Defence Minister, Krishna Menon, led the Afro-Asian Group in the Assembly in a vigorous and determined campaign against Portugal's candidacy and for Liberia, the African candidate.

I was not on the Irish Delegation at that Assembly – I was at home in the UN section of the Department – but a year later, sitting behind either Frank Aiken or, in his absence, one of my senior colleagues for long debates on disarmament in the First Committee, I came to know Menon, who sat across the room from us. Or at least to believe I did, though I fear it was only in the way that a small boy 'knows' a famous footballer whom he watches regularly from the stands. He was the Defence Minister of India but he seemed to be the regular leader of its delegation at the time. Earlier in his life, he had, I think, been a local councillor in a London borough, and later High Commissioner of India in London, accredited also as non-resident Ambassador to Ireland.

Menon was a forceful, vociferous man, with a great shock of greying hair that was almost as distinctive as Marge Simpson's blue beehive. He argued regularly in the Committee in favour of nuclear disarmament. For me at the time, naïve as I was, he epitomised what I thought of as the spirit of India – Nehru, Gandhi, pacifism and all that. He assumed really heroic stature for me when he returned to his seat in the Committee with a shaven scalp just one week after major brain surgery and began again to berate 'the nuclear powers' for their failure to stop nuclear testing and to begin on nuclear disarmament. But for many other delegations, and particularly for journalists, he was something of a hate figure. Understandable perhaps in the case of the journalists, since relations with the news media were not exactly his forte: according to legend – which may even be true – one day, in one of the lobbies of the UN, he seized by the throat a journalist who had pressed him with too many questions, and shook him vigorously before setting him down again. The press felt that their bitterness towards him was fully vindicated when, notwithstanding the pacific approach to international relations that he had seemed to espouse in the Committee, India annexed the Portuguese colony of Goa on its west coast by force in late 1961.

The campaign that Menon led in the Assembly in 1960 was strong enough to prevent Portugal's election to the Security Council, but it was not strong enough to win the seat for Liberia. At a subsequent meeting, the Western European Group, in its effort to 'save the seat', tried to find some Member State willing to run as a candidate instead of Portugal 'with the optimistic aim of being elected for two years and the compromise objective of eventually agreeing to a split term'.[3] Most Europeans drew back from this kind of split-term compromise. Eventually, after an approach in New York from the British representative, Aiken reported back to Dublin on 17 December for the information of the Taoiseach, Sean Lemass, that he was 'trying to find some other solution but that ultimately we may have no alternative but to agree to run'.

There must indeed have been significant pressure on the delegation for Frank Aiken to send such a message. I have no doubt that he was quite sincere in saying that he was 'trying to find some other solution'. I well recall his admirably modest and puritanical approach to 'office-seeking' by Ireland at the time – or at least to anything that involved expenditure or additional staff. It is true that he had approved Freddie Boland's candidacy for the prestigious post of President of the General Assembly in 1960; he released Conor Cruise O'Brien to be UN representative in Katanga in early 1961; and he must have also endorsed the appointment of General Sean McKeown to command ONUC, the UN peacekeeping force in the Congo, in that same year. But these were not appointments that would have involved large-scale expenditure by Ireland or entailed substantial additional staff in the Department of External Affairs.

On other matters, however, as we perceived it in the Department at the time, his three short years as Minister for Finance had deeply

---

3   Ibid., p. 175.

affected his thinking. To our disappointment, his first and instinctive response to any sounding about Irish membership of disarmament or other international bodies was to say 'no'. Rarely indeed did any such proposal or submission, especially one that would have led to a modest expansion of the Department, come back from his office with his customary laconic Ministerial annotation 'Aontaím' – that is to say, 'I agree'.

Michael Kennedy's paper confirms Aiken's reluctance about allowing Ireland to become a candidate for the Security Council and shows that it was shared at home. Con Cremin, the Secretary of the Department of External Affairs, who was the contact between Aiken in New York and the Taoiseach, Sean Lemass in Dublin

> informed Aiken that Lemass felt that if in Aiken's view 'it was necessary for us to accept, the Government would have no objection.' There was still great reluctance on Aiken's part to allow Ireland's name to go forward. Lemass left the final decision with his foreign minister, giving him the full support of the Cabinet and leaving Aiken in no doubt what his own views were. Lemass 'had requested the Minister for External Affairs … to avoid accepting Irish membership, if at all possible'. Lemass was as reluctant as Aiken to put Ireland forward, yet he realised that in certain circumstances Ireland might have no alternative.[4]

Those 'certain circumstances' came about very quickly, in the form of a further British approach to the Government – this time by the British Embassy in Dublin:

> Later on 17 December Cremin cabled Aiken with some revealing news: 'British have now put it to us strongly that we

---

4   Kennedy (2005) p. 176. In the absence of his Minister, Frank Aiken, in New York, Con Cremin, as Secretary of the Department of External Affairs, would have been reporting to the Taoiseach, Sean Lemass, and keeping Aiken informed by phone and by cable.

should accept Security Council seat in event of Norway feeling unable to do so … in the circumstances [the] Taoiseach considers [that] we should be more [than] ready to accept if [there is] no alternative. Have so informed British.'[5]

So Ireland, despite its reluctance, had been propelled forward to become a candidate. Having had no more than half a mind to run, it was now, in effect, to become a candidate for half a term. Quite a difference from 1980, when we conducted an intensive campaign for a seat on the Council for 1981–82; and a world, and more, away from the intensive four-year, all-out, 'life-or-death' campaign that gained Ireland its most recent seat on the Council for the years 2001–2002.

The vote in the General Assembly took place a day or two later. After a number of ballots the two leading candidates, Liberia and Ireland, were tied with forty-five votes each. A two-thirds majority, i.e. sixty votes, was necessary for election. After an adjournment for consultations between delegations, an informal agreement was reached: Liberia would be the only candidate that year; and, if elected, it would withdraw after one year, i.e. at the end of 1961, in favour of Ireland. The Assembly then duly elected Liberia and it took up its seat on the Council a fortnight later, on 1 January 1961.

The agreement that broke the deadlock, however, was an informal one. Even though Liberia had agreed to step down, it would still be necessary for Ireland to be elected formally to fill the vacancy at the Assembly the following autumn. By then I was in New York, serving as the most junior member of the delegation, and I

---

5 Ibid. Michael Kennedy in his essay sources these quotations to a cable of 17 December 1960 in file DFA PMUN 289 in the National Archives of Ireland. Since, as a very junior officer in the UN Section of the Department over this period I was left 'minding the shop' while my seniors were in New York with the Minister, I must have handled these papers, if only to put them on the appropriate file in the section after Con Cremin, the Secretary of the Department had dealt with them. However, I confess that at this stage I have no very detailed recollection of the sequence of events and I am correspondingly grateful to be able to draw here on the detailed annotated account given by Dr Kennedy in his essay in 2005.

followed, and reported on, the proceedings in the plenary session of the Assembly. The election took place on 30 October 1961 and Ireland was elected by 83 votes out of 97 to serve out the remaining year of Liberia's term. This elevation to the Council could be seen as the culmination of a period of great prominence for Ireland at the UN, following as it did Freddie Boland's Presidency of the General Assembly in 1960, General Sean McKeown's command of ONUC, the UN peacekeeping force in the Congo and Conor Cruise O'Brien's role as UN representative in Katanga in 1961.

Membership of the Security Council can indeed thrust a small Member State into unaccustomed prominence and responsibility in the United Nations system for a brief period. But it may also require it to take positions on world issues that it could otherwise quietly ignore. This may win it new contacts – or sour old friendships. As I recollect it, something of this kind happened to us for a time in 1962 over Kashmir.

The dispute over Kashmir dates back to the partition of the Indian subcontinent and the granting of independence to India and to Pakistan in 1947. At that time the rulers of the princely States spread over much of the subcontinent were allowed to opt to join their respective territories, either to India or to Pakistan. The Maharajah of Kashmir, a Hindu ruling over a majority Muslim population, dithered for a time, thinking of possible independence; and then, when Muslim tribesmen, encouraged by Pakistan, tried to take over Kashmir, opted quickly to join the territory to India. Fighting then erupted between the two countries and the outcome left the territory divided along a *de facto* ceasefire line. This was, and remains today, a very uneasy truce, punctuated sporadically by outbursts of violence. India claims that the choice was lawfully made in 1947 and that Kashmir is now rightfully part of India; Pakistan wants the people of the territory to have self-determination, believing that a majority would opt to join Pakistan; and India alleges that Pakistan supports terrorist insurgents in attacks on the part of the territory that is under Indian control.

There was a general expectation in the Department, as we prepared to take the seat from 1 January 1962, that Pakistan would seek to raise the Kashmir issue again in the Security Council. Some time before, I was sent over to the National Library in Kildare Street in Dublin to do some preliminary research for the brief that we would have to prepare. I had no great success with my assignment. The Library at the time seemed to me to be chronically starved of funds. Notwithstanding the serious conflicts that had taken place over Kashmir during the previous thirteen years, I could find nothing on that troubled region of later date than books with titles such as *Travels in Kashmir with a Donkey*, by Lieutenant Colonel Frobisher (or some such person), dating from 1876 (or some such date). Conor Cruise O'Brien once wrote, half-facetiously, of the UN's role in averting conflicts as something like that of helping to get a donkey down from the top of a minaret – today, he might find it more politically correct to add 'or a steeple'. But I doubted if Colonel Frobisher's nineteenth-century musings about his donkey would be of much help to Ambassador Boland in the Security Council seat in New York.

Pakistan did indeed bring the Kashmir issue to the Council that year. If my memory serves, Boland, speaking for Ireland in the debate that followed, expressed the hope that India and Pakistan would enter into talks on the problem. An unexceptionable – even laudable – sentiment it might seem to an outsider. But when States are in conflict, a call for 'talks' can sometimes be seen as favourable to the party that wants to reopen the question, and, conversely, as an unfriendly act by the other party to the dispute which wants the effort at reopening the issue to founder for lack of support. This seems to have been what happened here. Krishna Menon – for it was he who still spoke for India – took Boland's call for talks amiss, especially as it came from a country that he believed to have been historically sympathetic to India. In retaliation, he threatened Boland that he, Menon, would raise the partition of Ireland in the Council – something that the Irish Government would certainly not have thought helpful at the time. Pakistan, on the other hand, was pleasantly surprised at Ireland's attitude: it began to take a new interest in a country that had taken a position it had not expected; and, not too long thereafter, it accredited an Ambassador to Ireland on a non-resident basis.

'The Cuba bother' – if I may again borrow a phrase from Patrick Kavanagh – was much more serious. One of the more memorable confrontations of those dangerous days took place before the TV cameras in the Security Council in October of that year when the US representative, Adlai Stevenson, challenged his Soviet colleague to answer his charges and promised, if necessary, to wait for a response 'until Hell freezes over'.

In an earlier era, Cuba had been seen as almost an offshore island by the United States and US business interests. But relations soured in the mid-1950s when Castro's revolutionary forces took over; they deteriorated even further when Castro declared himself a Communist and confiscated American property in the island; and they reached their nadir in the early days of the Kennedy Administration when the CIA organised and funded the disastrous Bay of Pigs invasion by Cuban exiles.

In October 1962, American intelligence agencies detected moves by Khrushchev's Soviet Union to station offensive missiles with nuclear warheads and a range of several thousand miles in Cuba. Aerial photographs showed that Soviet naval vessels carrying these weapons were already on their way to Cuba. On 22 October, in a tense and dramatic television address to the nation, President Kennedy announced that the US was imposing, unilaterally, a naval and air quarantine of the island; and he threatened full retaliation if a missile were launched from there against the United States. He also announced that the US was asking for an emergency meeting of the UN Security Council; and he followed this up with a personal letter to Government leaders in other countries, including the Taoiseach, Sean Lemass, asking for their full support.

In his memoirs, U Thant, the Burmese Buddhist who was Acting

Secretary General of the United Nations at the time, recalls his reaction to Kennedy's television address:

> In my memory, it was the grimmest and gravest speech ever made by a head of state ...
>
> Never before had the lives of so many millions around the world been at the mercy of two men who had the power to make the ultimate decision. I was more deeply troubled than I had ever been in my life ... Never in the history of the United Nations did it face a moment of graver responsibility and grimmer challenge.[6]

On the night of 22 October after Kennedy's address, Adlai Stevenson, the US Permanent Representative, submitted a formal request to U Thant for an emergency meeting of the Security Council. The next morning, the Soviet representative, Zorin, who happened to hold the rotating Presidency of the Council that month, also asked for a Council meeting. He wanted the Council to examine 'the question of violation of the Charter and the threat to peace on the part of the United States'. Cuba, too, joined in: it asked for an emergency meeting of the Security Council to consider 'the act of war unilaterally committed by the United States' in ordering the naval blockade of Cuba.[7]

The Council met on the following day, 23 October 1962. Adlai Stevenson introduced a US draft resolution that called for the withdrawal of the Soviet missiles from Cuba under the supervision of UN observers. This would allow the US to lift its blockade of the Soviet ships, laden with missiles, which were still sailing for Cuba.[8] Many UN Member States urged U Thant to act; and on the following day, 24 October, in his capacity as Acting Secretary General he

---

6   I have drawn these quotations from several pages of his memoirs. See Thant (1978) pp. 155–158.

7   Ibid.

8   In this account I also draw on Skelly (1997) pp. 239–246.

sent identical messages to Kennedy and to Khrushchev, appealing for time. His message asked for

> on the one hand the voluntary suspension of all arms shipments to Cuba, and also the voluntary suspension of the quarantine measures involving the searching of ships bound for Cuba ... for a period of two to three weeks.[9]

Ironically, that very day was 'United Nations Day', which celebrates the entry into force of the UN Charter on 24 October 1945. U Thant records in his memoirs that the customary concert in the General Assembly hall that evening 'had to go on as originally scheduled' and he had to speak briefly at the concert. His messages to the US and the Soviet leaders, appealing for time, were on their way as he spoke. Later in the evening when the concert was over, the Security Council began its meeting.

I was not in New York that year, but I did attend that concert on United Nations Day in 1961 and again several times in the later 1960s and I know that it was customary for the orchestra to play Beethoven's 9th Symphony, with its great and stirring 'Ode to Joy' – a hymn to human brotherhood under God. *Alle Menschen werden Brüder*, the choir sings. It must have been a dramatic and poignant counterpoint to the meeting of the Council that night and the sombre events in the world outside.

The Taoiseach, Sean Lemass, was on a visit to Germany at this time. In a press conference in Bonn he expressed Ireland's support for the US position. He went on to say 'we are not in NATO, but that does not mean that we should be regarded as neutral. On the contrary we have emphasised over and over again that we are on the side of the western democracies.'[10] He had expressed similar sentiments even before the Cuban crisis broke. In a press conference on 5 September, he said:

9   Thant (1978) p. 460.
10   Quoted in Skelly (1997) p. 241.

We do not wish in the conflict between the free democracies and the communist empires to be thought of as neutral. We are not neutral and do not wish to be regarded as such, even though we have not got specific commitments of a military kind under any international agreements.[11]

Lemass phoned Aiken, who was in New York for the General Assembly session. They agreed between them that Ireland would speak, and vote for the US resolution in the Security Council.

Already in February of that year, Ireland had joined with the US and others in defeating an attempt by Cuba to have the Council consider a complaint about its expulsion by the OAS – the Organization of American States. In March it had also joined in voting down Cuba's request to have the Council ask for an advisory opinion from the International Court of Justice in The Hague about the legality of actions taken against it by the OAS, including expulsion and an economic boycott. The issue was whether a regional organisation could take enforcement action against one of its members without the prior authorisation of the Security Council. The normally cautious and mild-mannered U Thant later wrote that he thought Cuba fully justified in this request; and he described its rejection by the Council as 'a tragedy'.[12]

Aiken duly took the Irish seat in the Council and he addressed the Council on 24 October 1962. Though Ireland's voting position was not in doubt by then, particularly in view of its position in February and March, Aiken's speech in the Council is of some interest. Grave though the situation was at the time, he was still reasonable and moderate in what he said. His approach was not to attack the Soviet Union or Cuba but to express disappointment that

any small nation, no matter from what motives or under what provocation, should willingly become a new strategic base for

---

11 Denis Maher, *The Tortuous Path: The Course of Ireland's Entry into the EEC 1948–73*, pp. 156–157.

12 Thant (1978) p. 160.

the prosecution of the cold war or a spearhead in a nuclear conflict.[13]

He began with a short account of the origins of the bitter quarrel between the US and Cuba in which he recalled the confiscations of US interests in Cuba by Castro's Government, what he called the injection of the Cold War into relations between States in the Americas, and US retaliation against Cuba. He went on to express understanding for 'the concern that the Revolutionary Government of Cuba feel for their national security'. He continued:

> It is all the more understandable in view of the attempt made by Cuban refugee elements to invade their territory in April of last year. It is only natural that the Cubans should seek to strengthen their defences so as to be able to cope with any similar attack in the future. But it is a far cry from that to a military build-up of the kind which the Cuban Government now appears to have embarked upon with the massive assistance of the Soviet Union.

This, he said, was contrary to the growing hopes of many people that

> all the greater Powers, realising the immense responsibilities which the possession of nuclear armaments imposes, were seeking ways of withdrawing from foreign bases wherever they could, thereby relieving the tension which the maintenance of such bases tends to prolong.

He went on to draw a comparison with Ireland's neutrality during the Second World War. What he said was characteristic of his thinking in many ways, and it is worth quoting here at some length:

13   This and following extracts are taken from Aiken's speech of 24 October 1962 in the Security Council. Text is in Department of External Affairs (1962) pp. 23–30.

Our neutrality had as one of its fundamental bases a principle enunciated by the then leader of our Government, Mr. de Valera. That principle was that under no circumstances would we allow our country to be used as a base for attack against our neighbour, Great Britain. The principle is relevant to the case of all small countries threatened with involvement in conflicts or rivalries in which their powerful neighbours are engaged. It has special validity in the case of small countries placed beside powerful neighbours with whom they may have disputes or disagreements, as at the time of the Second World War we had – and indeed still have – with our neighbour, Great Britain, in regard to the partition of our country, but it is, we believe, a principle worthy of the consideration of the Government of Cuba.[14]

This was an interesting and sensible approach. A cynic might comment, of course, that on difficult issues representatives of States have latitude to express their principles in a moderate or sympathetic speech, provided the vote they cast in the end is 'right'. And there was no question but that in a world crisis of this magnitude and this danger, Ireland would vote with the United States, particularly since the US President, who had laid down the gauntlet so dramatically to Khrushchev, was John F. Kennedy. Lemass had already publicly said as much. He confirmed in the Dail on 6 November that this would indeed have been Ireland's position if the issue had come to a vote.

As Skelly notes, Ireland also responded positively to a US request on 23 October that it search any Czechoslovak planes that stopped at Shannon *en route* to Cuba to ensure that they did not carry munitions. Lemass personally agreed to do so, and the Irish authorities continued to carry out searches at Shannon over the next few weeks.[15] Sweden, in contrast, took quite a different line. According to U Thant's account:

---

14 Ibid., p. 26.
15 Skelly (1997) p. 244.

The Swedish government protested the U.S. naval blockade and in fact successfully tested it on October 26 by sending a ship, reportedly with a cargo from the USSR, through the interception zone to Havana.[16]

In the event, following a dramatic debate on the night of 24 October, the issue did not come to a vote in the Security Council. As the Soviet vessels neared the quarantine zone patrolled by the US Navy, U Thant sent his third message to Kennedy and Khrushchev. He urged both sides to allow a moratorium: this would mean that Khrushchev would keep Soviet ships from entering the interception area for a limited time; and Kennedy would instruct the US Navy to do all it could to avoid direct confrontation. Both leaders responded positively to his request. The confrontation between the Soviet Union and the United States continued, however, in direct exchanges between Kennedy and Khrushchev. Eventually, in face of the enormity of the threat of possible nuclear confrontation, Khrushchev backed down: he agreed to remove the missiles from Cuba and said he would be ready to discuss verification by UN representatives. [17]

By 28 October the worst of the crisis between the two super-powers was over. But they had reckoned without Cuba. Castro resented the Soviet readiness to withdraw the missiles as something agreed over his head. U Thant went to Cuba to try to persuade him. He was well received but Cuba maintained its position – though it offered to agree to UN inspection in Cuba if there were a similar inspection in the 'invasion camps' in Florida. There was no prospect that the US would concede on this. U Thant reports an interesting exchange during his visit. Castro asked him 'whether the demand of the United States for the dismantling of the launching pads was based on right or on a position of might'. 'I answered that it was not based on right, but based on apprehension.' As a good Buddhist, U

---

16   Thant (1978) p. 169.
17   I have drawn on U Thant's (1978) memoir in this and the following paragraphs.

Thant, in a very fraught situation, also maintained his practice of early morning meditation: 'I managed to practice *metta* (good will) and *karuna* (compassion) to all.'[18]

Gradually, due in some part at least to U Thant's creative combination of meditation with mediation, the crisis wound down. On 20 November 1962, President Kennedy announced that Khrushchev had agreed to withdraw the Soviet IL-28 bombers from Cuba within 30 days and to allow them to be observed and counted as they left. The statement went on:

> Inasmuch as this goes a long way toward reducing the danger which faced this Hemisphere four weeks ago, I have this afternoon instructed the Secretary of Defense to lift our naval quarantine.

The Cuban missile crisis was effectively over, but the shudder it had set off in the world continued long after.

It would be too much to say that the UN or its Acting Secretary General was central to the resolution of the crisis. U Thant does not make that claim. But the UN did serve as a useful forum, a channel and, to some extent, a point of reference that allowed both sides gradually to moderate the extremity of their positions. As he puts it:

> The settlement was an eloquent illustration of the usefulness of the United Nations to member states as a place for peaceful settlement of international conflicts. It is clear that direct, and almost daily, communication between President Kennedy and Chairman Khrushchev was mainly responsible for bringing to an end a most frightening confrontation between the two nuclear giants.[19]

Skelly puts it even better:

---

18 Ibid., p. 186.
19 Ibid., p. 191.

the UN had again performed one of its small but vital functions in the international system: providing the cover necessary for a leader to save face at home while extracting his country from a situation abroad that had spiralled out of control.[20]

As an elected member of the Security Council for that year, Ireland, though not centrally involved in the issue, was something more than a mere observer. During what was arguably the most dangerous crisis since the Second World War, it showed itself to be fundamentally supportive of the US in the face of what seemed to be a rash escalation of the threat posed by the Soviet Union. But in his address to the Council at the height of the crisis, Frank Aiken was still able to show some understanding of the security concerns of the Cuban Government and, finding some parallel in Ireland's own experience, he suggested a prudent principle that small countries placed beside powerful neighbours would do well to follow.

---

20   Skelly (1997) p. 243.

8

Apartheid

The achievements of the United Nations fall short in many respects of the high-minded aims proclaimed in 1945. But there are two areas, at least, where it has had notable success: the discrediting, and ultimately the ending, of colonialism; and the ending of the system of apartheid in South Africa, in which the UN played an important part. On both these related issues, Irish Delegations played an active role in the General Assembly in the years following Ireland's admission to UN membership. I will deal with our approach to the apartheid question in the present chapter and go on in the next chapter to consider the colonialism issue.

The United Nations came into being at the close of the Second World War. By then, the full horror of what racialist theories had led to in the concentration camps had become clear to the world. The universal revulsion at these revelations played a large part in the decision of those who drafted the Preamble to the Charter to have 'the Peoples of the United Nations' express their determination 'to reaffirm faith in fundamental human rights, in the dignity and worth of the human person, in the equal rights of men and women and of nations large and small'.

South Africa was a founder member of the United Nations. But a few years later its whites-only Government began to create the legal framework for apartheid, a system that elevated common prejudice and discrimination into a formal structure for governance that was the direct antithesis of the aim expressed in the Preamble to the Charter.

Happily that system has now been dismantled, and South Africa is now a democratic society where racial discrimination is no longer built into the system of government. In the Western-dominated UN General Assembly of the 1950s, however, it was not yet clear that things would go this way or even that the UN, an organisation of sovereign states, was entitled to engage itself in a direct effort to bring it to an end. Many Western countries at the time thought that the apartheid system was deplorable – indeed indefensible. But they saw the situation within South Africa as primarily an issue of human rights and they were dubious about the right of the UN to intervene. They believed that to do so would be contrary to Article 2.7 of the Charter, which bars the UN from intervening in matters that are 'essentially within the domestic jurisdiction of any State'. Ireland, however, took a strong stance on the issue from the earliest years of its UN membership, and considered that it was indeed right and proper for the UN to involve itself with the issue.

South Africa's racial policies were first discussed in the General Assembly as far back as 1946, when India raised the treatment of people of Indian origin in that country. The tendency in those years was to see the issue as one to be negotiated between India and South Africa, and in 1952 the General Assembly established a three-person commission to assist in such negotiations. By then it was assumed that three parties should be involved – India, Pakistan and South Africa itself. South Africa, however, declined to deal with the issue in any way under the UN Charter although it professed to be ready for direct negotiations with India.[1] It also rejected a resolution of the Assembly requesting it to suspend a new racial segregation law called the Group Areas Act.

The general approach of important Western countries to the domestic jurisdiction issue in those years is clear from their attitudes to this resolution. The United States decided to vote in

---

1   UN *Yearbook* (1995) pp. 52ff. For South Africa's refusal to deal with the issue under the Charter see p. 57.

favour, despite difficulties with parts of the text, but said that it was inadvisable for the Assembly to censure a piece of national legislation; the UK thought that parts of the text constituted intervention in matters within South Africa's jurisdiction; and Australia considered that the matter was outside the competence of the United Nations. On another resolution later that year Australia, Belgium, France, New Zealand and the UK 'supported, in general, the position of South Africa on the meaning of the Charter provision on domestic jurisdiction and the nature of international commitments on human rights'.[2] Even the Scandinavian countries Denmark, Norway and Sweden, which later took strong positions against apartheid, took the view at that time that the UN lacked jurisdiction to set up a fact-finding commission. They said, too, that the UN could make recommendations on matters of racial discrimination but that it was not competent to prescribe specific measures to be imposed on a State.[3]

South Africa remained obdurate, in no way deterred by these uncertain voices, and it continued throughout the decade to build up a legal framework for the apartheid system. By the late 1950s opinion in the Assembly had hardened considerably and the issue had moved well beyond South Africa's treatment of people of Indian origin. Many Western countries, however, though highly critical of South Africa's policies, continued to be dubious about the right of the UN to intervene directly in what they still saw as its 'internal affairs'.

In those years of the late 1950s, the Irish Delegation was active, with a small number of other countries, both in asking to have the apartheid issue inscribed on the Assembly agenda for discussion and in co-sponsoring resolutions in regard to it. These resolutions may seem to us now in retrospect to have been restrained in tone but, judged by the temper of the Assembly at the time, they were highly critical of South Africa's policies.

---

2   Ibid., p. 61, col. 1.
3   Ibid. p. 60, col. 1

The Minister, Frank Aiken, took a clear position on apartheid in South Africa in several of his speeches to the Assembly on other issues. In a speech in the Assembly on Tibet on 9 October 1959, for example, he rebutted in very clear terms the contention of some countries about the limitations on the competence of the Assembly to intervene on such issues:

> Wherever government action is directed towards the systematic violation of human rights, it is, we believe, the proper function of this Assembly to pronounce the judgment of world opinion on such a breach of the principles which all of us here are pledged to maintain and upon which our hopes of a just world order are based.[4]

He did not, however, devote any one speech solely to the question: that was, for the most part, a matter that other members of the delegation addressed each year in the detailed debates on the apartheid issue that took place in Committees of the Assembly. When I was Ireland's representative in the Special Political Committee during several sessions of the General Assembly in the latter part of the 1960s I dealt with the issue myself, and spoke out strongly on it. I recall that I was somewhat disconcerted – but also I suppose somewhat amused – to find that one such speech that I had made to the Committee calling for UN action on the issue was reported in one Irish newspaper under the rather dramatic headline 'Ireland warns South Africa', while another Irish paper, reading it differently perhaps, carried a report of the same speech under the no less dramatic headline 'Ireland warns the UN'.

From 1960 onwards the political balance within the Assembly changed rapidly: in the single month of September 1960 alone sixteen newly independent African States were admitted to the UN. As a consequence, the 'Afro-Asian' States, as they were usually called at the time, soon became a majority. They took over the

---

4   Department of External Affairs (1959) p. 25.

handling of the issue in the Assembly and pressed it to adopt resolutions that were much stronger than anything that it would previously have accepted. Over this same period, South Africa hardened its position. It was completely dismissive of the UN and it became inured to attack. In turn, it was treated as a pariah by many delegations that had become exasperated at its intransigence and at the apparent inability of condemnations by the Assembly to achieve any change.

As an example of the mood at the time, I can cite an episode from October 1961. I had been sitting in the Irish seat in the Assembly hall during a speech by the South African Foreign Minister, Eric Louw, in the annual General Debate. He was a man who had seemed tolerably urbane, the almost acceptable face that his country presented to the outside world. But his speech that day outraged many delegations. A semi-official letter in which I reported home to a colleague in the Department of External Affairs a few days later conveys something of the atmosphere:

> feelings boiled over immediately after Louw had spoken in the General Debate and Liberia moved – to thunderous applause – to have the whole speech expunged from the records. There was a very strong emotional current in the Assembly at that moment and almost anything might have happened ... Jaja Wachuku[5] pounded his desk, as did the ... delegate of Niger ... I found my [own] emotions rising as I listened to Louw's unfortunate speech. There seems to have been something doubly unhappy about the way it was delivered which may not come over in reading the text.

African countries in the Assembly reacted particularly strongly. My letter continued:

---

5   The Foreign Minister of Nigeria. He had been a student at Trinity College Dublin some years before

a proposal to adjourn the debate was carried and after lunch Liberia withdrew its proposal to expunge the speech from the records and substituted a loosely worded and hasty motion of censure which was passed – again in a very emotional atmosphere – by 67 to 1 with 20 abstentions and 12 non-participants. We abstained mainly because we felt that the censure motion was hasty, loosely-worded and unprecedented in the General Debate. On the earlier motion [to expunge the speech] we would have voted against on general principles.

Jaja Wachuku again pounded his desk and passed audible comments as the roll-call proceeded; there was some sardonic laughter from several delegations when Britain said 'not participating in the vote'; and amused laughter when Finland was found to be still in a huddle trying to make up its mind after its name had been called twice.

Some African delegations have said that they intend to propose specifically that South Africa be expelled but many Asian countries would not go along with this – Ceylon [now Sri Lanka] for example has said that it would oppose such a move on principle.

I should perhaps explain more fully why Ireland abstained that day on the motion of censure and indeed why Asian countries like Ceylon were prepared to oppose any move to expel South Africa – a position that the Irish Delegation would undoubtedly have shared if the issue had arisen. Ireland strongly repudiated South Africa's apartheid policy and wanted to see the Assembly condemn it. But we also held to certain fundamental principles: we wanted to uphold the provisions of the Charter, and, as far as possible, to maintain the universality of the UN; we could not agree to curtail the right of Foreign Ministers to speak freely in the General Debate, however deplorable, indeed outrageous, the sentiments they expressed; and we did not believe that it was within the power of the Assembly under the Charter to take it on itself to expel a Member

State by a simple vote to that effect. According to the UN Charter, it is for the Security Council to take the initiative on such an issue.[6]

There is a perception today that, even though Aiken remained Minister and leader of the delegation until 1969, Irish Delegations to the General Assembly in the later 1960s failed to show the courage and independence that their predecessors had shown in the 1950s. Certainly times changed. So did personalities – but Frank Aiken was still our Minister over the whole of the period in question.

Perhaps I am a bit defensive on this issue. I served myself on those later delegations – in each of the last four years of the 1960s. Not only that, but for several of those years I was the Irish representative on the Special Political Committee where the apartheid issue was debated. But then I can also claim to have spanned the two eras, to some extent at least, since I had earlier served in the UN section of the Department in 1960 and had been a member of the delegation to the 1961 Assembly.

I think it is fair to say that critics of Irish policy on apartheid and related issues during that later period do not allow sufficiently for the fact that the General Assembly itself was changing rapidly at about this time. As mentioned above, the membership grew dramatically during the 1960s, the decade of decolonisation, and there was a large influx of new member states from Africa in particular. They soon took over the initiative on African and on colonial issues. This meant that it was no longer necessary for some sympathetic countries outside Africa such as Ireland to ask to have apartheid put on the agenda and to propose draft resolutions in regard to it. African countries were now in a position to speak for themselves and for their continent, and they did so with increasing vigour and assertiveness.

The US and other Western Member States, on the other hand,

---

6   Article 6 of the Charter makes it clear that a Member State may be expelled by the Assembly only if the Security Council so recommends. The Article reads as follows: 'A Member of the United Nations which has persistently violated the Principles contained in the present Charter may be expelled from the Organization by the General Assembly upon the recommendation of the Security Council.'

had begun to take the Assembly less seriously than in the 1950s and were dubious about many of the proposals on the apartheid issue that were being pressed to a vote in the Assembly. Some of these States still tended towards a 'strict constructionist' interpretation of Article 2.7 of the Charter, which barred discussion of a state's 'internal affairs'. Other States, in part perhaps because they were economically engaged with South Africa, did not consider demands for sanctions against it to be a good approach; and many were dubious about declaratory resolutions and about the competence or the capacity of the General Assembly, as distinct from the Security Council, to impose sanctions or to enforce them if they were to be imposed. On the other hand, Soviet Bloc countries inevitably took advantage of the issue to embarrass Western countries for continuing their economic relations with South Africa.

By the mid-1960s the UN General Assembly was more radical, and at the same time taken less seriously by Western countries, than it had been in the early years of Ireland's membership. The new African members became increasingly frustrated at their inability, in the face of Western opposition, to secure action through declaratory resolutions forced through by a majority vote in the General Assembly. As they became more frustrated, the resolutions that they proposed became lengthier, and stronger and more vehement in condemning 'the major trading partners of South Africa' – that is those Western countries that refused to sever their economic relations with that country simply because of General Assembly resolutions recommending sanctions.

This frequently created a dilemma for Ireland, and for Scandinavian and other like-minded delegations. There were many of these draft resolutions that we agreed with and could support. But there were others that included paragraphs couched in language that it was difficult for us to accept. Sometimes, for example, these resolutions excoriated named Western countries in ways, and to an extent, with which we could not agree. Frequently, they aimed at the imposition of sanctions on South Africa in a way that was outside the competence of the General Assembly and likely to be ineffective and thus to discredit the very concept of sanctions.

Frank Aiken, much as he opposed apartheid, took a strong view on this latter point – largely, I think, because of his memories of the ineffectual efforts of the League of Nations to impose sanctions in certain cases in the 1930s. He believed strongly that sanctions would be ineffective unless they were fully implemented by all States. That meant that they had to be legally binding, which meant in turn that they would have to be imposed by the Security Council, the only body with authority to make mandatory decisions on such matters. Resolutions of the General Assembly, in contrast, are not binding and count only as 'recommendations'.[7] Aiken's view was that a scatter-shot approach by way of a General Assembly resolution, even one adopted by a large majority, would be counterproductive; it would not be fully implemented; it would not have any impact on South Africa; and it would do much to discredit the very idea of sanctions as a means of coercing recalcitrant Member States that were in breach of the Charter.

Quite often the sponsors of such resolutions, with majority support in the Assembly, refused to allow a separate vote on individual paragraphs. They were also ready to vote down any attempt to amend those paragraphs to make the resolution as a whole more acceptable. So what were the Irish, and other delegations, to do? Should we bite our tongues and vote in favour of these 'take it or leave it' resolutions to show our countries' abhorrence of apartheid? Or should we abstain, or even vote against, because of the unacceptable language of certain paragraphs and face criticism for being less than trenchant in opposition to the policy of apartheid?

In the later 1960s, Conor Cruise O'Brien, who had maintained a judicious silence in the first years after he resigned in 1961, began to write more critically of Irish policy at the UN, particularly in regard to South Africa. As a member of the Irish Delegation himself in the 1950s he had favoured what was then a strong line on apartheid,

---

7   Article 10 of the Charter.

judged by the standards of the time. As the 1960s went on, however, he began to argue that Ireland was no longer showing the courage and independence that had characterised its stance in those earlier years when he was on the delegation. He did not seem to realise how the temper of the Assembly had changed in the interim and how much further our position had moved in response to that change: Ireland was now voting for resolutions that went far beyond anything that he or the Irish Delegation were likely to have supported in an earlier era. His criticisms were taken up by others, including the very effective Irish Anti-Apartheid Movement organised by Kader Asmal. Naturally enough, they wanted to press the Minister and the delegation to take as forward a position as possible on the issue and it helped to have such a prominent and respected critic on their side.

To avoid misunderstanding, let me say clearly here that it was not at all the case that the Department of External Affairs or we, as officials involved in these issues, were unsympathetic to the Anti-Apartheid Movement or its aims. Contrary to what some might think, those on the inside of a Governmental system do not always regard the pressure generated by lobby groups outside it as unwelcome even if they must maintain a judicious silence about their own personal views. I would hazard a guess that, if we had not been constrained by our positions, some of us at the time might well have become members of the AAM ourselves and marched in its protests. I know that I would.

As the critics became more outspoken, Aiken, a man never given to active presentation of himself or his policies to the news media, became more taciturn. He was a man of courage and integrity but somewhat old-fashioned in his approach. It was simply not his style to engage in public debate on foreign policy issues, and he gave no public answer to criticisms of Ireland's voting position on the apartheid issue. Had he done so, he could at least have explained his position to the Anti-Apartheid Movement at home and let them see that he and the delegation shared their fundamental aims – though they would, no doubt, still have pressed him to go further.

However, in the absence of any defence from the Minister, who alone could defend policy publicly at home, the critics had it all their own way. The belief grew that Ireland was 'back-sliding' in a serious way from its past positions. Little account was taken of the fact that the General Assembly majority was now far more radical – and frustrated – than it had been in the late 1950s and that the resolutions that were being adopted were far stronger than anything that would have been proposed in the earlier period. The result, paradoxically, was that even though Ireland was voting far more radically on apartheid than it would ever have done in the period up to 1960, the received opinion at home was, and still remains, that the decade of the 1960s marked a major deterioration and failure of courage and independence in its stance at the UN.

For some of these years, as I noted above, I sat as Irish representative in the Special Political Committee where the apartheid issue was debated, and I always spoke strongly in the debate. I can also recall discussions within the delegation and with the then Permanent Representative, Ambassador Con Cremin, about the recommendations we should make to the Minister and to the Department at home in regard to our voting positions. Stung by the unanswered public criticism at home, we sometimes bent over backwards to find ways to rationalise voting in favour of resolutions that contained one or more paragraphs that we would ordinarily have thought unacceptable.

One regular problem, for example, was the regular condemnation – either of 'the main trading partners of South Africa' or sometimes, more specifically, of named Member States such as Germany, France and the UK – for continuing their 'collaboration' with that country. But since the Security Council, the only body with authority to take binding decisions on sanctions, had not done so, these countries could say that – so far as their UN obligations were concerned – they were fully entitled to continue trading with South Africa. Sometimes we swallowed hard and, having to take or leave the resolution as a whole, voted in favour.

Ireland's own trade with South Africa at the time was negligible and we could certainly feel virtuous about the issue. But that was according to Irish statistics. One day, freed for the moment from attendance in the Committee, I did some research in the UN Library. There I discovered, to my great surprise, that Ireland ranked quite high as a trading partner – fifth or sixth, so far as I recall – according to South African statistics. The explanation soon became apparent: our statistics excluded, and South African statistics included, the Shannon Free Airport area where a large South African company manufactured and traded in artificial diamonds. As someone who, as a small private personal gesture, had refused for years to eat 'Outspan' oranges, I was naturally somewhat put out at this. It seemed to me that we ought to ensure greater congruence between our voting position and our own approach to trade with South Africa – what the Fianna of Irish legend were reputed to have called *beart de réir ár mbriathar*; i.e. that we ought to match our actions to our words. Years later, in drafting an important foreign policy speech for a Minister, I wrote this point into the draft – without spelling it out too bluntly. Some colleagues took me to task afterwards for leading the Minister to suggest that Ireland should modify its principles to fit its interests. That was exactly the opposite of what I had intended: I had wanted the Minister to say that we should abide by our principles even when we feared that doing so might affect our interests.

The construction of the apartheid system from 1948 onwards was not the only flagrant breach by South Africa of the principles of the UN Charter which it had helped to write in 1945. It also tried to annex Namibia, then known as South West Africa, which had been entrusted to it as a 'mandate' by the League of Nations a quarter century before. Frank Aiken was particularly resolute in his opposition to South Africa on this point.

South West Africa had been a German 'protectorate' from 1890 until it was seized from Germany by South Africa during the First World War. After Germany was defeated, a number of former

German colonies were given to other countries to administer as 'mandates'. The Covenant of the League stipulated that in these territories 'the well-being and development' of the peoples concerned was to 'form a sacred trust of civilisation'. Under this system South Africa was given responsibility for South West Africa. It is true that the Covenant mentioned 'South West Africa' explicitly, along with 'certain of the South Pacific Islands', as territories that 'can best be administered under the laws of the Mandatory as integral portions of its territory'.[8] But it was still clear that what South Africa had been given was a mandate, and not a right to annex the area. However, when the League of Nations was wound up in 1946 after the Second World War, South Africa, rather speciously, began to claim that the mandate had lapsed and that it was not obliged to account internationally for the territory under the new Trusteeship system of the United Nations. In effect it planned to hold on to it for the future and make it part of South Africa.

This was a stance that most of the rest of the world saw as both outrageous and illegal. The International Court of Justice in The Hague declared in 1950 that South Africa had continuing international obligations in regard to the territory. Aiken strongly agreed. He believed that South Africa's claim was contrary to international law; and that, because of its obvious illegality, it was South West Africa, rather than the apartheid system as such, that was the real Achilles heel of racist South Africa. So, in speeches in the General Assembly, and in discussions with other UN Member States, he always argued that the question should be referred to the Security Council, which was the only UN organ that could adopt binding decisions and exercise coercive powers. South Africa, he said, had 'no right, legal or moral, to remain in occupation of the territory'. This was 'a clear case of aggression by a would-be colonial Power against a weak neighbouring people' and the freedom of South West Africa was 'a challenge to the United Nations … in particular to the wisdom of the Great Powers'.

---

8   Covenant of the League of Nations, Article 22.6.

In October 1966 the General Assembly formally terminated South Africa's mandate. Despite misgivings on the part of some members of the Afro-Asian group about the feasibility in practice of such an approach, it then appointed a United Nations Council for South West Africa that was to take on responsibility, including power to enact legislation, for the territory.[9] I was a member of the delegation that year and I was in the General Assembly when it voted to terminate South Africa's mandate. I particularly remember from those years the strength of Aiken's conviction on this issue.

Aiken and other members of the Irish Delegation had been actively involved in discussions with other delegations on the proposal before the General Assembly, but it is interesting that, precisely because of the depth of Aiken's concern, Ireland abstained on this resolution rather than voting in favour as might have been expected. This was because he believed that South Africa would remain obdurate and he knew that the Assembly was not in a position to ensure that its decision would be respected. So it must invoke the active cooperation of the Security Council. It would then be for the Council, the one UN organ with power to impose its decisions, 'to decide what further measures are to be employed and actions to be taken to secure compliance'.[10] If it were followed through, this approach would almost certainly lead to sanctions against South Africa. Without the involvement of the Security Council, however, it was Aiken's view that a resolution of the General Assembly on its own was likely to be ineffectual. This was quite an advanced position for a European Member State to take at the time.

In the event Aiken proved far-sighted in his approach: South Africa did indeed continue to defy the United Nations. The Security

9   Department of External Affairs, *Delegation Report on the Twenty-first Regular and Fifth Special Sessions of the United Nations General Assembly 1966 and 1967*, pp. 27–34.

10   The quotations are from the Minister's speech in the General Assembly on 4 May 1967. See Department of External Affairs (1967) pp. 11–16. There are also two other speeches on the issue in this volume.

Council took up the issue in 1969 and declared the continuing presence of South Africa in the territory to be illegal – a view upheld in an Opinion by the International Court Justice in The Hague in 1971. But South Africa still proved intransigent; it still held on to the territory; and it forcibly suppressed opposition by SWAPO, the South West African People's Organisation.

Ten years further on, in April 1981, I had a more direct personal involvement in the issue of Namibia, as it had come to be called by then, during Ireland's two-year term as an elected member of the Security Council when I was myself the Irish Permanent Representative to the UN. Ireland held the rotating Presidency of the Council for that month and I found myself not just speaking in, but presiding over, a very fraught debate on Namibia. But that is another story. Here I will limit myself to saying that the story did not end even then. Seven more years were to pass before South Africa agreed to free elections under UN supervision in the territory. This was the prelude to the emergence of Namibia to full independence as a sovereign state in March 1990 and its admission to membership of the United Nations one month later – on 23 April 1990. It would have been nice if Frank Aiken had lived to see it but he died in 1983, five years before.

9

Colonialism

Colonialism today is dead and discredited, but in the 1950s and for part of the 1960s it was very much alive. Some important European countries still maintained colonies in Africa and elsewhere at that time and believed in their right to do so.

The UN Charter does not flatly rule out the holding of colonies – that would not have been acceptable to important Member States such as the UK and France at the time it was drafted in 1945. Nevertheless, Chapter XI of the Charter, headed 'Declaration regarding Non-Self-Governing Territories', in speaking of 'territories whose peoples have not yet attained a full measure of self-government' implies strongly that colonialism, although tolerated for the moment, is eventually to be brought to an end. Furthermore, an Article in that Chapter required Member States responsible for what it describes as 'non-self-governing territories' to transmit information regularly to the Secretary General on 'economic, social and educational conditions' in those territories.[1] Some colonial powers were prepared to do this; others flatly refused. Some European countries even went so far as to deny that the territories they held in Africa and elsewhere were colonies: they argued that they were either an integral part or an 'overseas department' of their metropolitan territory. France, for example, took this position in relation to Algeria, as Portugal did in relation to Mozambique and Angola. Even those countries that accepted that their colonies should ultimately be allowed to exercise self-determination tended to argue at the time

---

1   Article 73e.

that it would be wrong for the colonial power to withdraw 'precipitously' and 'without adequate preparation' from territories that they had governed in some cases for a century or more.

It was natural that the attitude of the Irish delegation to the whole question of colonialism should reflect their sense of Ireland's own historic experience. In December 1960 the Minister for External Affairs, Frank Aiken, who led the delegation, adopted a particularly strong and distinctive position on what came to be seen as a landmark resolution of the General Assembly – Resolution 1514 (XV). This was the 'Declaration on the Granting of Independence to Colonial Countries and Peoples'. It asserted flatly that 'all peoples have an inalienable right to complete freedom'; and it solemnly proclaimed 'the necessity of bringing to a speedy and unconditional end colonialism in all its forms and manifestations'. The use of the word 'unconditional' in this resolution was particularly significant because it was an implicit rebuttal of the argument advanced by some European countries at the time – that a colonial power could defer granting independence if it considered that the people of a colony were not yet ready to govern themselves. Some might argue, of course, that the unfortunate events in the Congo following its ill-prepared launch into independence, which were happening even as the resolution was adopted, ought to have been seen as a counter-example.

Aiken warmly endorsed the text of the draft resolution in a speech in the General Assembly on 5 December 1960 and he welcomed what he described as the constructive approach of the 43 African and Asian countries that had co-sponsored it. While uncompromising in his support for decolonisation, he also gave credit where he thought it was due: he spoke positively of 'the widening of freedom ... through the wise and realistic statesmanship of the colonial Powers'.

In his speech he urged that the resolution on the ending of colonialism should be 'as universal in its application as is the Universal Declaration of Human Rights'. The rights it proclaimed:

should be applicable to all peoples in all parts of the world, east or west, north or south … whether the oppressors and the oppressed were of the same race, creed or colour or of different races, creeds and colours; whether the oppressed peoples came under the domination of an outside power many centuries ago like my own country, or in the last century like many countries in Africa, or in recent years like Tibet.[2]

He also managed a suitably eirenic reference to the situation in Ireland. Having noted that one paragraph in the text described 'the partial or total disruption of the national unity and the territorial integrity of a country' as incompatible with the principles of the UN Charter, he went on:

We have every hope that, with the growth of good will and better understanding, the unity of our country will be recovered with reasonable speed and in a peaceful and orderly manner, in keeping with the interests of the Irish nation as a whole, and of Great Britain as well.[3]

A number of Western countries were dubious about the draft resolution. They were particularly concerned about the principle that decolonisation should be immediate and that lack of adequate preparation was not to be a pretext for delay. Nevertheless, in the end they refrained from voting against it. The resolution was adopted by 89 votes to none on 14 December 1960. However, nine 'Western' countries, including the US, the UK and France abstained.[4] Ireland voted in favour. In view of its sense of its own history, and its policy approach at the UN, it could not well have done otherwise. Aiken's speech was strong and it showed clearly that this was a deeply felt, personal position.

---

2   Quotations are taken from his speech of 5 December 1960. For the text see Department of External Affairs (1960) pp. 47–53.

3   Ibid., p. 53.

4   United Nations (1995) p. 187.

While this established Ireland's support for the principle of bringing colonialism to a 'speedy and unconditional end', the specific case of Algeria, a territory that was at that time still engaged in a bloody war to gain its independence from France, was a more difficult issue for the Irish Delegation. On one hand, Ireland had always had good relations with France, and the French Government made strong diplomatic representations to Ireland and other countries each year to gain support and understanding for its position. On the other hand, the Irish Delegation could not accept the contention of France that Algeria was really a part of France's metropolitan territory and not a colony; and it sympathised strongly with the case for self-determination for the people of Algeria.

The resources of the Department of External Affairs were limited enough at the time but I remember that in the small Political/ United Nations section, where it fell to me to maintain files based on reading and monitoring various journals and publications, we followed the Algerian struggle for independence as best we could. We also had regular reports from our Ambassador in Paris, William Fay. Understandably perhaps given his position, his reports tended to reflect the French viewpoint to what I and my colleagues in Dublin considered too great a degree. I should add however that, to his credit, he had the prescience to maintain occasional contact with General de Gaulle during his years of self-imposed internal 'exile' – a link that proved useful later when de Gaulle returned to power.

But we had at least some other sources of information on the conflict. In addition to the main French newspapers, *Le Monde* and *Le Figaro*, the Department subscribed to a small Algerian French-language weekly called *El Moujahid* that I and another colleague read regularly. For some odd reason the word *wilayet*, which I met frequently in its pages, sticks in my memory even today: my recollection is that it was the word for a province or governmental subdivision of the country, equivalent perhaps to a *Department* in France. *El Moujahid* was the newspaper of the FLN, the organisation that led the Algerian independence struggle. It had begun in 1956 'in a scruffily roneo'd format ... distributed secretly through the Casbah'.[5] Today it is a large and prominent daily paper owned by the Algerian Government.

When Frank Aiken first addressed the question of Algeria in the course of his General Debate speech in September 1957, he took a clear stand. He referred to himself as one of the 'friends and admirers of the great French nation', and went on:

> But the nature of the conflict there is one that leaves a country with Ireland's traditions no choice. As this case is due to be considered by this Assembly, we cannot do otherwise than support self-determination for Algeria.[6]

At the time there was a substantial and long-established population of French settlers in Algeria – the so-called *pieds noirs* – as well as a minority of Algerians who had worked with the colonial administration and felt that their interest lay in close links with France. The French Algerian settler population had considerable support in France, and successive French Governments waged a prolonged war to suppress the Algerian independence movement. The war dragged on for nearly eight years with great brutality on both sides: it toppled six French Prime Ministers[7] and it deeply divided both France and the French military.

The divisions in France culminated in the 'revolution' of May 1958 which, in effect, ended the Fourth Republic and brought the country close to civil war. At this point, Charles de Gaulle, revered by many as France's saviour in the Second World War, came forward again to take a central role. For much of the 1950s, he had lived in a kind of sulky internal exile – biding his time, as some said – in the little French village of Colombey-les-Deux-Eglises. His position on the Algerian issue was enigmatic. Nevertheless, he was voted into

5   Alistair Horne, *A Savage War of Peace: Algeria 1954–1962*, p. 133.
6   Speech of 20 September 1957. See Department of External Affairs (1957) p. 24.
7   Horne (1977) p. 14.

power by a divided National Assembly that accepted his terms – full powers to rule by decree for six months and a mandate to submit a new constitution to the country for approval. This was approved in a referendum and the Fifth Republic was established with de Gaulle as its first President.

One historian of the Algerian conflict puts it succinctly: 'De Gaulle had let the country go to the very edge of the abyss and gaze down on the ultimate catastrophe of civil war before putting out a hand to pull it back'.[8] In June 1958, shortly after his inauguration as President, de Gaulle travelled to Algeria where he was warmly welcomed by French generals and by the French Algerian population. Flanked by the leading French general, Salan, he addressed a wildly enthusiastic crowd of French Algerians from a balcony in Algiers. He assured them that he understood them – *je vous ai compris* – a Delphic utterance that added to the shock they felt later when he cut the Gordian knot that was strangling France, and disengaged from Algeria. Three months later, in an address to the nation on 16 September, he began what was to be a long and painful process by solemnly accepting the right of the Algerian people to self-determination.

I have recounted these events at some length in order to evoke something of the atmosphere in which the issue was debated at the time in the UN General Assembly and to explain the background to the position taken by Aiken. In his General Debate speech of 20 September 1957, he urged the French Government to concede the right of self-determination to Algeria 'absolutely and unequivocally' and to abandon 'the theory that Algeria is an integral part of France'. But he also urged 'the revolutionaries of Algeria, for their part, to cease fire forthwith' and to accept peacefully the result of free elections and negotiations. They should also declare that, if they won those elections, they would be 'not only just but generous' to all European settlers who wished to remain and would compensate those who wished to leave.[9]

---

8   Ibid., p. 299.
9   Department of External Affairs (1957) pp. 24–25.

Addressing the issue again in 1960, Aiken welcomed de Gaulle's 'progressive and constructive declarations' which recognised 'the right of the people of Algeria to determine their future according to their own freely expressed will'; and he hoped that de Gaulle, 'with the overwhelming majority of the French people behind him, will negotiate a just and friendly settlement with all possible speed'. There should be 'international supervision of any election or referendum to be held to determine the free will of the Algerian people' to ensure that the result would not be open to question. He made no direct reference to Ireland but it is obvious that he had Ireland in mind when he spoke strongly against any attempt to partition Algeria:

> I wish to emphasise that, in our view, no minority has the right to defeat the will of the majority of the Algerian people by attempting to partition Algeria. At the same time we believe that minorities wishing to remain in Algeria are entitled to constitutional guarantees, and that any of them who may wish to leave when self-determination has been implemented have the right to just compensation.[10]

Aiken's statements to the General Assembly and how the Irish Delegation would vote on the question of Algeria from year to year were, understandably, matters of some concern to the French Government of the day. As I recall it, the French Ambassador in Dublin regularly made representations on the issue to the Secretary of the Department, Con Cremin, in which he usually emphasised the 'delicacy of the present situation' and sometimes the hope, or even the imminence, of some kind of settlement talks. Junior though I was at the time, I had a sense that the Taoiseach, Sean Lemass, was susceptible to these arguments; and possibly, he was just a little nervous about what his colleague, Frank Aiken, was doing and saying in the Assembly on the issue.

---

10   Department of External Affairs (1960) pp. 54–57.

By 1961, however, direct contacts between French and Algerian representatives raised real hope of a settlement. In his speech on the issue in the Assembly in December, Aiken said he would again vote for the resolution that was before it that year. But he regretted that it did not recognise more specifically the importance of the bilateral discussions for 'the just satisfaction of Algerian national aspirations and the establishment of lasting peace and fruitful cooperation between the two peoples'. Is it extravagant to suggest that this language may perhaps have seemed to him to echo faintly the phrasing used in the September 1921 correspondence between his own leader, Éamon de Valera, and Lloyd George, which established a basis for the negotiations that led eventually to the Anglo-Irish Treaty of 1921?[11]

Following the signature of the Evian Agreements in March, Algeria eventually emerged to independence on 5 July 1962. Ireland, as it happened, was serving a one-year term as an elected member of the Security Council that year, as I have explained in an earlier chapter. When Algeria's application for membership of the United Nations came before the Council in October, Frank Aiken took the Irish seat for the occasion and had the satisfaction of joining in co-sponsorship of the resolution that approved its application. In addressing the Council he spoke of Algeria's struggle for independence in words that seemed to evoke poignant memories of his own experiences half a century before:

no one knows what such a struggle can mean in terms of sacrifice and suffering, hardship and anguish, better than those who have had to endure the experience themselves ... National struggles such as those of Algeria, once begun, are not easily ended. To end them calls for the qualities of vision, courage and foresight which go to make statesmanship of the very highest order.

11 To 'enter a Conference to ascertain how the association of Ireland with the community of nations known as the British Empire can best be reconciled with Irish national aspirations' – see Fanning *et al.* (1998) p. 266.

He warmly praised the statesmanship and unshakeable resolve that de Gaulle had shown, but ended by drawing a lesson from Algeria's struggle for freedom:

> It reminds us that, as past history has so often shown, the spirit of nationalism, once aroused, cannot be crushed by force of arms. It may meet reversals, it may even suffer temporary exhaustion, but sooner or later it will reassert itself and no military force, however powerful, can hope in the long run to destroy it or to deny its just demands.[12]

It was the speech of an old fighter for freedom turned statesman himself.

In this book I have been dealing with Ireland at the United Nations in the 1960s. Frank Aiken was Minister for External Affairs for virtually all of that period – he left office finally in March 1969. In the two final chapters of the book I will deal with one further episode from the decade of the 1960s: in August, some months after Aiken had gone, his successor, Dr Patrick Hillery appeared before the Security Council to ask for a peacekeeping force for Northern Ireland. Before I do so I think that I ought to offer my own overall assessment of 'the Aiken years' – an era that covered almost all of the first decade and a half of Ireland's membership of the UN.

Frank Aiken was Ireland's Minister for External Affairs for twelve continuous years, and for all of my own first nine years in the Department. He led the Irish Delegation to the UN General Assembly every year from 1957 to 1968; and he sat on the Security Council on several occasions during Ireland's one-year term as a member in 1962. It was a long and honourable record.

Under his leadership, the Irish Delegation to the UN showed a considerable degree of independence in its approach – as is evident from his own and other speeches and the record of the votes it cast in the General Assembly. The independence was rather greater in

---

12   Department of External Affairs (1962) pp. 15–17.

the early years than later, though it continued to some extent into the 1960s. But it would be an exaggeration to believe that, even in the earlier period, Ireland always judged issues entirely on their merits and took absolutely no account of its own national interest or of relations with important countries such as the USA. No Government could afford to be so quixotic. This is not to say that it lacked courage when this was needed, but – particularly in the latter part of the period, when Sean Lemass took over as Taoiseach from Éamon de Valera – courage, on occasion at least, was tempered with prudence and realism.

The balance tipped a little more towards prudence on certain matters once the Irish Government under Lemass decided to apply for full membership of what was then the European Communities, the EEC, in 1961. It was by no means a foregone conclusion that Ireland would be accepted as an applicant capable of taking on the role of a full member – after all, it had been describing itself internationally as 'underdeveloped' only a short time previously. It was important therefore to maintain good relations with, and indeed to court, the six founding Member States of the EEC. The stance of the Irish delegation in New York on such issues as the Algerian struggle for independence from France, which I have just described, became a matter of concern to Lemass, who feared that the result would be to antagonise a country that was crucial to the success of Ireland's application for EEC membership.

I recall also the very considerable nervousness in Dublin, which emanated ultimately I think from Lemass himself and filtered down even into my level in the Department, about the active role that Conor Cruise O'Brien played in New York over the South Tyrol/Alto-Adige question at the 1960 General Assembly, a year before our EEC membership application.

This was an area that had been transferred from Austria to Italy after the First World War. In 1946 Austria and Italy signed an agreement that guaranteed respect for the rights of the population, two-thirds of whom were German-speaking, and provided for a measure of autonomy for the region. Over the following years, Austria became dissatisfied with Italian policies in the area and it complained that the agreement was not being fully observed. In 1960 it took the issue to the UN General Assembly but failed to find there the sympathy that it had expected. Conor was instrumental in helping it to get off the hook without too great a loss of face. This was done by way of a resolution that called for talks to achieve a 'friendly solution'.

Though this may seem innocuous enough, in context it was helpful to Austria and, for that reason, less than welcome to Italy. The Department in Dublin, as I recollect it, reflecting a measure of concern on the part of Lemass about possible offence to Italy, would have preferred Conor to hold back from too active an involvement in the issue. But, with the support of his Minister, Frank Aiken, who was with him in New York, Conor continued. As he put it in his *Memoir* many years later, 'With the full support of all who now counted in our delegation, I intervened in the debate with some confidence.' Conor obviously attached some importance to the phrase 'all who now counted in our delegation'. It included his Minister, Frank Aiken, of course, but somewhat to his surprise it also included the Ambassador, Freddie Boland.[13] He may perhaps not have been fully aware that some who counted at home, at the highest Government level, had been rather nervous.

A year later, after Conor had left for Katanga, Austria asked to have the issue put on the agenda again for the 1961 General Assembly. Aiken advised the Austrians not to do this because he doubted if they could get a result which would be any better than that they had achieved the year before. Lemass, too, did not think it wise for Ireland to take an initiative on the issue and he told Aiken so. His prudence is understandable since he knew he would need

13   O'Brien (1998) p. 197. The account that he gives there is somewhat tendentious in that he attributes Freddie Boland's lack of opposition to his activities to a wish to curry favour with newly admitted non-aligned member states in order to further his chances of election to the Presidency of the General Assembly. This is strange, as Boland, having been elected on the opening day of the session, was already President of the General Assembly at the time these events took place.

Italy's support for the application by Ireland for membership which he had submitted to the EEC two months previously. Late in that General Assembly session, however, events took a new turn. As Skelly explains, by November 1961 talks between Italy and Austria had stalled and the Italian Foreign Minister, no less, asked the Irish Delegation to help, with others, in drafting a compromise resolution. The eventual outcome was a bland resolution calling for 'further efforts between the two parties concerned to find a solution to the problem'. It was adopted unanimously by the General Assembly and it helped to remove the issue from its agenda.[14]

More generally, Skelly, from a close study of the documents of the period,[15] has shown that Lemass – like de Valera before him – followed quite closely what Ireland was doing at the UN on major issues. This is borne out by Dr Michael Kennedy in an essay on Ireland's decision to run for election to what proved to be a one-year term on the Security Council in 1962, to which I have already referred.[16] Mine was a much more limited view at the time: I can only say that it sometimes appeared to me in those years as if Ireland had, in effect, two Foreign Ministers: Lemass as Taoiseach seemed to be 'Minister for Europe' while Aiken, because of his stature within the Government as one of the major figures in the War of Independence, close to de Valera, was largely given his head in his long-standing role which might be described as 'Minister for the United Nations'. Certainly Aiken seemed to take little direct interest in European issues. While he did not speak out explicitly on the matter, I think it is fair to say that he was more than dubious about the decision to apply for EEC membership and did not wish to be associated with it.

In an earlier chapter, I said that some people tend to recall those early years of Ireland's UN membership as a kind of golden age. To

14   Skelly (1997) pp. 222–226.
15   Ibid., pp. 170–171.
16   Chapter 6 entitled '"Persuade an alternative European candidate to stand": why Ireland was elected to the United Nations Security Council in 1961', in Kennedy and McMahon (2005).

call it that would be an exaggeration. But re-reading Aiken's published speeches at the UN has brought home to me that he deserves enormous credit as a concerned Minister, of great integrity, who was often creative and sometimes quirky in his thinking. It is true that this was largely declaratory diplomacy, proclaimed more often through speeches than through direct action by the State – though the resolution in regard to the spread of nuclear weapons that he introduced and promoted led on to a most important international treaty. But Ireland's contribution to the work of the UN in the Aiken years – and indeed since – was not limited to thoughtful speeches and a positive voting record: when asked, Ireland has always been ready to supply contingents of its Defence Forces for UN peacekeeping operations. This began in Aiken's early years as Minister: as I recounted in an earlier chapter, we sent unarmed observers to Lebanon in 1958 and full peacekeeping battalions – at one time close to one-ninth of our Defence Forces – to serve with the UN in the Congo in the early 1960s. In 1964, shortly after the end of the Congo operation, Ireland undertook a new commitment to UN peacekeeping in Cyprus.[17] For a time in late August of that year it had as many as 1,033 members of its Defence Forces serving with UNFICYP, the United Nations Interim Force in Cyprus. It has regularly supplied peacekeeping contingents to many other UN operations elsewhere in the world since then.

But the speeches, too, were good – better on re-reading them today than I had remembered. Much of the credit for their quality in the early years may have been due to the drafting skills of Conor Cruise O'Brien, but the quality continued long after Conor left the Irish foreign service in 1961. In the later years some of my colleagues and I would work on drafts for 'an tAire' as we always called him, but as the years went on Aiken himself more often than not would write the first draft and offer it to us for comments – a reversal of what a civil servant would normally expect.

17   Katsumi Ishizuka, *Ireland and International Peacekeeping Operations 1960–2000*, p. 82.

All in all, it seems to me now that Frank Aiken as I and my colleagues knew him over that decade was a good and decent man of great integrity. He had time to establish a good record as Minister, and deserves to be well remembered for doing so.

A UN Peacekeeping Force
for Northern Ireland?

In August 1969 Ireland, for the first and only time, tried to raise the Northern Ireland issue formally at the United Nations. Frank Aiken had left office after serving twelve years as Minister for External Affairs. His successor, Dr Patrick Hillery, who was only months in the post, was sent to New York by the Government to ask the Security Council to authorise a UN peacekeeping force for the area.

This request to the Council by the Irish Government inevitably cast Britain and Ireland into opposing roles. Even so, the issue at the UN was handled by the representatives of both Governments in a way that made it quite unlike other disputes that come before the Council: it was conducted with courtesy and with a degree of that adversarial restraint that has often characterised Anglo-Irish relations, even at moments of high tension. Dr Hillery did not get what he had asked for, since the Council did not take up the issue formally. Nevertheless, the episode had positive consequences in some respects; and, two years later, the writer of a book about the UN Security Council concluded that the handling of the issue made it a 'model from which students of diplomatic technique can learn much'.[1]

Today, there is a cordial partnership between the British and the Irish Governments and they have worked closely together to bring the long and winding peace process in Northern Ireland to a

---

1   Andrew Boyd, *Fifteen Men on a Powder Keg: A History of the UN Security Council*, p. 329.

successful conclusion. In contrast, in the late 1960s, at the start of the Troubles in Northern Ireland, the relationship between the two Governments was a good deal more distant – and sometimes strained. Now that times have changed it is of interest to look back at this largely forgotten episode to see how and why the Irish Government decided to look for a UN peacekeeping force and how the issue was handled by both sides when it came to a head in New York.[2]

Although the Northern Ireland question had never been raised formally before that time, it had been alluded to by Irish representatives on many occasions. In one of his earliest addresses to the UN General Assembly which I mentioned in Chapter 2, Frank Aiken referred to what he called 'the great master principle of self-determination' and spoke of the hope that Ireland's entry to the UN might help to secure its application to 'Our own outstanding problem – the division of our country'.[3] During his twelve years as leader of the Irish Delegation he referred to the partition issue from time to time in speeches; other members of the delegation sometimes touched on it in debates in Committees on other issues.[4]

---

2 This chapter and Chapter 11 taken together are a somewhat shortened version of a paper I contributed to Kennedy and McMahon (2005). Re-publication here is by kind permission of the IPA. I should add, perhaps, that, although I did not consult him in advance, the account that I gave in that paper was seen both in draft and in its published form by the late Dr Hillery. He phoned me on two occasions and expressed his approval.

   As I note in the next chapter, eleven years after these events the Irish Permanent Representative at the UN at the time, the late Ambassador Cremin, wrote an interesting but cautious account of the handling of the request in New York. More recently, Professor Ronan Fanning of UCD, working from the archives and from interviews, has given a broader and more comprehensive account of the response of the British and Irish Governments to the Northern Ireland crisis over the whole of the two-year period 1968–69 ('Playing it cool: the response of the British and Irish governments to the crisis in Northern Ireland, 1968–9').

3 Department of External Affairs (1957) pp. 23–24. He clearly assumed that the entity that should have the right to self-determination would be the island taken as a whole and not simply Northern Ireland.

4 Conor Cruise O'Brien, for example, gave a lengthy analysis of 'this general question of partition' in a debate on Korea and Vietnam in the Special Political Committee on 14 October 1957. He spoke at some length about 'self-determination' in a First

But the Irish Government showed no inclination to raise the issue formally at the UN over this period – even though Aiken as Minister received letters from time to time in the mid-1960s from some Irish-American groups pressing him to do so.

As a member of the delegation in those years, I remember helping to draft replies to these letters for the Minister's signature. Those were the years of the Lemass and Lynch meetings with Terence O'Neill, the Prime Minister of Northern Ireland. It was a time of 'hands across the border' and the replies we drafted focused on this approach. In Irish Government circles there was also a memory of the unfortunate and unsuccessful 'sore thumb' policy followed at the Council of Europe where the partition issue had been raised constantly in the early 1950s. That policy had achieved little other than contributing to the boredom and irritation of other delegations. In this later period, Aiken preferred to focus on establishing a respectable record for Ireland as 'a good UN member'.

Did he have in mind that, once this had been done, Ireland might then raise the issue in some way in the UN? I may be imputing later thinking to him but I am inclined to doubt it. I think that, as a Northerner himself, who had fought for Irish independence in an earlier period, his instinct would have been that the Northern Ireland question was essentially a matter for the people of Ireland, and of Britain and Ireland, to resolve between themselves: taking it

---

4   *contd.* Committee debate on Cyprus on 11 December 1957. He told the Committee on that occasion that 'Self-determination, as applied by the United Kingdom, in our experience is an elastic doctrine. It can cover the whole of the British Isles and cause them to be so called, or it can cover the North-Eastern corner of one of the islands. What it does not cover is what one would naturally and normally expect it to cover – self-determination for the people of the island of Ireland.' The partition of Ireland was also touched on by the Permanent Representative, Freddie Boland on 21 February 1957 in a First Committee debate on Cyprus and on 26 November 1957 in a debate on West Irian. Other members of the delegation also referred to it on occasion in other Committees. In more recent times, the practice was for the Minister for Foreign Affairs in his General Debate speech at the start of each annual session to report, generally in positive terms, to the General Assembly on progress in the peace process.

to an international forum would have been a confession of failure that would achieve nothing.

If the issue of the partition of Ireland as such had been raised formally in the General Assembly in those years, it would in any event have been difficult to get support for Ireland's case. One problem would be the Agreement of 1925: after the collapse of the Boundary Commission, the then Government of the Irish Free State had in effect accepted partition in return for a financial settlement. That Agreement was signed before the Fianna Fáil party entered the Dáil; and Éamon de Valera's Government in 1932, like all later Fianna Fáil Governments, refused to accept its validity. However, if the partition issue became a matter of legal argument internationally, or if it were ever submitted to the International Court of Justice in The Hague, then the issue would be judged on legal and not on political grounds. In that case the existence of that Agreement would be a serious obstacle from the viewpoint of the Irish Government.

It might seem, of course, that playing it as a colonial issue at the UN would prove a trump card. But, equally, that argument, if not carefully handled, could go wrong: many newly independent countries, which themselves had had to live with the division of whole peoples separated by the illogically drawn borders of the colonial era, would be wary of the idea of changing borders now, especially after an interval of fifty years. In any case, most Member States would see it as essentially a dispute about the territory of Northern Ireland: should it remain part of the United Kingdom or become part of a new united Ireland? In such cases, there is a strong tendency to look to the wishes of a majority of the population in the territory in question – an approach that, in the case of Northern Ireland, would serve to confirm and consolidate the Unionist position.

Another possibility might have been to raise the question solely as an issue relating to the human rights – or more specifically the civil and political rights – of the minority in Northern Ireland. This would certainly have drawn attention to the problem. But in Ireland we were too prone in the past to believe that if wrongs could only be brought to world attention, they would be righted. Sadly, this is far from being the case. It certainly was not so in the late 1950s and early 1960s. It seems to me questionable whether 'internationalising' the issue in this kind of adversarial way – and probably having to return to it regularly at each annual session – would have achieved much more in practice than the futile 'anti-partition' campaign of the early 1950s at the Council of Europe. It would also have meant relying on general provisions in various Articles of the Charter. In those years, negotiation of what is today quite a dense network of UN Conventions on human rights issues, with provisions for peer review by other Member States, was only just beginning. And, as I explained in Chapter 8, some important Western countries took the rule in the Charter against intervention by the UN in a State's internal affairs so seriously that they had even been dubious for a long time about voting for resolutions that called for action against apartheid in South Africa.

In early 1958, however, Conor Cruise O'Brien, who was then responsible for the UN Section in the Department in Dublin, and the Permanent Representative, Freddie Boland, responding from New York, did exchange memoranda about the possibility of asking to have the issue of Irish unity placed on the agenda of the General Assembly. Interestingly, in view of his later position, it was O'Brien who promoted the idea while Boland opposed it strongly. O'Brien even went so far as to draft a possible resolution.

The preamble to the resolution he envisaged would have the Assembly

[recognise] that the principle of self-determination is applicable to the people of Ireland; [note] that the island of Ireland is a historical as well as a geographical unit; [note] also that the present division of Ireland is contrary to the wishes of the great majority of the inhabitants.

In a single operative paragraph the proposed resolution would then call

> on all those concerned, including the Governments of Great Britain, of Ireland, and of Northern Ireland, to discuss the problem, with a view to making progress towards a peaceful, just and democratic solution.[5]

The practice in the General Assembly is to assign various items on its agenda, according to subject matter, for debate in one or other of seven specialised Committees on which all Member States are represented. When a resolution, after detailed debate, has been adopted by a Committee, it is referred onwards to a Plenary meeting of the General Assembly for final approval. O'Brien's view was that if Ireland placed the issue on the Assembly agenda, it would be referred for debate to the Special Political Committee. He believed that it would be possible to get that Committee to adopt the kind of resolution he envisaged but that it would not be possible to get it through a Plenary session of the Assembly. So he proposed a somewhat convoluted procedural approach. Once the Committee had adopted the resolution, Ireland would approach Canada and India informally and ask them to propose a compromise resolution that would delete the preambular paragraphs about self-determination from the Irish draft resolution. This would leave only the operative paragraph calling on the three Governments to enter into discussions about 'a peaceful, just and democratic solution'. The General Assembly would then approve this text.

This, he felt, would bring 'the problem of Partition' to the forefront of world attention; possibly bring movement; and, in any case, give new heart to the minority in Northern Ireland. But it would be necessary also, he thought, to tell the United Nations that there was no question of coercing the Northern Ireland majority. To meet this point, the resolution would need to avoid calling for an

---

5   Taken from a copy of the text in the possession of the author.

all-Ireland plebiscite; it would have to be clear that no solution would be imposed on a recalcitrant local majority; and there would be a new emphasis on economic cooperation between North and South. In this way, so he argued, it would be possible to combine a 'cooperative' with a 'United Nations' approach to the Northern Ireland issue.

Boland, responding a month later, took a diametrically opposite view: he argued that it would simply not be possible to combine the two approaches; and in any case, a positive case for raising the issue, as O'Brien had proposed, had simply not been made. There was no certainty that a resolution would even get through the Special Political Committee. Even if Ireland did eventually get a resolution advocating talks through the Assembly, it would have to report back to the UN a year later that the talks had got nowhere. It would then be fated to continue pursuing the issue, vainly, year after year. In any case, the Unionist majority in Northern Ireland would see the initiative as a new form of coercion by the South; and in any debate, the British Delegation would rest their case on the 1925 Agreement and offer, if necessary, to submit the issue to the International Court of Justice in The Hague where it would be decided on legal and not political grounds. This was something the Irish Government could not accept.

This exchange of memoranda across the Atlantic between two heavyweights in the Irish Foreign Service was, to my knowledge, the only serious consideration given at any level to putting the issue of Northern Ireland formally on the agenda of the UN over the fourteen-year period between our admission to UN membership and 1969. I have sometimes wondered if it is just possible that Conor made the proposal simply in order to have Boland shoot it down – what a billiards player might call a cannon, which would glance off Boland but really be aimed at Aiken. On balance I very much doubt this. In any case, his proposal to raise the issue formally was never pursued. It is hard to believe that it would have been successful if it had been.

By the summer of 1969, however, the whole situation had changed. Leaders of the Nationalist minority in Northern Ireland were agitating vigorously for civil rights; reforms envisaged by the Northern Prime Minister, Terence O'Neill, were slow in coming and opposed by many Unionists; and there had been sporadic violence against civil rights marchers and others of the minority. In August 1969 the situation became extremely serious. The Apprentice Boys parade in Derry on 12 August led to violent disturbances; the trouble spread; and Nationalist areas in Derry and Belfast came under attack. Policing by the RUC was inadequate at best; at worst, it appeared that some of the police in Derry and in Belfast had themselves been among the attackers. The British Government decided to deploy troops on the streets in both cities to protect Nationalists, and refugees from Belfast were crossing the Border to seek safety in the South. Emotions were high in the South as well as in the North; in Dublin, as we now know, the Taoiseach, Jack Lynch, faced serious divisions within his own Government about what was to be done.[6]

Already, before the parade, the Irish Government was apprehensive about what might happen.[7] Dr Hillery, who had been appointed Minister for External Affairs only two months before,

---

6   Ronan Fanning, who interviewed Dr Hillery on 20 June 2001, gives a graphic account of the atmosphere in the Irish Cabinet (Fanning, 2001, pp. 73–74): 'When Hillery got back to Dublin Lynch warned him that his Cabinet colleagues were "very excited"': Lynch 'was particularly surprised at Lenihan'. Hillery likened one of the subsequent emergency Cabinet meetings to 'a ballad session … They were all talking patriotic … I remember being sure our Army was not as well armed as the B Specials, not to talk of the British army.'

7   In the account that follows I draw directly on documents in my possession which are also available in the National Archives of Ireland as I have indicated in relevant footnotes. While Professor Ronan Fanning's theme in his paper 'Playing it cool: the response of the British and Irish Governments to the crisis in Northern Ireland, 1968–9' is the broader one of the response of the respective Governments to the emerging crisis over the whole of that two-year period, his paper also includes a good and carefully documented account of the events of August 1969, including the Hillery–Chalfont meetings, which I describe here. He was also able to interview two people who were prominent then and later and who are now deceased – the Minister, Dr Patrick Hillery and a senior official, Mr Eamon Gallagher.

travelled to London on 1 August.[8] There he had a meeting at the Foreign Office, kept private at the time, with the Foreign Secretary in the Labour Government, Michael Stewart. Hillery warned the Foreign Secretary that the Apprentice Boys parade of 12 August had been 'deliberately stepped up': there would be some seventy bands as against seventeen in previous years. Derry, he said, had become 'a powder keg' and something might start there that it would be very difficult to contain.[9] He would prefer to see the parade banned, but if this was not possible, the sponsors should at least be required to limit it to the normal size and keep it to a particular area; the B Specials should not be allowed a role in policing it; and the British Government should send observers.

The Foreign Secretary, to say the least, was not very receptive. It was better to control the parade than to ban it, he said – this was an approach that had proved correct recently in Bermuda. Although the British Government kept in close touch with the situation, responsibility for the area lay with the Northern Ireland Government. There were now some hopeful signs that that Government was taking steps towards reform. In any case, he had to say that 'there is a limit to the extent to which we can discuss with outsiders – even our nearest neighbours – this internal matter.'

Although Dr Hillery was clearly dissatisfied with this response, he had to conclude that there was no possibility of taking the matter further with the British side at that point. He concluded the discussion with a warning of the danger of 'a spill over into violence': if this happened he would come under increasing pressure to act. His predecessor (Frank Aiken), he said, had gone to the UN during a previous outbreak of trouble in Derry although he did not raise

8 At this point his title in English was still 'Minister for External Affairs', which had been the usage in countries of the Commonwealth. Dr Hillery himself was later responsible for the change in the title of the post to 'Minister for Foreign Affairs', although, interestingly, the title in Irish – 'Aire Gnóthai Eachtracha' – has remained unchanged.

9 National Archives of Ireland DFA 2000/6/557, 'Notes of a discussion at the Foreign Office, Friday 1 August 1969'.

the problem formally before any UN body. However, if violence should occur in Derry and spill over into the South, then he, as Minister, would have to deal with the situation and 'it might have to be raised.'

In speaking of Aiken having gone previously 'to the UN', Dr Hillery was referring to an episode in late April 1969. At that point, the Irish Government was already concerned about growing trouble in Derry, following the Burntollet and other civil rights marches, and it had sent Aiken, as Minister for External Affairs, to brief the Secretary General, U Thant, on the situation. In the event this was to be his last visit to New York as Minister, as he left office shortly afterwards.

In view of what happened later, it is interesting to look back at the press conference that Aiken gave in New York on 23 April 1969 after his meeting with the Secretary General. He first laid out for journalists, at some length, what was then the standard Irish account of partition, with quotations from Asquith and Churchill about its impermanence. He recalled that 'not even one Irish member [of Parliament] voted for the Partition of Ireland – for the 1920 Act.' He expressed his hope for 'the restoration of Irish unity' by peaceful means and for a continuation of 'the evolution that has gone on amongst the Unionists in the North … [so that] we can have a settlement in the mutual interests of all the people of all parts of Ireland'. Having laid out this standard background, however, he made it clear that his focus was not on ending partition but on civil rights and on the need for reform in Northern Ireland. When asked whether he might bring the issue at some stage to one of the UN bodies that dealt with the remnants of colonialism, he responded that 'the best way … is to settle this between ourselves'; when pressed about bringing it to one of the UN Human Rights bodies, he stressed that the only purpose of his visit was to keep the Secretary General – 'the principal officer of the international organisation for peace' – informed.

Perhaps his most interesting response, in the light of later events, was his answer to a journalist who asked whether he had discussed with the Secretary General 'the possible use at any time of a UN Peacekeeping Force to maintain the peace in Northern Ireland'. Aiken replied, 'I didn't. The Government have taken no decision to ask for a Peacekeeping Force and I think there is sufficient wisdom if it can only be energised in our section of the world, in these islands off the North West of Europe, to settle this problem.'[10]

By August 1969, however, Aiken, a wise head on Northern Ireland matters, was out of office; and in a deteriorating situation the view of the Irish Government on this point had changed, as Dr Hillery had warned Michael Stewart obliquely on 1 August that it might.

On Tuesday, 13 August 1969, the day after the Apprentice Boys parade, there was an emergency meeting of the Irish Government. That afternoon, while the Government was still meeting, it sent word to the Secretary of the Department of External Affairs[11] to issue an instruction to the Irish Ambassador in London: he was 'to convey immediately to the British Government the request that they arrange for the immediate cessation of the police attacks on the people of Derry'.[12] The Ambassador was on leave so, in his absence, the Chargé d'Affaires, Kevin Rush, acting on the instruction, sought an appointment with the Foreign Secretary. He too was on leave, so Rush met late that afternoon with Lord Chalfont, Minister of State, who was handling business at the Foreign Office during the holiday month of August.

It is interesting to note the speed with which this meeting was arranged. It may indicate that the British Government, in a change from the Foreign Secretary's complacency of 1 August, was by now seriously concerned. Rush received the instruction from Dublin at 3.30 pm: an hour and a half later he was received by Chalfont in his room at the Foreign Office.

---

10 Quotations are taken from a verbatim transcript of Aiken's press conference in New York on 23 April 1969, published by the Department of External Affairs (of Ireland) as 1/69 in the series 'Statements and Speeches'.

11 Hugh McCann.

12 NAI 2000/9/2 G.C. 13/11, 13 Aug. 1969.

Rush brought with him an *aide-mémoire* setting out the text of the message he had been asked to convey. However, while he was in an ante-room at the Foreign Office waiting to be taken in to Chalfont, he received another telephone call from the Department in Dublin. This was presumably the result of a further decision of the Cabinet. Rush was now

> to also request the British Government to apply immediately to the United Nations for the urgent dispatch of a peace-keeping force to the Six Counties of Northern Ireland and [to say that] the Government has instructed the Irish Permanent Representative to the United Nations to inform the Secretary General of the foregoing[13]

Immediately thereafter he was taken in to see Chalfont. He handed over the *aide-mémoire* that he had prepared on the basis of the earlier instruction and supplemented it orally by reading out the text of the later message that he had just received by telephone in the waiting room. The Foreign Office official acting as note-taker duly noted this text.

Chalfont was courteous enough in his response but he main-tained the standard position of the British Government at the time: he would note all that had been said and convey it to the Home Office, which was the responsible Department; personally, he could not for a single moment accept that the police were attacking the people of Derry; and as to the United Nations, the issue was 'an internal affair of the United Kingdom, it was not a matter which it would be appropriate to raise at the United Nations'. When showing Rush out, the Foreign Office note-taker confirmed with him his own impression of what Rush had said: the Irish Government was requesting the British Government to take up the matter of a peacekeeping force with the United Nations – the Irish Government was not proposing to do this itself.

---

13   Ibid.

On the following day, Wednesday, 13 August 1969, two days after the Apprentice Boys parade, the Taoiseach, Jack Lynch, in a television statement expressed his 'deep sadness' at the tragic events in Derry and elsewhere. He noted that the Irish Government had 'acted with great restraint for several months': it had made its views known to the British Government on a number of occasions but had been 'careful to do nothing that would exacerbate the situation'. It was clear now 'that the present situation cannot be allowed to continue … [and] clear, also, that the Irish Government can no longer stand by and see innocent people injured and perhaps worse'.[14] Lynch went on:

> It is obvious that the RUC is no longer accepted as an impartial police force. Neither would the employment of British troops be acceptable nor would they be likely to restore peaceful conditions – certainly not in the long term. The Irish Government have, therefore, requested the British Government to apply immediately to the United Nations for the urgent dispatch of a Peace-keeping Force to the Six Counties of Northern Ireland and have instructed the Irish Permanent Representative to the United Nations to inform the Secretary-General of this request.

Lynch announced that the Government was sending Army field hospitals to the border to cater for those of the injured who did not

---

14 NAI 2000/5/12. The popular memory has it that Lynch said that the Irish Government could no longer stand *idly* by (emphasis added), but the word 'idly' does not appear in the copy I have of the text released to the press at the time or in the collected volume of Lynch's statements and speeches at this time (Government Information Bureau, *Speeches and Statements on Irish Unity, Northern Ireland, Anglo-Irish Relations August 1969–October 1971*, p. 2). From television footage of the time which is still available today it is quite clear that Lynch did not use the word 'idly'. However, Professor Ronan Fanning, in his paper on the response of the British and Irish Governments to the crisis (2001, p. 73), notes that a draft prepared by the Department of Foreign Affairs for possible use by the Taoiseach did include the word 'idly'.

wish to be treated in Six County hospitals; and he went on to raise the possibility of talks about reunification:

> Recognising, however, that the re-unification of the national territory can provide the only permanent solution for the problem, it is our intention to request the British Government to enter into early negotiations with the Irish Government to review the present constitutional position of the Six Counties of Northern Ireland.

The next day, 15 August, Dr Hillery, who had been recalled urgently from a holiday in the West of Ireland, travelled to London to meet his British equivalent.[15] After some delay he was received eventually at the Foreign Office by Lord Chalfont, Minister of State at the Foreign Office and Lord Stonham, his counterpart at the Home Office. This was the holiday period and the Foreign Secretary, Michael Stewart, was still away. Chalfont was reluctant and far from gracious about the meeting. He began by saying that he considered it 'useful' to have discussions on these matters. But he qualified this with what seemed like a slight reproof: 'I am personally sorry that it was not possible to have a prior agreement regarding your visit.' He maintained the official position that 'anything happening there [i.e. in Northern Ireland] is an internal matter to be dealt with by the Home Department [i.e. the Home Office]'.[16]

Dr Hillery recalled that he had told the Foreign Secretary on 1 August that the Irish Government was seriously perturbed about what might happen if the Apprentice Boys parade went ahead in Derry on 12 August. 'On that occasion I accepted that the control of the situation was at present in your hands but not that it is solely your affair.' Now, he went on, 'There is trouble for all of us – serious, grave trouble.' He told Chalfont and Stonham that

---

15   Professor Ronan Fanning, who interviewed Dr Hillery in 2001 for his paper 'Playing it cool', mentions that the Minister was on a painting holiday in Achill (p. 72).

16   NAI 2000/6/558, confidential report of discussion at the Foreign Office, London, 15 August 1969.

this situation is not one that can be handled by a partisan peace-keeping force. So perhaps your troops and ours could be combined together to form a peace-keeping force acceptable to both sides or alternatively, there could be a UN force.

Chalfont accepted that there was concern on the part of the Irish Government and he understood why they were anxious to discuss the matter. But the maintenance of law and order in the UK was

primarily our [i.e. Britain's] concern. This responsibility is exercised in concert with the Government of Northern Ireland ... As regards the need for a UN or international intervention, we consider it is simply not necessary. It is well within our capacity to deal with the situation not only for juridical reasons, but because we are confident we can deal with it in an impartial way. The presence of any international or joint force in the area would be totally irrelevant and here I might add that our view is shared by the Secretary-General of the United Nations.

Later Chalfont, apparently responding to what the Taoiseach had said on television on the evening of 13 August, said

I find it irrational although perhaps psychologically predictable, to say that the presence of troops is intolerable to anybody. How can the presence of troops in towns of the United Kingdom be intolerable to anyone except the people in those towns? It isn't anyone else's business.

Hillery asked to talk to the Prime Minister, Harold Wilson, but he was on holidays in the Scilly Isles. Chalfont said he would report to him, and to the Home Secretary, what Hillery had said, but he could not hold out any hope of talks with the Prime Minister.

   It is interesting that Chalfont could say to Hillery that the UN Secretary General, U Thant, shared the view of the British

Government on the question of an international force. So far as I know, there is no evidence that the Irish side were aware that U Thant had been consulted on such a proposal at this stage. However, the UK, like the other four Permanent Members of the Security Council, enjoys something of a special status at the UN: one might surmise that Chalfont had received a report from the British representative, who may perhaps have sounded out U Thant privately after Lynch's statement of 13 August.

Did the Irish Government at this point really expect that the British Government would agree either to set up a joint peace-keeping operation with the Irish side or to request the UN to send a peacekeeping force? In retrospect it seems unlikely. But in any event, the proposal had now been put and rejected. The Irish Government was under severe pressure at home and, as we now know, it was internally divided between 'hardliners' and those who favoured a more 'level-headed' approach to the Northern crisis. So on his return to Dublin, the Government decided that the Minister for Foreign Affairs, Dr Hillery, should go at once to New York to ask the Security Council for such a force. He left for New York on the afternoon of Saturday, 16 August 1969.

The Government had met earlier that same day – a Saturday meeting was a most unusual event – and it had considered a 'Memorandum for the Information of the Government' prepared by the Department of External Affairs under the heading 'Bringing the Situation in the North of Ireland before the UN'.[17] This document considered various options for both the approach that might be taken and the UN body in which it could be raised.

As to how to approach the question, it said that there were three possibilities: it could be raised as a threat to the peace; as an issue of self-determination; or as a human rights question. As to where to raise it, the Memorandum, in what seems like an excessive attempt to be exhaustive, suggested that that could be done in any one of five main organs of the UN – not only in the Security Council or the

---

17   NAI 2000/6/558.

Assembly but also in the Economic and Social Council, or with the Secretary General or at the International Court of Justice. Of these, it suggested, the most relevant seemed to be the Security Council, which would make it necessary to imply in some way that there was a 'threat to the peace'; or, alternatively, the General Assembly, where the main emphasis would probably have to be on 'human rights'. The Memorandum then gave an estimate – presumably on the basis of a report from Cremin in New York – of what the reaction in the Security Council would be if an effort were made to raise the issue there: the 'maximum affirmative vote' in the Council in favour of placing the issue on the agenda would be eight, whereas nine positive votes would be needed. In view of later events, it is interesting that it advised the Government that

> Ireland would have no right to participate in the discussion about the placing of such an item on the Security Council Agenda and only if it were to be admitted to debate would we be invited to participate, without vote, in the subsequent discussion.

For this reason, the Memorandum concluded, raising the issue in the General Assembly 'seems to be the most profitable course'. However, this did not preclude raising it (later?) in the Security Council 'although such action has practically no prospect of success, if for no other reason because of the British attitude and the fact that Britain has a veto'.

It is clear from this that there was some awareness in Dublin of the difficulties, at least among External Affairs officials with a good knowledge of the UN. I can vouch personally for the fact that this was the case.

At the time I was home on leave from the Embassy in Washington where I was First Secretary, and, while I was not as centrally involved as my colleagues based in Dublin, I too was drawn in to a certain extent to help out for a few days. So far as I recall it now, my own personal view, for what it was worth, would have been close enough to that in the memorandum – that an attempt to take the issue to the Security Council had little prospect of success.[18] After all, Con Cremin, a meticulous Ambassador with many good contacts, had done a head-count in New York and he had reported that the *maximum* affirmative vote (emphasis added) would fall short by one of the number required to put the issue on the agenda.

But, granted the attitude of the Government and the widely felt emotions of the time, some way of responding to the Government's wish to 'take it to the UN' had to be found, whatever doubts may have existed among officials with some knowledge of the UN. So the memorandum tried to steer the Government towards the General Assembly, where it should at least be possible to ensure that it would be debated. The Government, however, wanted something more than this. So within hours, Dr Hillery, a new Minister with no experience of the UN who had taken over from Frank Aiken only two months earlier, was on his way to New York to raise – or seek to raise – the issue with the UN Security Council.

---

18 However, in thinking this I may have been focused mainly on the fact that the UK, as a Permanent Member of the Council, had the right of veto. I am not sure that I took fully into account the point that, as I explain at the beginning of the next chapter, if the issue were to be raised under Chapter 6 of the Charter ('Pacific Settlement of Disputes') rather than under Chapter 7 ('Action with Respect to Threats to the Peace, Breaches of the Peace and Acts of Aggression') the veto would not apply.

A Well-Managed Scenario

On the face of it, it should have been obvious that Dr Hillery's mission to seek a peacekeeping force for Northern Ireland was a difficult one that was unlikely to be successful without the support, or at least the acquiescence, of the government of the United Kingdom. The UK was, after all, a Permanent Member of the Council with the right of veto. It is true that the request for a peacekeeping force would be submitted under Chapter 6 of the Charter, which deals with 'Pacific Settlement of Disputes', rather than under Chapter 7, which deals with 'Threats to the Peace'. The distinction is important: when the Council takes a decision under Chapter 6, 'a party to a dispute shall abstain from voting'; in a vote under Chapter 7, on the other hand, the veto right applies, so the UK would be able to block a decision.

The first question, however, was whether the Council would even agree to consider the question. The UK would certainly argue strongly that Northern Ireland was a purely internal matter; and it would point to Article 2.7 of the Charter, which states clearly that the UN is not authorised 'to intervene in matters which are essentially within the domestic jurisdiction of any state'. Indeed, in arguing that it was an internal matter, the UK might conceivably call the UN Charter itself in evidence: the Charter explicitly names 'The United Kingdom of Great Britain *and Northern Ireland*' (emphasis added) as one of the five Permanent Members of the Security Council. At that stage, UK Governments took a rigidly legal approach to the constitutional position of Northern Ireland within the United Kingdom: they had not yet come to accept, as they did from 1973 onwards, that, whatever the formal legal position, the Irish Government must have a substantial role to play in any settlement of the Northern Ireland Troubles.

Even if the Council did agree to debate the issue, a further question would follow from the argument that Northern Ireland was an internal matter for the UK. The principle that a UN peacekeeping force could operate only with consent was clearly established by then: in 1967, U Thant had felt obliged to withdraw UNEF I, the UN force in Sinai, when Egypt withdrew the consent it had initially given for its presence. How then could the Council agree to send a peacekeeping force to Northern Ireland if Britain objected to its going there?

Even if those considerable difficulties could be overcome, further questions would arise. Would the UN be willing to involve itself in an internal policing role of indefinite duration in a developed country of Western Europe? UN peacekeeping at the time was still, in some ways, on a very uncertain footing, especially as regards financing. When the Security Council agreed five years previously to send a UN peacekeeping force to Cyprus, for example, France and the Soviet Union had both abstained on the key paragraph of the resolution setting up the force – even though the force would have the consent of Cyprus itself, as well as of Greece, Turkey and the UK.[1] It was true that the UN force in the Sinai, interposed between the organised forces of Israel and Egypt with their consent, had been successful enough before its withdrawal in 1967. But the Congo experience of the early 1960s, on the other hand, had shown how difficult – and even dangerous – it was for the UN to be drawn into dealing with a chaotic situation within a State. There were other questions too: who would take part in such a force? How would it

---

1   See United Nations Yearbook (1995) p. 76. The resolution as a whole was adopted unanimously by the Council but the USSR, France and Czechoslovakia abstained on operative paragraph 4.

be received in a divided society where the majority community would probably oppose its very presence? How long would it remain? And, even if welcomed initially, would it soon become part of the problem itself, subject to attack from both sides, as indeed happened later with the British Army?

Looking back now, more than a generation later, we might ask a further question about this episode: was its basic aim to obtain, or merely to be seen to ask for, a UN peacekeeping force? No doubt the Irish Government at the time believed in a broad and general way that a UN peacekeeping force could help. But to those who knew the UN, the odds were against getting such a force. As I noted in the previous chapter, the Memorandum for the Government from External Affairs of 16 August, basing itself on Cremin's reporting from New York, had concluded, bluntly enough, that 'such action has practically no prospect of success'. Undoubtedly, the 'hardliners' in Government, with little knowledge of the UN, would have discounted this assessment by what they would think of as the faint-hearted officials of External Affairs. But we can see now that yielding to the hardliners to the extent of being seen to 'take the issue to the UN' served a useful purpose in itself in helping Jack Lynch to ride the turbulence in the Cabinet and, more generally, to defuse tension in the South. It also, to a degree, added to the pressure on London to bring needed reform to Northern Ireland. A cynic might perhaps also think that it was intended to provide a basis from which the Irish Government could say 'I told you so' later, if it felt a need to criticise the role or the actions of the British Army in Northern Ireland.

In retirement, eleven years on, the late Con Cremin, who had succeeded Freddie Boland as Ireland's Permanent Representative (that is, Ambassador) to the United Nations in New York, published an account of this whole episode.[2] It is accurate and correct, as anyone who knew Con Cremin would expect. But it is also carefully written and circumspect: those of us who knew him would expect

---

2   Cremin (1980) pp. 67–73.

no less. It does not quite convey the enormity of the task that faced Dr Hillery, and the degree of improvisation that necessarily followed the sudden decision to send him to New York to appear before the Security Council; and it is cautious too about referring to some of what the Irish representatives learned at the time about the likely attitude of countries represented on the Council.

In his published paper, Cremin recounts how he, as Irish Permanent Representative, wrote on Sunday 17 August 1969 to the Spanish Ambassador who was President of the Council for that month to ask for an urgent meeting. This was Jaime de Pinies: a strong and colourful character who was reputed to have served, at different times, on both sides in the Spanish Civil War. He spent most of his career as Spain's UN representative and at one point was elected to serve for a year as President of the General Assembly. At this time, he represented Franco's Spain. I came to know him well later as a colleague on the Security Council, to which Spain was again elected, along with Ireland, in 1981–82, and we often consulted together on the work of the Council. At that stage, he spoke, with equal conviction, for a new democratic Spanish Government. He told me many times of the large part that he personally had played in securing a hearing for Dr Hillery. No doubt he was moved to do so because he felt that there is an affinity between Spain and Ireland. In any case, Spain had its own long-standing dispute with Britain about Gibraltar and he may have seen some points of similarity between the two issues.

The Presidency of the Security Council rotates alphabetically, on a monthly basis, among the fifteen Member States on the Council. While the representative holding the Presidency cannot impose his or her views on other Member States, a good President will consult widely with colleagues and seek to promote agreement. De Pinies, in his capacity as President at this time, took an active approach to his role.

Ambassador Cremin's memoir, published eleven years later, mentions that Dr Hillery had conversations with each member of the Security Council and that he kept in very close touch with the President (de Pinies) and the Secretary General, but does not go into detail on any of these exchanges. In fact Dr Hillery and he met informally with de Pinies at his residence that Sunday morning before Cremin sent his formal letter requesting a meeting of the Council.[3] De Pinies was helpful to his Irish visitors. He advised them on the terms of the letter that Cremin was later to send to him in his capacity as President of the Council for that month: it should stress the 'urgency' of the situation and also the possibility that events in Northern Ireland would lead to 'international friction'. This echo of a phrase in Chapter 6 (Article 34) of the Charter, which deals with the 'Pacific Settlement of International Disputes', would, he said, help to bring the question more clearly within the remit of the Council.

Cremin's letter, carefully drafted to take account of these suggestions, was duly sent to de Pinies early that Sunday evening. De Pinies lost no time in consulting, as he was required to do, with other Member States about the Irish request to hold a meeting of the Council. He was able to tell Cremin shortly after ten that Sunday evening that he had spoken to all but one of the fifteen repre-sentatives.[4] There seemed to be general agreement that a meeting should be called, but this of course was only a first step – it did not mean that the Council would necessarily agree to discuss the issue. De Pinies' own thinking at this stage, which he may have discussed with his French colleague, seems to have been that the issue would be placed on the agenda of the Council and, after both sides had been heard, he would propose that the members of the Council would wish to reflect on what had been said. Speaking as President, he would then express the Council's concern about the situation and its hope that all concerned would refrain from anything that might

---

3   In the account that follows I draw on a memorandum by Ambassador Cremin dated 16 October 1969, a copy of which is in my possession.

4   He could not reach the Ambassador of Paraguay but seems to have spoken to his Deputy.

aggravate it. He would then adjourn the meeting and leave the date of any future meeting to be determined in consultations.

I think we may conclude from this that de Pinies probably realised already from his consultations that Sunday evening that it was very doubtful if the Council would ever agree to send a peace-keeping force to Northern Ireland. The procedure he had in mind, however, would seize the Council of the issue, formally at least, and allow it to express concern in a very general way, while saving face and honour all around.

On that same Sunday evening, 17 August, Lord Caradon – the British Permanent Representative, who had been away – telephoned Cremin at his residence and remonstrated with him, gently enough, for not telling him, Caradon, in advance that Ireland was going to raise the Northern Ireland issue in the Security Council. Cremin replied that he had assumed that after Hillery's meeting with Chalfont on 15 August he, Caradon, would have been fully briefed by London. Caradon then suggested that he meet Dr Hillery. They met at noon on the following day, Monday, in an area between two of the delegates' lounges in the UN building.

Caradon – a large, agreeably benevolent man – was at the time a major figure at the UN, where he had represented the United Kingdom since 1964. He had an apartment on a lower floor in the same building as Cremin, his Irish colleague. As Sir Hugh Foot, he had been the last British Governor of Cyprus and he now had the rank of Minister of State in Harold Wilson's Labour Government. He was a brother of Michael Foot, later leader of the Labour Party and one of three Foot brothers, known affectionately as 'the three left Feet'. As I remember it, he had a disarming way of responding to criticism of Britain's colonial record by boasting that it had given 600 million people their independence in his lifetime. As I heard him repeat this many times in UN debates I sometimes wondered if he ever thought of the corollary – if it was Britain that granted them independence, then it must have been Britain that deprived them of that independence in the first place. He was popular at the

UN, however, and I do not recall that anyone ever picked him up on the point.

The atmosphere at the meeting, as noted later by Cremin, was 'rather cold'. Caradon did most of the talking. He spoke of the danger of initiating action without knowing precisely where it might end up. He held firmly to the British position that the issue could not appropriately be discussed by the Security Council: Article 2.7 of the Charter precluded UN intervention in internal affairs, and Northern Ireland was an integral part of the United Kingdom. Thus far, it seems, he was making his formal position clear. But he then went on to say that the Irish letter had been sent so the question now was how to resolve the matter with least detriment. The letter would of course have received worldwide publicity and this, he thought, would meet one of the Irish side's possible objectives: it could remain on file and be followed later by other explanatory documents. What he was implying was that, once Ireland had gained some publicity for its initiative in raising the issue, it should decide not to pursue its request to the Council further. He must have known that that would hardly be sufficient.

He then went on to float a second idea, which evoked no immediate reaction from the Irish side. In retrospect, however, we can see it now as highly significant in that it foreshadowed the way in which the issue was actually dealt with later in the Council. An alternative to his earlier suggestion, Caradon said, could be that, since the Minister had come to New York and since it was impossible to have the item placed on the agenda of the Council, the Minister might still be given an opportunity of making a statement. This might meet many of the considerations that lay behind the Irish request to the Council. Dr Hillery listened quietly but did not respond on this point.

On that Monday evening, 18 August, in the course of a reception, there was another significant exchange. Ambassador Max Jakobson, the representative of Finland, which had a seat at the time on the Council, phoned Cremin during the reception and told him that he had been thinking about a possible procedural approach that the Council might take and he had found wide acceptance for his idea. Jakobson was a distinguished UN figure who was a candidate for the post of Secretary General in 1971, two years later. He might well have been elected – and he would have been a good choice – but it was said that the Soviet Union would not find him acceptable because it believed that his Jewish background would make him unsuitable to deal with the problems of the Middle East. During his phone call, Jakobson outlined to Cremin an approach that, in fact, he went on to propose in the Council two days later. His proposal was that, in a departure from normal procedure, Dr Hillery should be allowed to address the Council at the initial procedural stage when it was considering whether or not to accept the issue on to its agenda.

A short time later, de Pinies, who was also at the reception, met quietly in a corner with Hillery and Cremin and told them that as a result of his consultations with other Council members, he had concluded that it was now improbable that Ireland would gain the nine votes necessary to place the issue on the agenda of the Security Council. In these circumstances, the best formula to follow would be that outlined already by Jakobson on the phone to Cremin. Significantly, de Pinies thought that the idea for such an approach had originated with the UK. If true, this would mean, in effect, that it had been suggested to Finland by Caradon. The fact that Caradon had outlined an idea very close to this to Dr Hillery earlier that same day makes it plausible to think that this was indeed what happened.

On the following day, Tuesday, 19 August, Jakobson phoned Cremin again and said that he doubted if the Irish request would receive enough votes to be placed formally on the agenda. He again outlined to Cremin the procedural approach that he had in mind. He said that he had now polled all members of the Council and had found that such an approach would have general support – although Britain did not like it and wanted to have the Irish request rejected. He asked Cremin to let him know during that afternoon whether or not Ireland would find it acceptable. Cremin later noted that he and the Minister, Dr Hillery, 'were quite satisfied by then that we did not have the requisite number of votes'. So he phoned Jakobson about 3.00 pm to say that the Irish side would not object.

At lunchtime that day, de Pinies had confirmed to the Irish side his own earlier estimate of the position. He told them that his private head-count had shown only seven votes in favour of the Irish request to place the issue on the agenda, two short of the necessary nine. Pakistan, Spain, China, Paraguay and Colombia would probably vote in favour; the Soviet Union and Hungary were reticent but he thought that they too would do so; he was doubtful about Senegal and Zambia; and he thought that the third African member of the Council, Algeria, would not vote in favour. Jakobson later suggested to Cremin that the position of the African members on this kind of issue would be influenced by their concern about the effort at secession by Biafra, which had led to the civil war then raging in Nigeria.[5]

Cremin also learned from Ambassador Yost of the US that he had received instructions to abstain – because, in the American view, the issue was one of domestic jurisdiction, it was not a threat to international peace, and Britain was taking measures to improve the situation. Cremin's French colleague, Berard, was helpful enough in private, advising that the key thing for Ireland was not to suffer a defeat. But at a meeting with the Irish side on Monday, 18 August, Berard also drew attention to the strong position that France had traditionally taken in regard to the bar in Article 2.7 of the Charter on intervention by the UN 'in matters which are essentially within the domestic jurisdiction of any state'. In retrospect one can surmise that, because of its attitude to that Article, it is most unlikely that France would have gone so far as to vote in favour of the Irish request to put the issue on the agenda. Finland too, if it came to it, would abstain: Jakobson in his phone call had told Cremin this. The

---

5   That is to say that they might be wary of any talk of Irish unity since, in their eyes, it would seem to involve 'secession' by Northern Ireland from the UK.

UK of course would oppose. As to the fifteenth member of the Council, Nepal, Cremin had kept in touch with its representative, General Khatri, but de Pinies' view was that he was very erratic.

Later in the afternoon of Tuesday, 19 August, de Pinies confirmed that the meeting of the Council had now been fixed for the following day. He also told his Irish colleagues that there was agreement among the members of the Council by then to follow the procedure suggested by Finland. The UN Legal Counsel was perturbed, he said, because he feared that it could open the door to abuse of Council procedures. However, de Pinies said that they could take it that the meeting would follow the Finnish approach: he thought this would be the most satisfactory result from an Irish viewpoint. Dr Hillery confirmed that the Irish side had already told Jakobson that Ireland would not object to this procedure. Still later, about 8.45 pm, de Pinies phoned Cremin again to urge that in Dr Hillery's speech to the Council the next day, there should be an emphasis on the tension and friction along the border in Ireland. This was necessary, he said, because several Council members had told him privately that they were not satisfied that Cremin's original letter requesting a Council meeting had shown sufficient evidence of a threat to *international* peace (my emphasis). Cremin noted this but said that they would have to be careful not to overstate the case, as 'this might serve to nourish tension'.

Following all of these exchanges, de Pinies called a Council meeting for Wednesday morning to consider the Irish request to put the item on the agenda. (Initially the meeting was to take place on Tuesday, 19 August, but the Council was still preoccupied at that point with a complaint by Lebanon against Israel.)

Over the days before the meeting Dr Hillery had also been in contact with the Secretary General, U Thant, who tells us of these meetings in his autobiography:

> I met with the Irish Ambassador and Foreign Minister several times in 1969 and offered to mediate the dispute. Specifically

I proposed that, if both Dublin and London agreed, the question could be looked into by a third party, with or without my involvement. I had in mind the names of two statesmen who were universally recognized to be impartial: Lester Pearson, former Prime Minister of Canada, and Earl Warren, former Chief Justice of the United States. While Dublin appeared receptive to the idea, however, London remained silent. And later, while not referring directly to my proposal, London many times reiterated its position that 'the matter does not lend itself to intervention from outside.'[6]

The Council eventually convened to consider the issue about lunchtime on Wednesday, 20 August. Ambassador Cremin's letter of the previous Sunday was the only item on its provisional agenda. The agenda at this stage, however, could only be provisional: the first business for the Council would be to agree to its adoption. For this, a positive vote from at least nine of the fifteen members would be necessary. This meant that an abstention by any Council member would have the same effect as a vote against.

At the start of the meeting Lord Caradon, the British representative, objected to the formal approval of the draft agenda. He said he would not discuss the substantive issues raised in the Irish letter to the President of the Council – he would keep to the principle that the UN could not intervene in matters of domestic jurisdiction. Northern Ireland was an issue within the domestic jurisdiction of the United Kingdom; and, in consequence, the UN was precluded from dealing with it under Article 2.7 of the Charter which, he said, overrides any other Charter provision. The UK Delegation had always believed that the Council should consider all issues properly raised before it but this issue could not properly be raised.

---

6   Thant (1978) p. 55. Con Cremin (1980, p. 68), in referring to U Thant's memoirs, adds that U Thant also mentioned Dr Ralph Bunche, Under-Secretary General and holder of the Nobel Peace Prize.

Immediately after Caradon had finished, Jakobson, the Finnish representative, intervened to make the proposal that he had outlined to Cremin on the previous day. He noted that Dr Hillery as Irish Foreign Minister had come to New York to explain the situation and present his case in detail; and he suggested that before deciding on the agenda the Council should hear him as a courtesy in case the draft agenda might eventually not be adopted.

Caradon responded that this was a most unusual procedure for which there were few, if any, precedents. Nevertheless, he said,

> for the reasons and on the basis which has been proposed by the Ambassador of Finland, and as a matter of courtesy to the visiting Foreign Minister who is with us, I would certainly raise no objection to this proposal and I look forward to hearing what the Foreign Minister has to say to us.[7]

The scenario, first mentioned in passing by Caradon to Hillery two days previously, and picked up later by Jakobson of Finland who may perhaps have been encouraged privately by Caradon, was now beginning to play itself out in public in the Council. As a result, Dr Hillery was centre stage and in the spotlight, and he now had a full chance to explain the position of the Irish Government in relation to Northern Ireland.

Surprisingly in retrospect, if my recollection is correct, he had travelled alone to New York with no officials to help in the preparation of the address to the Council in which he was to challenge the position of the UK, a Permanent Member. The speech had to be prepared in the Irish Permanent Mission to the UN once he arrived in New York.[8]

---

7   Provisional Verbatim Record of the 1503rd meeting of the Security Council, S/PV 1503, 20 August 1969.

8   My memory is that this was done largely by the Permanent Representative Ambassador Con Cremin and Paddy MacKernan, a junior colleague drawn in for the occasion from the Irish Consulate General in New York – though no doubt other officials in the Irish Mission helped. Paddy MacKernan, who was then

Notwithstanding the short time available, the speech would have to be carefully drafted – and it was. For an Irish domestic audience it had to maintain consistency with the 'theology' of Irish nationalism at the time by situating the whole problem of Northern Ireland against the background of the partition of Ireland in 1920–21. But it also had to avoid treating partition as such as the issue to be brought before the Council. Instead it had to focus on discrimination and the slow pace of reform in Northern Ireland. It had somehow to show that Article 2.7, which bars the UN from intervening in 'matters which are essentially within the domestic jurisdiction of any state', was not a barrier to consideration by the Council: it did this by citing the cases of Cyprus and apartheid in South Africa. It also had to explain the point of the initiative of the Irish Government: its conviction that, for historic reasons, the British Army, then deploying on the streets of Belfast and Derry, would not be acceptable there in the longer term and that a UN peacekeeping force was needed instead.

When Dr Hillery had set out all this at length, Zakharov, the Soviet Union representative, supported his request that the issue be accepted formally on to the agenda of the Council. Zakharov spoke briefly, and somewhat inaccurately, of discrimination in Northern Ireland as shown, he said, 'by the fact that the right to form a government ... belongs only to one religious community, the Protestants'. In addition to taking measures 'to put an end to the persecution' of those fighting discrimination, the British Government, he said, must 'see to it that the necessary conditions are created for the solution of problems in conformity with the wishes of the people of Northern Ireland'. It was an intervention –

---

8   *contd.* Deputy Consul-General, was subsequently Irish Ambassador in Washington and in Paris, Permanent Representative to the EU and, like Cremin well before him, Secretary (General) of the Department of Foreign Affairs. Other diplomats in the Permanent Mission of Ireland at the time who may have helped were the late Paddy Power, who was Deputy Permanent Representative, and Declan Connolly, whose name was mentioned to me by Dr Hillery when he read an earlier version of this chapter.

the only such intervention – that at least had the merit of supporting the request that the issue be put formally on the agenda. Dr Hillery no doubt welcomed support from any source, but he could be forgiven if he swallowed hard at the terms in which that support was expressed by the Soviet Union. *Non tali auxilio* …

Caradon then responded, following, as we might now surmise, the choreography required by the Jakobson procedure. Dr Hillery's speech, he said, was 'careful and restrained', but of course he could not possibly agree with a lot of what had been said. He did not want to be drawn into a debate on the substance. Nevertheless, he went on to deal with the issues raised.

As to the constitutional position, he said, this was not an international matter: 'the Irish Republic had, over the years, recognized the fact of partition and had accepted its consequences'. There had for example been meetings between the Prime Minister of the Republic and the Head of Government in Northern Ireland to discuss such matters as cooperation on tourism and electricity supply. He acknowledged that the Irish Foreign Minister shared 'the purposes of reconciliation and the reduction of intense feeling and the restoration of order'. But he should be aware of the dangers of intervention. Now that British troops had been deployed on the streets in Northern Ireland, there was a peacekeeping force already there – and there could be no better or more impartial force. 'Talk about introducing a peacekeeping force against the wishes of the country concerned [was] a contradiction in terms.' He agreed with Dr Hillery about the importance of human rights; and he cited in full the statement issued by Downing Street about that aspect that had been issued after a meeting on the previous day between the Prime Minister, Wilson, and the Northern Ireland Prime Minister, Chichester-Clark. He noted too that 'the Civil Rights Movement in the North is directed not to the transfer of Northern Ireland from the United Kingdom but to internal reform.' The programme of reform was under way.

At the close of his speech he stressed again to members of the Council that to breach the principle of domestic jurisdiction would have the most serious consequences.

> We have gone out of our way and departed from established practices in order to pay respect and courtesy to the visiting Foreign Minister and enable him to speak to us today.

He had, he said, heard a suggestion in consultations that having heard the Minister, the Council might wish to adjourn the meeting. He would have expected it to vote in the normal way on the adoption of the provisional agenda. However, he went on:

> I would say to you, Sir, that we would not complain if the Council decided to adjourn. But I should make it very plain that we should accept such a decision on the clear under-standing that the wish of the Council is not to accept and proceed with the item proposed.

This was a very clear hint to the other Members of the Council that the UK was ready to accept the scenario canvassed privately by Jakobson, the Finnish representative – which, indeed, Caradon may have had a hand in suggesting to him in the first place.

The next step in the careful choreography was taken by Ambassador Muuka, the Zambian representative. He intervened to say that 'It is our feeling, a feeling which is shared by other members of the Security Council, that in the light of the statements made this morning it might be wise of the Council to adjourn a decision on whether or not to adopt the agenda. Accordingly, he proposed formally that the meeting be adjourned.

Cremin in a later report home said that he and the Minister had been told afterwards by de Pinies that this approach had been discussed in advance in private 'consultations' that morning between members of the Security Council.[9] It was understood among the members at this point, even before the formal meeting started, that the Zambian representative would make this proposal and he (Muuka) had been 'very annoyed' that Caradon had mentioned it first at the formal session. This raises a question: had the Zambian been encouraged privately in advance to make this proposal? If so, by whom – by de Pinies, by Jakobson, perhaps even by Caradon? At this stage we cannot know. But if he had indeed been encouraged by Caradon, then his subsequent annoyance at Caradon's 'jumping the gun' in public himself would be understandable.

Jaime de Pinies as President recalled for the Council the rule that required him to put such a proposal to the vote immediately, without debate. Noting quickly that there had been no objection to the Zambian proposal, he said he would declare it unanimously adopted. He then adjourned the meeting. The music stopped; the elaborately choreographed dance – if indeed that is what it was – was over. The Council did not take up the issue again – then or since.

Dr Hillery, before leaving New York for home, did not have another opportunity to meet with Lord Caradon but, at Hillery's request, Cremin later told Caradon that while Hillery did not agree with the substance of the British position, he was grateful for the way Caradon had handled the issue. Caradon thanked him warmly for this. Later still, Cremin was told by a contact in the British Mission that Caradon had been very impressed by the Minister. There was honour, it seems, on both sides, between opponents – or should they be described as, in some degree at least, partners:

---

9 It was, and is, the practice for the representatives of the Member States of the Security Council to hold private 'consultations' before meetings of the Council in an effort to reach agreement. These consultations are held in a small room behind the Council chamber. They are informal; they take place in English, without interpretation; and there are no TV cameras, records or note-takers present. Some believe that they can be helpful at times in working out an agreed scenario and avoiding polemics in the Council chamber; others deplore them as allowing the five Permanent Members of the Council to avoid taking responsibility publicly for the positions they take, which may include a threat to veto a proposed draft resolution.

constrained by the situation, and by their own dispositions, to join in what became a carefully arranged dance?

I was based in the Irish Embassy in Washington at the time. One month later, I went to New York to join the Irish Delegation to the annual session of the General Assembly, as I had done for each of the previous three years. Dr Hillery as Minister came out again from Dublin to lead the delegation in the opening weeks of the session. By then what we can now see as the underlying objective of the Government's initiative of mid-August had been achieved: the issue had been seen to have been 'taken to the UN', and Dr Hillery had had a hearing for his case. In any event, the immediate crisis had eased somewhat. The issue now at the UN – though this would not have been admitted, or perhaps even recognised by the Irish side at the time – was how to withdraw gracefully to a less exposed position.

This judicious and necessary withdrawal was achieved under cover of what appeared to be, and may even have been intended by some to be, another advance. A formal letter was sent by the Irish Permanent Representative, Ambassador Cremin, to the Secretary General requesting that the issue that Dr Hillery had sought to raise with the Council should now be placed on the agenda of the annual session of the General Assembly, which was due to open in mid-September.

When the General Assembly met, it, like the Council, had first to consider a 'provisional agenda' and then to decide which items on that provisional list should be accepted formally for debate by the Assembly. In the case of the Assembly this is done by a twenty-five-person 'General Committee' comprising the Assembly President and Vice-Presidents and the Chairmen of the main Committees.

Dr Hillery duly appeared before this Committee on 17 September 1969 to argue the case for adding the issue to the agenda as Cremin's letter had requested. In addressing the Committee, he focused mainly on a procedural question – the competence of the Assembly to deal with such an issue. In a reprise of events in the Security

Council four weeks previously, Lord Caradon replied. He pointed to the urgency with which the British Government was pressing ahead with reform and argued that while human rights issues could be discussed in the Assembly, the Irish request went well beyond that: it should be withdrawn. The Soviet Union again supported the proposal to put the item on the Assembly's agenda. The US said that it found itself in an 'unhappy dilemma', and it waited to hear Dr Hillery's response to Caradon's statement.

I recall sitting in the meeting hall listening to these exchanges with colleagues (who, like me, had helped to prepare the material) and feeling a degree of surprise at hearing Dr Hillery's measured response. The core of it was not a renewal of the argument for debate in the General Assembly that he had made in his opening statement but rather an acceptance of Caradon's personal good faith in saying that reforms in Northern Ireland would be put into effect urgently. Dr Hillery told the Committee that he would reflect on this. In such a meeting, a willingness 'to reflect' is an important signal for those alert to hear. On this occasion the signal was heard: Nigeria proposed that further consideration of the request to put the issue on the agenda should be suspended for a period to be decided by the Chairman. This proposal was accepted by the Committee. So the Irish request remained formally on the table. It was never raised again. Whether or not this was the intention – and no doubt some of those involved would deny that it was – a graceful withdrawal had been achieved: Ireland had retreated in relatively good order from its exposed position of mid-August.

Was it a defeat?

In describing the incident in his book on the Security Council that I cited in the previous chapter, Andrew Boyd saw it on the contrary as a well-judged and well-executed example of how the UN should be used as a point of reference and a help in defusing tensions that might otherwise lead to conflict.[10] It is possible of course that Boyd exaggerated the extent to which the participants

---

10   This is my summary of his views – see Boyd (1971) p. 329.

at the time had consciously choreographed, rather than extempor-
ised, the dance in which they engaged in the Council chamber.[11]

Con Cremin would have been in a good position to judge. In his
1980 paper he commended Boyd's account, published eight years
before, as 'interesting' and 'well done'. But in a circumlocution of a
kind that those who knew him will recall with affection, he added
a qualification: 'one statement could be interpreted to have an
implication which would not be valid.' This was a very polite way of
saying that it was not correct. He was referring to Boyd's comment
that Caradon and Hillery in a 'quiet talk … evidently found that …
they could trust each other to play their parts in the Council with
dignity and what may be termed "style".' Cremin acknowledged that
Caradon and Hillery did indeed have a talk, but he rejected 'any
inference that they, as it were, worked out a scenario for the Council
session'.

This is no doubt, strictly speaking, true: they did not explicitly
work out a scenario. But experienced politicians and diplomats do
not always need to be literal or heavy-handed in their approach –
nuance is everything for those with ears to hear and interpret. It is
significant that Cremin's own account of their meeting to which I
referred earlier mentions that on that Sunday evening, 17 August,
Caradon floated to Dr Hillery an idea for how the issue might be
handled that was virtually identical to that proposed later by
Finland's Jakobson. Cremin's report records that 'the Minister
listened quietly' but it appears that he did not offer any reaction.
However, that was indeed the approach that the Council eventually
followed three days later.

I wonder now whether Caradon was instructed from London to
take the position he did. Or was it rather that he, a political figure
of some substance, felt free to interpret his instructions with greater

11   I think Boyd was friendly in earlier years with some members of the Irish
     Delegation such as Conor Cruise O'Brien and that he had a very sympathetic
     attitude towards Ireland. It may even have been he who was responsible for the
     leading article that appeared in *The Economist* in 1960 under the rather extravagant
     heading 'The Afro-Irish Assembly', which I mentioned in Chapter 2.

latitude than a career diplomat might have done? Personally, although I have no evidence, I feel that the latter is more likely.

In summarising the whole episode, I think I should quote again from Boyd:

> in this case the 'defusing' potential of the Council was exploited with unusual deftness. The Irish Government at home, faced a general demand that it should do something, and a specific demand that it should take the matter to the United Nations. Its action enabled it to claim that it had responded to both these demands; that it had pushed its case as far as the Council would allow it to go; and that it had thereby added to the pressure on the British government to put the right kind of pressure on the Ulster Unionists. Yet it could not be accused by any level-headed person of having further inflamed an explosive situation. The brief and measured exchanges in the Council (and the marked silence of no less than eleven of its fifteen members) had the opposite effect.[12]

The eventual outcome of all that had happened was that no decision was ever taken by the Security Council on the request by Ireland for a peacekeeping force because the issue was never formally inscribed on the agenda of the Security Council. If it had been, there was no chance in practice that the Council would have agreed to send a UN peacekeeping force to Northern Ireland over British objections. But, nevertheless, with the acquiescence of the British representative, Lord Caradon, the Irish Foreign Minister Dr Hillery had been allowed to present his case in full to the Council when the preliminary procedural issue of whether or not to put the item on the agenda was being debated. That was the important thing at the time for the Irish public at home, who had a generally positive view of the UN but were not likely to be well-versed in the niceties of UN procedure.

---

12   Boyd (1971) p. 328.

Now, more than forty years on, with the heightened passions of the time largely spent, we can also see it as one of a series of steps through which successive Irish Governments were able gradually to establish that they had a substantial role to play in relation to Northern Ireland – contrary to the initial British view that 'the Irish Question' had been settled definitively in 1921–22 and that, in consequence, the Republic was now a 'foreign country'.

This is not to say, of course, that later developments could have been foreseen in 1969. 'Taking the issue to the UN' was largely one of the responses by a divided Government in Dublin to the need to be seen to 'do something' in a time of crisis that they could do little to resolve directly. But as one of several steps that helped at least to channel, though not wholly to defuse, tension in the South, the decision to send Dr Hillery to New York, and his handling of the issue there, must be seen now as having been a reasonable success. He did not get what he had been sent to ask for – a UN force. He did not even succeed in getting the question put formally on the agenda of the Security Council. But he did get something that seemed important at the time – a chance to present the Government's case on the Northern Ireland issue before the world forum.

Conor Cruise O'Brien wrote long ago about the useful role that the UN can serve in ritualising conflict as a way of avoiding real bloodshed. These events in which Ireland was involved as the 1960s drew to an end, and 'the Troubles' in Northern Ireland began in earnest, may have been a good example of that role. No doubt the good reputation that Ireland had earned for itself in the UN over more than a decade under Dr Hillery's predecessor, Frank Aiken, helped in winning it friends who played a helpful role in the handling of the issue before the Security Council.

In any event, the episode is now history; after much futile bloodshed times have changed; and relations within Northern Ireland, between North and South in the island of Ireland, and between Britain and Ireland are set today on a much happier course.

Bibliography

Aiken, Frank: *see under* Department of External Affairs, Dublin

Bendiner, Elmer. *A Time for Angels: The Tragicomic History of the League of Nations* (Alfred A. Knopf, New York, 1975)

Boyd, Andrew. *Fifteen Men on a Powder Keg: A History of the UN Security Council* (Stein and Day, New York, 1971)

Brown-Scott, James (ed.). *Texts of the Peace Conference at The Hague, 1899 and 1907* (Ginn and Company, Boston and London, 1908)

Chossudovsky, Evgeny M. 'The origins of the treaty on the non-proliferation of nuclear weapons: Ireland's initiative in the United Nations (1958–61)' in *Irish Studies in International Affairs*, Vol. 3, No. 2, 1990 (Royal Irish Academy, Dublin), 111–135

Claude, Inis L. Jr. *Swords into Plowshares: The Problems and Progress of International Organization* (3rd ed., revised) (Random House, New York, 1964, seventh printing 1968)

Commission on Global Governance. *Our Global Neighbourhood* (Oxford University Press, Oxford, 1995)

Coogan, Tim Pat. *De Valera: Long Fellow, Long Shadow* (Hutchinson, London, 1993)

Covenant of the League of Nations, see pp. 162–166 of *The League of Nations 1920–1946: Organization and Accomplishments; A Retrospective of the First Organization for the Establishment of World Peace* (United Nations, New York and Geneva, 1996)

Cremin, Con. 'Northern Ireland at the United Nations August/September 1969' in *Irish Studies in International Affairs*, Vol. 1, No. 2, 1980, 67–73

Cremin, Con. 'United Nations Peace-Keeping Operations: an Irish Initiative 1961–1968' in *Irish Studies in International Affairs*, Vol. 1, No. 4, 1984, 79–84

Crowe, Catriona, Fanning, Ronan, Kennedy, Michael, Keogh, Dermot and O'Halpin, Eunan (eds). *Documents on Irish Foreign Policy*, Vol. IV, 1932–1936 (Royal Irish Academy, Dublin, 2004)

Department of External Affairs, Dublin. *Éire ag na Náisiúin Aontaithe: Ireland at the United Nations* (Brún agus Ó Nualláin Teo, Dublin, 1957, 1958, 1959, 1960, 1961, 1962, 1964, 1967) – a series of booklets containing the speeches of the Minister for External Affairs, Mr Frank Aiken, TD, at the United Nations, published annually over a number of years

Department of External Affairs, Dublin (internal). *Delegation Report on the Twentieth General Assembly of the United Nations 1965*

Department of External Affairs, Dublin (internal). *Delegation Report on the Twenty-first Regular and Fifth Special Sessions of the United Nations General Assembly 1966 and 1967*

Department of External Affairs, Dublin. 'Statements and Speeches' 1/69 (verbatim transcript of Aiken's press conference in New York on 23 April 1969)

Dorr, Noel. 'Ireland at the United Nations' in Ben Tonra and Eilís Ward (eds) *Ireland in International Affairs: Interests, Institutions and Identities. Essays in honour of Professor N.P. Keatinge FTCD, MRIA* (Institute of Public Administration, Dublin, 2002, pp. 104–128)

Fanning, Ronan. 'The Anglo-American alliance and the Irish application for membership of the United Nations' in *Irish Studies in International Affairs*, Vol. 2, No. 2, 1986, 35–61

Fanning, Ronan. 'Playing it cool: the response of the British and Irish Governments to the crisis in Northern Ireland, 1968–9' in *Irish Studies in International Affairs*, Vol. 12, 2001, 57–85

Fanning, Ronan, Kennedy, Michael, Keogh, Dermot and O'Halpin, Eunan (eds). *Documents on Irish Foreign Policy, Vol. I, 1919–1922* (Royal Irish Academy and Department of Foreign Affairs, Dublin, 1998)

Fanning, Ronan, Kennedy, Michael, Keogh, Dermot and O'Halpin, Eunan (eds). *Documents on Irish Foreign Policy, Vol. II, 1923–1926*

(Royal Irish Academy and Department of Foreign Affairs, Dublin, 2000)

Fisk, Robert. *In Time of War: Ireland, Ulster and the Price of Neutrality 1939–45* (Andre Deutsch, London, 1983)

Fry, M.G., Goldstein, E. and Langhorne, R. (eds). *Guide to International Relations and Diplomacy* (Continuum, London, 2002)

Gageby, Douglas. *The Last Secretary General: Sean Lester and the League of Nations* (Town House, Dublin, 1999)

Gavshon, Arthur L. *The Mysterious Death of Dag Hammarskjöld* (Walker and Company, New York, 1962)

Government Information Bureau, Dublin. *Speeches and Statements on Irish Unity, Northern Ireland, Anglo-Irish Relations August 1969–October 1971* (1971)

Horne, Alistair. *A Savage War of Peace: Algeria 1954–1962* (Viking, New York, 1977)

Ishizuka, Katsumi, *Ireland and International Peacekeeping Operations 1960–2000* (Cass, London, 2005)

Kagan, Robert. *Paradise and Power: America and Europe in the New World Order* (Atlantic Books, London, 2003)

Kalb, Madeleine G. *The Congo Cables: The Cold War in Africa – from Eisenhower to Kennedy* (Macmillan, New York, 1982)

Kennedy, Michael. *Ireland and the League of Nations 1919–1946: International Relations, Diplomacy and Politics* (Irish Academic Press, Dublin, 1996)

Kennedy, Michael and McMahon, Deirdre (eds). *Obligations and Responsibilities: Ireland and the United Nations, 1955–2005. Essays Marking Fifty Years of Ireland's United Nations Membership* (Institute of Public Administration, Dublin, 2005)

Kennedy, Michael and Skelly, Joseph Morrison (eds). *Irish Foreign Policy 1919–1966: From Independence to Internationalism* (Four Courts Press, Dublin, 2000)

Keogh, Niall. *Con Cremin: Ireland's Wartime Diplomat* (Mercier Press, Cork, 2006)

Li Thian-hok. 'The China impasse: a Formosan view' in *Foreign*

Affairs: An American Quarterly Review, Vol. 36, No. 3, April 1958

Macmillan, Harold. *Pointing the Way: 1959–1961* (Harper and Row, New York, 1972)

Maher, Denis. *The Tortuous Path: The Course of Ireland's Entry into the EEC 1948–73* (Institute of Public Administration, Dublin, 1986)

Mitchell, Arthur and Ó Snodaigh, Pádraig (eds). *Irish Political Documents 1916–1949* (Irish Academic Press, Dublin 1985)

Moynihan, Maurice. *Speeches and Statements by Eamon de Valera 1917–1973* (Gill and Macmillan, Dublin and St. Martin's Press, New York, 1980)

O'Brien, Conor Cruise. *To Katanga and Back: A UN Case History* (New York, The Universal Library, 1962)

O'Brien, Conor Cruise (text) and Topolski, Felix (illustrations). *The United Nations: Sacred Drama* (Simon and Schuster, New York, 1968)

O'Brien, Conor Cruise. *Memoir: My Life and Themes* (Poolbeg Press, Dublin, 1998)

O'Halpin, Eunan. *Defending Ireland: The Irish State and Its Enemies since 1922* (Oxford University Press, 1999)

O'Neill, John Terence and Rees, Nicholas. *United Nations Peacekeeping in the Post-Cold War Era* (Routledge, London and New York, 2005)

Parsons, Anthony. *From Cold War to Hot Peace: UN Interventions 1947–1994* (Michael Joseph, London, 1995)

Ross, Alf. *The United Nations: Peace and Progress* (The Bedminster Press, Totowa, NJ, 1966)

Skelly, Joseph Morrison. 'Ireland, the Department of External Affairs and the United Nations 1946–55: A new look' in *Irish Studies in International Affairs*, Vol. 7, 1996

Skelly, Joseph Morrison. *Irish Diplomacy at the United Nations 1945–1965: National Interests and the International Order* (Irish Academic Press, Dublin, 1997)

Thant, U. *View from the UN* (David and Charles, Newton Abbot and London, 1978)

United Nations. *United Nations Review,* Vol. 8, No. 10 (October 1961)

United Nations. *Yearbook of the United Nations: Special Edition: UN Fiftieth Anniversary 1945–1995* (Martinus Nijhoff, The Hague, 1995)

United Nations. *'We the Peoples': The Role of the United Nations in the Twenty-First century.* Report of the Secretary General of the United Nations 2000

United Nations. *In Larger Freedom: Development, Security and Human Rights for All.* Report of the Secretary General (UN document series A/59/2005) 21 March 2005

Urquhart, Brian. *Hammarskjöld* (Alfred A. Knopf, New York, 1973)

Urquhart, Brian. *A Life in Peace and War* (W.W. Norton and Company, New York and London, 1987)

Index

Page references followed by 'n' indicate footnotes.